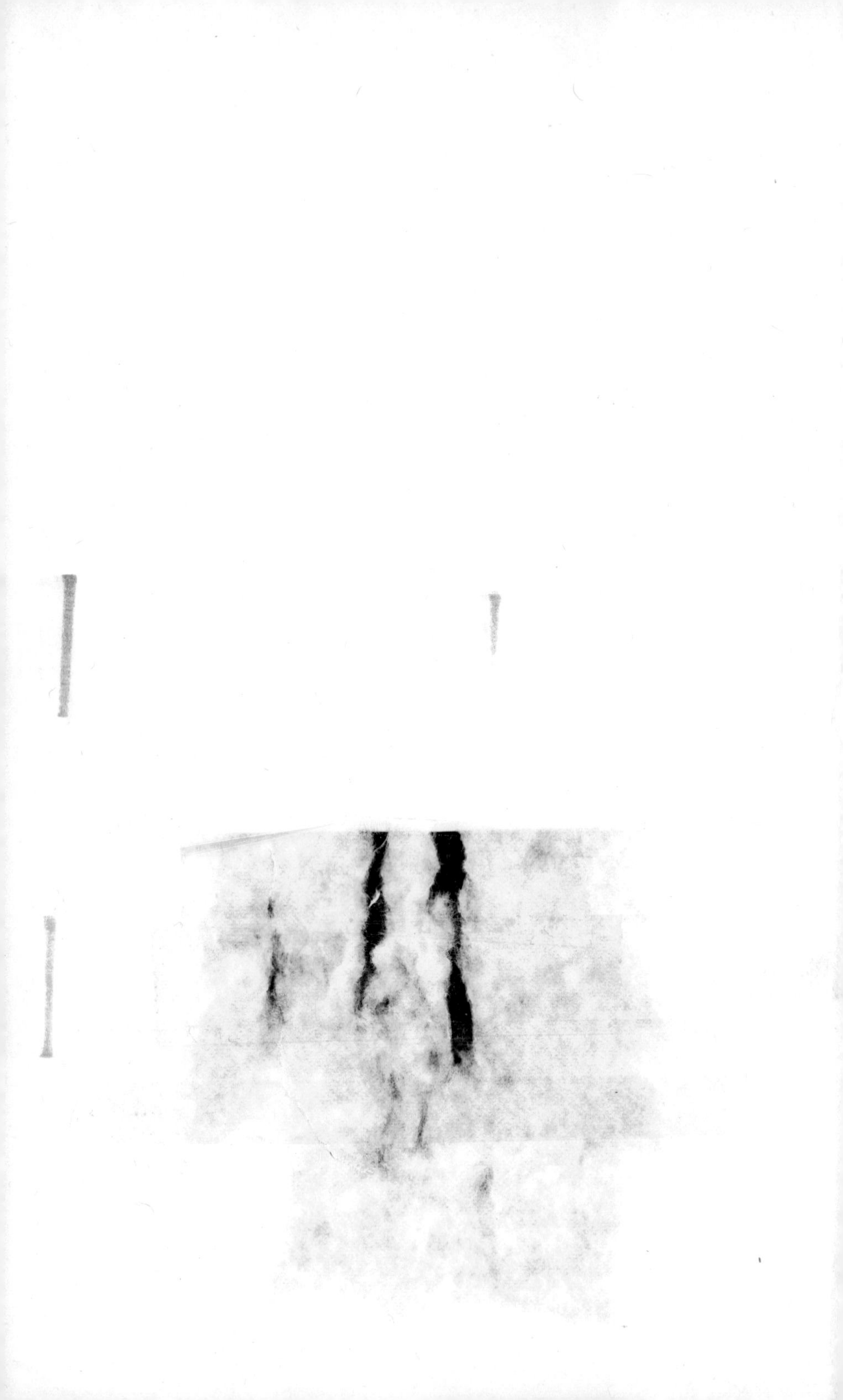

Willa Cather's Imagination

Willa Cather's Imagination

David Stouck

University of Nebraska Press • Lincoln

Portions of the discussions of Willa Cather's fiction have appeared in somewhat different form in the journals listed on pages 247–248, which constitute an extension of the copyright page. Acknowledgments for permission to quote from the works of Willa Cather appear on the same page.

The publication of this book was assisted by a grant from
The Andrew W. Mellon Foundation.

Library of Congress Cataloging in Publication Data

Stouck, David, 1940–
Willa Cather's Imagination.

Bibliography: p.
Includes index.
1. Cather, Willa Sibert, 1873–1947—Criticism and Interpretation. I. Title.
PS3505.A87Z86 813'.5'2 74–81363
ISBN 0–8032–0848–0

For my grandmother
MILDRED HAMILTON

Contents

Willa Cather's Imagination

Introduction

Wright Morris introduces his collection of critical essays, *The Territory Ahead,* by pointing to the tendency of American writers to "start well then peter out." There is a special ring of truth to this generalization because Melville, Fitzgerald, Sherwood Anderson, and even Hemingway never seemed to realize fully the brilliant promise that characterized the outset of their careers. Wright Morris's thesis, however, does not hold for his fellow Nebraskan Willa Cather, who published one of her finest novels, *Death Comes for the Archbishop,* relatively late in her career (she was then fifty-three). Moreover, Willa Cather's imagination, in contrast with that of many of her more flamboyant contemporaries, was always developing in terms of its emotional and intellectual needs and in the manner of its esthetic expression. Her last novel, *Sapphira and the Slave Girl,* with its figurations of life from the viewpoint of a five-year-old child, was as experimental in form as her first attempt at epic in *Alexander's Bridge* or her use of the sonata form in *The Professor's House.*

The extent of her development as an artist is reflected in the broad range of modes, forms, and themes to be found in her fiction. The novels from the first half of Willa Cather's career are written in different imaginative modes: *O Pioneers!,* with its vision of a new land and heroic settlers, has the qualities of an epic; *My Ántonia,* with its rural setting and its journey through memory, is a pastoral; while *The Professor's House,* which chronicles an ugly tale of human greed and ambition, is largely satirical in intention. The novels of Willa Cather's maturity explore the moral possibilities of traditional literary forms: *Death Comes for the Archbishop* is a saint's legend and *Shadows on the Rock* is a historical novel. And while thematically her novels range from the pioneer experience in America to the history of Catholic civilization, the one theme germane to all great art, the relationship between art and life, informs her fiction throughout. In her last books Willa Cather took up the question which confronts every artist—that is, whether or not art is valid as a way of life. Indeed, very few American writers have explored the archetypal dimensions of the imagination so fully.

The chief purpose of this study is to illustrate the unusual range and depth of Willa Cather's imagination. Too often Willa Cather is identified exclusively as the author of *My Ántonia* and as the elegist of American pioneer life. While her memoir of a prairie childhood is certainly one of her finest achievements and an indisputable classic, the materials of her art and the scope of her imagination reach considerably beyond nostalgia for a way of life that has vanished. This can be illustrated by *My Ántonia* itself and that favorite Cather image of the plow silhouetted against the sun, which yields so many symbolic meanings. Literally the plow is magnified by the setting sun so that it attains heroic physical proportions; it becomes the epic symbol of creativity and the founding of a new country. However, in the context of Jim Burden's memory the image acquires a nostalgic dimension, for memory directs our attention to the fact of the sunset and to reflecting on a way of life that has irretrievably passed away. But in the still larger context of the whole novel a critical content adheres in the image as well—a submerged recognition that the plow is the first instrument in that inevitable series of forces which will change the face of the prairie, which will cut down the beloved cottonwoods and bring highways across the graves of the first settlers. Indeed, in the novels that follow *My Ántonia* Jim Burden's lament for a way of life that has disappeared mutates into a bitter denunciation of materialistic progress. But the plow against the sun is also an emblem of the esthetic impulse in Willa Cather's imagination. The symbolic plow as artifact (Jim describes it as "picture writing on the sun") reflects the artist's desire to transcend the limitations of experience and to create images or pictures which resist time and change. From this single image as it unfolds one begins to perceive something of the complexity of Willa Cather's imagination, something of the artful purpose and sophisticated invention that lie beneath the simple classical prose.

Following roughly the chronological development of Willa Cather's career, I have divided this study into three parts, each of which examines the author's imagination from a different critical vantage point. Part I attempts to illustrate the breadth of her imagination by considering the various modes through which her fiction moves. It looks first at *Alexander's Bridge* and *O Pioneers!* and two early stories in the light of the epic imagination; it then considers *My Ántonia, A Lost Lady,* and numerous short stories as pastorals; and finally it examines *One of Ours* and *The Professor's House* as satires, or works of the critical imagination. In each case I have sketched out a brief working definition of mode, designed to illuminate certain qualities in the books discussed. The approach through mode is not exhaustive (in most cases I have not rehearsed the findings of other critics, and much remains to be explored in these books), but this approach does have the advantage of pointing to the archetypal imaginative patterns which adhere in these American narratives and which relate them, as one of Willa Cather's characters might have said, to the two or three human stories that "go on repeating themselves as fiercely as if they had never happened before."

Part II explores the depths of Willa Cather's imagination in terms of her moral vision. The focus falls on the author's use of traditional narrative forms in which moral states are implicit or by which they are approached most directly: *My Mortal Enemy* as a novella incisively dramatizes an experience of consuming hate and self-damnation; as a saint's legend *Death Comes for the Archbishop* holds up a paradisal vision; and *Shadows on the Rock* as a historical novel gives us a glimpse of man's purgatorial suffering in a world burdened with time. I believe that when Willa Cather wrote these three novels she experienced and came to understand most fully the nature of the good and evil instincts within herself.

Part III looks at the theme of art in relation to life, which runs throughout Willa Cather's fiction. First are considered those stories of artists (especially *The Song of the Lark*) in which art is viewed most positively as giving life its highest kind of dignity and purpose. These earlier narratives are then contrasted with

Willa Cather's last four books (*Obscure Destinies, Lucy Gayheart, Sapphira and the Slave Girl,* and *The Old Beauty and Others*), in which doubts are expressed as to art's redemptive power and in which life values are given supremacy.

This study is not strictly speaking biographical; however, Willa Cather practiced an art which often had its source in personal memories (she once described it as "cremated youth"), so at times I have approached the elusive statements beneath the smooth surfaces of her prose by bringing her life and art into some conjunction. The modes in which her books are written, I think, can be more fully appreciated and understood when related to some of the decisive experiences in her life. The heroic and pastoral novels about the Midwest are the products partly of the author's growing up in pioneer Nebraska and seeing that period and that way of life recede into history. Her novels of disillusionment and frequent bitter attack written in the 1920s derive, I believe, from a number of complex sources, including a violent reaction to the material values that dominated the decade, changes in her friendship with Isabelle McClung, and more broadly, but perhaps most importantly, the general disaffection of middle age. The serenity of *Death Comes for the Archbishop* reflects something of the equilibrium she was able to achieve once more in her life, while the last books are marked by unhappy changes in the life of her family and by the advance of old age. My interest is not with the details of Willa Cather's life as such (that is a matter for biographers), but with what they can reveal to us about the nature of her imaginative vision. Similarly, the concern of this study is not with Willa Cather as a woman or as an American, but with Willa Cather as an artist and with the universal dimensions of her imagination.

PART I

Modes

CHAPTER ONE

Epic

Willa Cather and the Epic Mode

The circumstances of Willa Cather's early life would seem to have determined that she sound the epic note in her writing. The author was born in Virginia on December 7, 1873, but when she was nine years of age her parents moved the family to Webster County, Nebraska, where other branches of the Cather family had taken up homesteads.[1] The Nebraska experience is obviously crucial as it forms the backdrop for so much of Willa Cather's fiction; but perhaps more important to the special mode of her early novels was the move itself from the restrictive social order in Virginia to the open pioneering life on the plains. In Virginia the Cather families, including the author's grandparents, were farmers with small holdings, and in the tightly knit social and economic organization of the colonial state there was little opportunity for them to improve their station in life. The move to Nebraska meant leaving behind the physical and spiritual amenities of civilization, but in return the relocation to the prairie, where there were still scarcely any human landmarks, provided the opportunity of beginning life over again. The special climate of mind bred by the early pioneer experience—the exhilarated, forward-looking attitude, the strong optimism of creativity, and the necessary confidence in one's own endeavors—characterizes, broadly speaking, Willa Cather's early novels which are stories of growth, struggle, and conquest in the epic mode. As she was growing up the author observed first hand the development of a civilization in the West, knew intimately the day-to-day struggles of the pioneers with the land, shared their hopes for the future. Although Willa Cather left Webster County behind when she was seventeen, first to attend university at Lincoln, subsequently to pursue a writing career in Pittsburgh and New York, she returned frequently for long visits with her family there and she returned imaginatively to her childhood home for the setting of six of her twelve novels.

The influence of the Nebraska experience on the early stories and novels was coincident with another source of creative inspiration for Willa Cather—her friendship with Isabelle McClung. Miss McClung was the daughter of a wealthy, conservative Pittsburgh judge and the two women apparently met backstage at a theatre sometime in 1899 when Miss Cather was working on the Pittsburgh *Daily Leader.* They became close friends and Miss McClung, who preferred the company of artists to fashionable society, invited Willa Cather to live at the McClung mansion. Miss Cather's residence at 1180 Murray Hill Avenue lasted nearly five years during which time she taught high school and wrote and published her first two books: *April Twilights* (1903), a volume of verse, and *The Troll Garden* (1905), a collection of short stories. According to friends, Isabelle McClung was an exceptionally handsome woman and an entirely frank and generous person; to Willa Cather she was a rare and perfect human being and the author loved her deeply for the rest of her life.

In 1906 Willa Cather left Pittsburgh to join the staff of *McClure's Magazine* in New York, but in the following years (from the time the author was thirty-two until she was forty-two) she frequently returned to Pittsburgh for holidays with Isabelle and periods of work in the special room set aside for her in the McClung mansion. The creative feelings inspired by the friendship are expressed in the dedicatory poem to Isabelle which appeared in the first edition of *The Song of the Lark:*

> On uplands,
> At morning,
> The world was young, the winds were free;
> A garden fair,
> In that blue desert air
> Its guest invited me to be.

The mood of youthful aspiration that Isabelle McClung inspired in the author combined with her pioneer memories of genesis in the West to leave an indelible imprint of confidence and creativity on the first three novels: *Alexander's Bridge* (1912), *O Pioneers!* (1913) and *The Song of the Lark* (1915). The protagonists in these novels are strong, creative characters who strive for perfection in the life's work they choose, whether it be bridge-building, cultivating the wild prairie, or achieving excellence in art. Success in these novels is realistically qualified (Alexander's greatest engineering feat ends in disaster symbolic of his personal life; Alexandra Bergson loses the much-loved brother for whom she has worked so hard; Thea Kronborg, the opera singer, becomes impersonal and hardened by success), but the emphasis, nonetheless, in these novels is on creative achievement. The names Alexander and Alexandra deliberately evoke images of conquest on an epic scale.

There are in some of Willa Cather's earliest stories characters of exceptional physical strength, such as Canute Canuteson in "On the Divide" or Serge Povolitchky in "The Clemency of the Court," and there are descriptions of the prairie which awaken the reader to a sense of its elemental power and beauty; but the first piece of writing which creates and sustains the epic feeling as an integral part of its total effect is a love story entitled "Eric Hermannson's Soul,"[2] published in 1900 after the author had moved to Pittsburgh. The two central figures in this story are both larger than life—the man for his vitality and primitive strength, the woman for her beauty and sophisticated enterprise. Although their story is a form of romance and they individually suffer considerable inner turmoil, they have been given a grandeur of conception which is commensurate with the setting on the vast, open plains.

Until he came under the spell of the Free Gospel religion and Asa Skinner, Eric Hermannson was known as "the wildest lad on the Divide." He is described, in phrases which endow him with epic stature, as a giant, as "the flower of the Norwegian youth," as "a dragon slayer"; the heroine's brother suggestively nicknames him Siegfried. Everything in Eric's life assumes a mythic scale of reference: his sinful dalliance with Lena Hanson, an immigrant woman of doubtful reputation, is terminated in allegorical fashion when Eric spies a rattlesnake coiled on her doorstep; even his religious converter, Asa Skinner, a former train gambler, "from the most debauched of men . . . had become the most ascetic." Into Eric's chastened existence comes Margaret Elliot whose beauty and sophistication suggest to Eric another unearthly kingdom of the soul. There is a playful touch of the classical epic manner when the narrator states that Margaret Elliot had no reason to be in the West: "But ah! across what leagues of land and sea, by what improbable chances, do the unrelenting gods bring us to our fate!" The heroine, whose life in the East is characterized by a preciousness and fashionable ennui, is awakened through Eric to a world of primitive instincts and powerful sexual feelings that she has never known with her fiancé. She feels that on the plains with Eric she has come into the presence of life's most powerful and ennobling forces, and she says to her brother: " 'I think if one lived here long enough one would quite forget how to be trivial, and would read only the great books that we never get time to read in the world, and would remember only the great music, and the things that are really worth while would stand out clearly against that horizon over there.' "

As in many of Willa Cather's best pieces of writing there is little plot as such in "Eric Hermannson's Soul"; the story achieves its effect through character, setting, and allusion fused into an organic whole by three sequences of symbolic action. The first of these is the dramatic conversion of Eric at the gospel meeting where he renounces earthly pleasures by smashing his violin. The most powerful scenes portray the physical passion that the two lovers feel for each other: the encounter with a herd of wild ponies is a magnificent dramatizing of sexual energies, and the ascent to the top of the windmill after the dance symbolizes both the heightening and the sublimating of sexual passion. The full imaginative power of the story derives from the juxtaposition in Eric and Margaret of everything that is irreconcilably opposite—East and West, civilization and barbarism, thought and feeling. Heightened appreciation of the epic, elemental quality of life on the prairie is created through these contrasts. The overrefined, almost decadent character of life in Eastern cities is epitomized by Margaret's fiancé; we glimpse part of a letter he has written to her in which he describes not his passion for his absent lover but two purchases of art he has recently made. Even in the description of the paintings, which represent the couple's respective tastes in art, there is a contrast operative: between the pale pastoral scene by Puvis de Chavannes (further contrasted with the vigorous rural setting of the story itself) and the more florid, sensual landscape by Constant. The world of fashionable cynicism and depleted energies so pointedly evoked by the letter is in direct contrast to the rugged life of the immigrants on the plains. Again the epic hardihood of their existence is underscored by mythic allusions: at the farewell dance for Margaret and her brother the music, made up of folk songs from the North, suggests to Margaret the landscape of *Peer Gynt,* and the old men are described keeping time to the music "with the vigor of old Silenus." And Eric, in contrast to Margaret's fiancé with his high, white forehead and drooping shoulders, is a passionate giant with shoulders "like those of the stone Doryphorus" and arms that "could have thrown Thor's hammer out in the cornfields." The mythic allusions are apotheosized in the Nebraska landscape—in the plains described as "a scented sea of cornland bathed in opalescent air and blinding sunlight," and in the great Western sky "which seemed to reach around the world" and about which in the dusk there lingered "a pale, white light, as of a universal dawn." The descriptions of Eric with his hair "yellow as the heavy wheat in the ripe of summer" and his eyes "like the blue water between the ice packs in the North Sea" make him a physical part of that elemental landscape.

The passion between Eric and Margaret embodies a dialectic of energies as old as human history. We are told that in Margaret's presence Eric felt "as the Goths before the white marbles in the Roman Capitol"—a contrast between the barbarians at the dawn of their civilization and the last magnificent edifices of a civilization that has passed through its zenith into decline. Margaret recognizes that Eric's life is still one with nature, whereas she herself belongs to "an ultra-refined civilization which tries to cheat nature with elegant sophistries." In Margaret's reflection is embodied a fundamental truth about life and human values which persists throughout Willa Cather's fiction—namely, that what is natural will ultimately prevail. Margaret reflects that one generation or two may rise above or sink below nature—Jerusalem or Sodom—but in the end nature restores her balance: " 'I made the world, I rule it, and I am its destiny.' " (Margaret's idea expresses an intellectual belief Willa Cather held about the cyclical nature of human civilization. As early as 1895, in one of her critical articles, the author argues that when a civilization becomes refined and effete, it is invariably overwhelmed by a more primitive race that will destroy the decadent world and thereby renew life: "Some day, perhaps, when our civilization has grown too utterly complex, when our introspection cuts off all action . . . then the savage strength of the Slav or the Bushmen will come upon us and will burn our psychologies and carry us away into captivity and make us dress the vines and plow the earth and teach us that after all nature is best." The image she uses to describe the Roman-Barbarian conflict is that of Thor's hammer crushing the defiled altars of Aphrodite, an image which illuminates something powerful in the conception and the allusions of "Eric Hermannson's Soul.")[3]

Ultimately Margaret recognizes that she cannot return to a primitive existence herself and so she goes back to her effete fiancé in the East, leaving Eric to the great, untamed landscape and to Asa Skinner. Eric's imagination has an epic scope which corresponds to his fundamental grasp of life. In a moment of impassioned sacrilege, he pictures Margaret as an angel from the heavens whom he loves "more than Christ," and afterwards he envisions himself as damned in hell but joyfully "treading down the tempest of flame, hugging the fiery hurricane to his breast." In a final flourish of defiance towards Asa Skinner he murmurs to himself in consolation for his day of passion: " ' "And a day shall be as a thousand years, and a thousand years as a day." ' "

Alexander's Bridge and Literary Epic

"Eric Hermannson's Soul" is the only early story Willa Cather wrote in the epic mode, but when she came to the composition of her first novel, *Alexander's Bridge* (1912), she very consciously turned to the idea of epic to give her modern tale universal significance and weight. In years to follow Willa Cather wrote disparagingly about *Alexander's Bridge:* in a brief discussion of her first two novels written for the *Colophon* in 1931 she referred to *Alexander's Bridge* as a "studio picture," implying that it was a literary exercise and a good deal contrived;[4] and in her preface to the 1922 edition she described its composition as the building of a story externally, to be distinguished from the kind of story that shapes itself instinctively and inevitably in the writer's mind.[5] There is a distinctly literary or "invented" quality to *Alexander's Bridge,* apparent when the book is compared to a novel like *O Pioneers!;* however, a literary quality to a novel is not in itself negative, but indicates a different kind of writing. C. S. Lewis is helpful here when he distinguishes in his *Preface to Paradise Lost* two kinds of epic which he calls primary and secondary.[6] The subject matter of a primary epic such as *Beowulf* is drawn from the legends and experiences of the artist and his society and is informed by a cyclical vision of human existence. Beowulf's rise to power through his victory over Grendel and his defeat in old age by the dragon are seen as phases of a career subject finally to the rise-and-fall pattern of nature's cycles. (I will treat primary epic more fully in the discussion of *O Pioneers!.*) A secondary epic such as Virgil's *Aeneid,* on the other hand, has a literary source and its conflict involves a historical rather than cyclical vision of human destiny; the *Aeneid* draws together from its many sources a narrative of events which take place only once in human history. When Willa Cather was writing *Alexander's Bridge* she was probably not thinking about epic in this light, but by looking at *Alexander's Bridge* as a secondary, or literary, epic we can appreciate more fully, I think, the kind of book she did write. One should add here that the author's judgment should not be entirely credited. For one thing, she overlooks the genuine craftsmanship in the story; but more importantly the novel contains much of her essential imaginative material—particularly the motif of returning to childhood—and when the novel strikes this vein it speaks, as Edith Lewis has suggested, with passion and authority.[7]

Willa Cather clearly conceived of Bartley Alexander as an epic hero, for the flaw in his personal life—his love for an actress and desire to return to youth—brings about the collapse of the most important piece of bridge-building going on in the world. Alexander's achievements have historical importance: his old university professor describes his last project as one of the " 'bridges into the future, over which the feet of every one of us will go.' " Like the archetypal hero of epic and romance, Alexander is self-engendered and self-sustaining; we are given no details about his origins except that he spent his boyhood in the "old West" and as a youth worked his way to Europe on a cattle boat. Alexander's name of course is suggestive of his heroic stature and he is described as a man of extraordinary talent and energy:

> There were other bridge-builders in the world, certainly, but it was always Alexander's picture that the Sunday Supplement men wanted, because he looked as a tamer of rivers ought to look. Under his tumbled sandy hair his head seemed as hard and powerful as a catapult, and his shoulders looked strong enough in themselves to support a span of any one of his ten great bridges. [P. 7]

To heighten Alexander's stature further he is seen through the eyes of his former professor, Lucius Wilson, a man of wholly sedentary instinct. In the prophetic manner of literary epic (with its vision of man's destiny), Wilson foresees Alexander's downfall —with a big crack zigzagging across his facade, " 'then a crash and clouds of dust' " (p. 9). Alexander's historic significance as an engineer is underscored throughout the novel by glimpses of him from the public eye: newspapers publish accounts of his daily affairs in New York; on board ship his fellow passengers watch him from a respectful distance, assuming that he is brooding over his new cantilever bridge in Canada; and at the end of the novel his wife first learns of his death from the newsboys crying it in the streets.

After the first chapter has established Alexander's epic stature through the viewpoint of his wife and former professor, the novel's perspective changes and we look at the story through Alexander's eyes. As the public view of Alexander yields to a private one, so the mode of the novel shifts its emphasis from epic to romantic, although Alexander's private story retains a curiously prophetic quality because it sets forth for the first time an imaginative dilemma central to Willa Cather's fiction. Alexander's crisis turns on material and public success which fails to satisfy—one of the powerful, recurrent themes of American literature. A boy of obscure origins but distinguished by "a powerfully equipped nature," Alexander becomes through desire and tremendous effort one of the world's most important men. But he achieves power and fame at the expense of his instinctual nature and becomes a classic instance of the man divided against himself. He wishes to become a boy again before the dream of success was tarnished, but that is impossible; unable to move backward or to go forward, he is destroyed by the progress of the machine he set in motion.

Alexander's dilemma is dramatized in his relations with two women: his wife and his former lover, who is now an actress. Alexander's wife, Winifred, is a handsome woman of both culture and means and is a symbol of her husband's ambitions and achievements; she is appropriately described by such adjectives as "proud," "handsome," "hard," "self-sufficient," "composed." In the novel's imagery she is repeatedly associated with stars, planets that are cold, bright, and that give direction. As she and Professor Wilson sit down to tea in the first scene, the evening star is visible through the bare trees. When he is young and feels life's challenge issuing from the mountains and the stars, Alexander answers that challenge with his wife's name; and when years later he thinks of their courtship, he remembers a big white house on a hill under the moon and the "cold, splendid stars" (p. 95). Business takes Alexander to London where he chances to meet again Hilda Burgoyne, an actress with whom he was very much in love when he was a student in Paris. He sees her first on stage in one of the hit plays of the season, and memories of their youthful affair revive in him his old feeling for her. Like Jim Burden in *My Ántonia* whose dilemma is similar, Alexander hesitates to see Hilda again in person: "Remembering Hilda as she used to be, was doubtless more satisfactory than seeing her as she must be now—and, after all, Alexander asked himself, what was it but his own young years that he was remembering?" (p. 30). Seeing Hilda awakens the dissatisfaction in Alexander which ultimately destroys him. Again like Jim Burden he comes to feel cheated both by his dreams of success and by the passage of youth: "How quickly it had passed; and, when it had passed, how little worth while anything was. None of the things he had gained in the least compensated" (p. 31). Similar disillusionment is experienced by Godfrey St. Peter in *The Professor's House* and Henry Grenfell in "Before Breakfast."

However, when Alexander does meet Hilda in person she quickens in him a renewed desire for life and he falls in love with her again. In her person and manner Hilda is the antithesis of Winifred Alexander: she is "soft," "supple," "round," "girlish," "eager"; her apartment is full of flowers and lit by candles and soft lamplight. She is associated in the novel's imagery with the moon of romantic love. When Alexander first sees her on stage she sings a song called "The Rising of the Moon," and when he goes to search her out again in the city there is a "grimy moon" and he describes himself as "mooning about" (p. 36). The image delineates his crisis when he tries to free himself from his love for Hilda: he compares himself to the boy who drank from the brook and became a stag, an allusion to the legend of Actaeon, who was destroyed after he looked on the nakedness of Diana, the moon goddess. Hilda is also associated through a subtle network of allusions with Helen of Troy, another classical female figure who left ruin in the wake of love. Alexander is a variant name for Paris, the Trojan prince who stole Helen away from the Greeks. Bartley Alexander, who we are told "caught the wind in his sails early," says to Hilda the last time they are together, " 'You can love as queens did in the old time' " (p. 90), and at the end of the novel Wilson questions that " 'out of so many conquests and the spoils of conquered cities' " (p. 108) Hilda could miss an old professor. Alexander himself is associated with the sun. When he tells Hilda he has been mooning about, she counters comically with a reference to his honors in Japan: " 'What was it, Commander of the Order of the Rising Sun?' " The sun in the sky reflects his moods; at a bright sunrise he feels all his old power and his desire to conquer, but at sunset (which is also moonrise) his thoughts are filled with Hilda and childhood. These images are particularly prevalent on his winter voyage to England and during his subsequent exhilarating stay.

For most of the novel Alexander is torn between his self-preserving instinct, embodied in his wife, career, and reputation, and his instinctual desire to become a carefree youth again in erotic dalliance with Hilda Burgoyne. In this divided state Alexander is closest to Godfrey St. Peter among Willa Cather's other characters. Like St. Peter, Alexander married a woman of means, and her fortune coupled with his success as an engineer has brought obligations and restraints rather than freedom and a sense of fulfillment. Like St. Peter, he finds himself "living exactly the kind of life he had determined to escape" (p. 32). There is also the curious parallel that Alexander is happier in his study than anywhere else (p. 82). But most significant of all in relating the two books is the fact that Alexander does not fall in love with Hilda again for herself, but because she suggests to him a way of recovering his own youthful self. In her presence he feels the survival of his youth: "This feeling was the only happiness that was real to him, and such hours were the only ones in which he could feel his own continuous identity—feel the boy he had been in the rough days of the old West, feel the youth who had worked his way across the ocean on a cattle-ship and gone to study in Paris without a dollar in his pocket" (p. 33). Hilda is essential to his quest, for, as he says to her, " 'I'm growing older, and you've got my young self here with you,' " but it is important to stress that in the end it is his young self he seeks and not Hilda:

> He walked shoulder to shoulder with a shadowy companion—not little Hilda Burgoyne, by any means, but some one vastly dearer to him than she had ever been—his own younger self, the youth who had waited for him upon the steps of the British Museum that night, and who, though he had tried to pass so quietly, had known him and come down and linked an arm in his. [P. 34]

Like the Professor, whose roles as a historian and a family man have eroded his sense of original identity and his integrity, Alexander too seeks to reassess his life by returning for a time to boyhood and his original dream of the world. This is Willa Cather's own theme, the roots of which go much deeper than the novel's literary invention; it gives the book its authority in the Cather canon.

In the last chapter Willa Cather deftly weaves together the two threads of her story: the epic theme of Alexander the bridge-builder and the romantic theme of Alexander the lover and boy. Alexander's two selves will not mesh. Because he is with Hilda in New York he does not receive in time the telegram warning him of the trouble with his bridge, and when he reaches Moorlock he is destroyed with the collapse of his great flawed structure. The progress of Alexander's life is artfully suggested in the last chapter by images of bridges—bridges which have always led him into the future. At sunset the train passes over a weather-stained wooden bridge, beneath which a group of boys are seated around a fire. The scene takes Alexander back in memory to childhood—"to a campfire on a sandbar in a Western river, and he wished he could go back and sit down with them" (p. 94). The image occurs several times in Willa Cather's poetry and fiction ("Dedicatory" to *April Twilights,* "The Enchanted Bluff," *My Ántonia*), and denotes a way of looking at the world when life is still untried and bespeaks only the excitement and wonder of the future. The image brings into focus Alexander's self-destructive desire to recapture his youth. Then the train comes to Allway where Alexander built his first bridge and where he met his wife. The bridge and the man who built it—a man in the first flush of power and success—no longer seem part of him; he recoils from crossing over that bridge again and from remembering the kind of man he was then. To Winifred the bridge still has a romantic, bridal aspect, suspended in mist and clouds over a wild Canadian river; but to Alexander it has a sinister dimension, for just as strong as the exaltation of love associated with the bridge is the foreboding of death. As the bridge which led Alexander to a successful future, it also led to the death of his spirit and imagination. The third bridge, the engineering feat at Moorlock, symbolizes in direct fashion Alexander's internal crisis and his defeat. Both the bridge and its creator are under a strain they cannot support. Because Alexander has succumbed to the temptations of his instinctual nature, the bridge, which was to have been the acme of his achievements, crumbles and destroys its negligent creator. The narrator, fusing the epic and romantic themes together, says in summary: "When a great man dies in his prime there is no surgeon who can say whether he did well; whether or not the future was his, as it seemed to be. The mind that society had come to regard as a powerful and reliable machine, dedicated to its service, may for a long time have been sick within itself and bent upon its own destruction" (p. 106).

The epilogue, in which Alexander is seen again through Professor Wilson's eyes, restores something of the epic perspective and gives the novel a symmetrical form. It also dramatizes vividly once more the nature of the division in Alexander's soul. Hilda Burgoyne, who promised Alexander the pleasures of recovered youth, mourns his loss with the resigned but empty feeling that " 'nothing can happen to [her] after Bartley' " (p. 112). But Winifred, whose love denoted Alexander's power and conquests in the world, finds that death permits her for the first time complete possession of her husband. She seems to recognize that death gave to her what life would have taken away; in her sorrow she is truly fulfilled. Professor Wilson tells Hilda (note the images) that as he and Winifred watched the sunset burn on the river, he realized that her mourning gave her " 'a fixed star to steer by' " (p. 110). When he was drowning beneath his crumbled bridge, Alexander felt his wife was there with him; (on the mythic level perhaps it reminds us that Paris-Alexander's wife, Oenone, was a water nymph). In actuality the workmen were dragging Alexander down in the water, but when he gave up his last breath he felt that his wife had finally let him go. His original feeling that death was coexistent with his love for Winifred (his dedication to power and success) is fulfilled in the image of his wife's death lock and by the final image of Winifred replete in sorrow.

After Willa Cather had completed *Alexander's Bridge* in the fall of 1911 she arranged for a leave of absence from *McClure's* and in the following months she wrote three long stories, all of which were set in Nebraska and were invested with an epic feeling for the land and the people of her childhood. The first of these stories to be published was "The Bohemian Girl"; on finishing it Willa Cather at once felt it was the best thing she had done.[8] The next two stories, "Alexandra" and "The White Mulberry Tree" (later woven together to form *O Pioneers!*), were written with the additional inspiration of a trip to Nebraska in the summer of 1912. The subject matter and form for all three stories was not "literary," as it had been with *Alexander's Bridge,* but came directly from the author's expriences in the West. Their special heroic feeling relates to what C. S. Lewis would designate as primary epic.

"The Bohemian Girl"[9] is actually a blending of several imaginative modes. In the foreground of the story is the *romance* between Nils Ericson and his brother's wife, Clara Vavrika, the Bohemian girl. Their illicit affair, however, in direct contrast to the innocent simplicity of pioneer life, is conducted in a spirit of *irony* and sophistication. At the same time, the story is for Nils a *pastoral* for it involves his return from a European city to the scenes of his country childhood and a revival of old memories. But the most powerful element in the story, in counterpoint to the witty, ironic love affair, is the *epic* backdrop with its great sweeping plains and hard-toiling pioneers.

As a love story "The Bohemian Girl" occupies a unique place in Willa Cather's fiction. The story is similar structurally to both "Eric Hermannson's Soul" and *O Pioneers!* in that it combines the love affair between a Scandinavian man and a girl of vital spirits (Marie Shabata in *O Pioneers!* is also a Bohemian like Clara Vavrika) with a profound feeling for the plains and the pioneers of the West. But whereas the attraction between Eric Hermannson and Margaret Elliot is a primitive sexual instinct and the romance of Emil and Marie in *O Pioneers!* is essentially childlike, the affair between Nils and Clara is a witty, sexual duel, opposing two clever, equally matched adults. Moreover, unlike the other pairs of lovers, they find happiness together in the end. (Other equally matched couples in Willa Cather's fiction who struggle for mastery either end hating each other, like the Treffingers in "The Marriage of Phaedra" and the comic-grotesque Wick Cutter of *My Ántonia,* or separating, like Don Hedger and Eden Bower in "Coming, Aphrodite!.") The special mark of the affair between Clara and Nils is the way in which pleasure is intimately allied, in the Keatsian manner, with pain. Clara, self-willed and discontented, is both a sexual temptress and a cruel mistress. On his return from Norway, Nils first sees her, a slender figure riding across the plain at dusk; when her horse shies she strikes the animal and curses in Bohemian. In free, rhythmical gallop she rides on and becomes silhouetted against the skyline. This powerful initial image of Clara which suggests both her attractiveness and her fiery nature is substantiated in the description of her at home the next morning. She is a dark beauty with "a touch of dull salmon red in her cheeks" and an Oriental slant to her eyes. Spoiled by her doting aunt, she is often sullen and bored, but when animated she becomes mocking and sarcastic. She is contemptuous of her husband and his family; her marriage to Nils's stolid older brother, Olaf, was motivated by her desire to spite Nils, who deserted her twelve years before. Her only pleasure in marriage is to taunt the Ericson family and flaunt her intellectual superiority over them. Nils says to her: " 'This is a perfect ferret fight here; you live by biting and being bitten.' " These images reflect the special temperament of the lovers in the story. Clara with her fiery eyes and riding whip is to Nils like a wild bird or a wild tune; but Nils himself is no sad, pale victim, rather he is every bit a match for her. In a playful bit of dialogue between Nils, Clara, and her father, Joe Vavrika, Nils insists on mastery in the battle of the sexes. When Joe asks Nils when he will marry, Clara interjects that perhaps he has not got enough to keep a wife:

> Nils looked at her coolly, raising one eyebrow. "Oh, I can keep her, all right."
>
> "The way she wants to be kept?"
>
> "With my wife I'll decide that," replied Nils calmly. "I'll give her what's good for her."
>
> Clara made a wry face. "You'll give her the strap, I expect, like old Peter Oleson gave his wife."
>
> "When she needs it," said Nils lazily, locking his hands behind his head and squinting up through the leaves of the cherry tree.

In the same mood he remembers squeezing cherry juice on Clara's clean dress when they were children and how they always fought and played together as equals.

Their teasing courtship becomes increasingly animated at Olaf's barn-raising. In high spirits Clara makes fun of all the Ericsons by playing the opening grand march, led by Olaf and his mother, with mock solemnity. In a playfully sarcastic mood, Nils in turn dances with all the homely Swedish girls. When they eventually dance together, Nils again reminds Clara that they were most in love with each other when they used to fight. He recalls to her how she would pinch: " 'Your fingers were like little nippers. A regular snapping turtle' "; and when she speculates on what kind of woman he will some day marry he replies: " 'She'll be a snapping turtle, and she'll be a match for me.' " When Nils finally persuades Clara to run off with him, his mastery of her is presented in an image of male sexuality that culminates the motif of erotic pain: "He kissed her slowly. He was a deliberate man, but his nerves were steel when he wanted anything. Something flashed out from him like a knife out of a sheath. Clara felt everything slipping away from her; she was flooded by the summer night." In this story pain is the acme of pleasure, the heightened accent in a dynamic sexual union.

The love affair between Nils Ericson and Clara Vavrika is played out against an epic backdrop of pioneer life. The background filled with so many simple, hard-working people gives appreciable depth to the ironic attitudes and the sophistication of the two lovers. But the author's fictive loyalties are not exclusively with her two engaging protagonists. The miles of great plain with its golden wheat and tin-roofed houses winking in the sun has a powerful imaginative pull. Nils feels it on his return (it makes him homesick), and even haughty Clara feels it when she must choose whether to remain or run away with Nils. The strong epic figure in the story is Nils's mother, Mrs. Ericson, mother of ten sons and nearly seventy, who still manages her land and drives one of the first automobiles in the country. The barn-raising supper and dance is the great epic scene in the story, with its rows of guests seated about the barn and tables laden with provisions. Again it is the old women especially who are seen in a heroic light.

> They were a fine company of old women, and a Dutch painter would have loved to find them there together, where the sun made bright patches on the floor and sent long, quivering shafts of gold through the dusky shade up among the rafters. There were fat, rosy old women . . . with brown, dark-veined hands; and several of almost heroic frame, not less massive than old Mrs. Ericson herself. Few of them wore glasses, and old Mrs. Svendsen, a Danish woman, who was quite bald, wore the only cap among them. Mrs. Oleson, who had twelve big grandchildren, could still show two braids of yellow hair as thick as her own wrists. Among all these grandmothers there were more brown heads than white. They all had a pleased, prosperous air, as if they were more than satisfied with themselves and with life.

Nils reflects on "the Herculean labors" their hands had performed —the cows they had milked, gardens planted, children tended, and mountains of food cooked.[10]

In the end Nils leaves with Clara for his shipping business in Norway, but imaginatively the decision to leave is not a simple one. Willa Cather gives us a final scene in the story in which Nils's younger brother, Eric, must choose between joining his brother in the old country or staying in Nebraska. After starting on his journey east, he goes back to the farm and the protective roof of his aging but stalwart mother. We cannot help feeling that his choice involves the author's deepest sympathies and emotional preference.

O Pioneers! and the Epic Imagination

When Willa Cather put together her novel *O Pioneers!* she was again working with materials taken directly from her own experience, so that if we continue to use the classification of C. S. Lewis the heroic qualities of the book are those of primary epic. The imagination in primary epic expresses itself in the creation of public myths. The artist articulates in his work his society's most fundamental and cherished values, giving voice to the quest and aspirations of a whole people. An epic is nationalistic for it makes its appeal to a whole people by defining a common enemy; consequently, it tends to be simplistic in terms of both the struggle it presents and the moral values it affirms. Primary epics generally appear in the earlier, more creative phases of a culture's development, at a time when the artist can most effectively participate in the growth of his country (or a popular new art form) by giving expression and endorsement to those values which are its source of strength and growth. The urge to be a vital part of the dynamic young American democracy informs all of Whitman's epic poetry. Similarly, it was in response both to a new society and to a new popular art form that Griffith and Eisenstein created their classic epics of the cinema.[11]

The focus in epic rests on the figure of the strong man or woman who defends the people and their values against forces which threaten chaos. Such a figure tends to be one-dimensional because the imagination responds to him largely in terms of his strength as a leader. Consider the larger-than-life but static characterizations of traditional epic heroes such as Odysseus, Beowulf, or Milton's Christ. Sometimes the artist embodies himself in his work in the form of a weaker figure needing the protection and guidance of the strong leader. This weaker figure may suggest a depth of character and a measure of inner conflict, but the epic hero himself seldom develops or changes. The struggle in which he is engaged serves finally only to heighten our admiration for his strength and moral virtue.

Because its appeal is to people of every class (but particularly the common man), epic is highly rhetorical and conventional in style. The fundamental human emotions expressed in epic are most effectively aroused by heavily rhythmic patterns and by set pieces which call forth a familiar and uncritical response. The concrete physical realism of epic also derives from this demand for the familiar and uncomplicated, while the catalogues and repetitive enumerations (the single image multiplied as in serried ranks of arms and warriors) fulfill a vision of the identity and equality of a united people. We have already seen an example of this aspect of the epic style in "The Bohemian Girl" where Willa Cather describes the great quantities of food prepared for the barn-raising dance and the rows of old pioneer women who had performed such "Herculean" labors during their lifetime. Finally, because epic evokes a simplistic response to life that suppresses all critical distinctions, its tone is humble and eulogistic and its vision (that of the people) is sentimental.

In writing about the settling of the Midwest in *O Pioneers!* Willa Cather chose her subject, as Melville had earlier, from the classical matter for American epic—the struggle of man against nature. As much as from revolution and civil war, America came into being and achieved its identity from the struggle of the common man to subdue the lonely and terrifying wilderness around him. Miss Cather herself apparently referred to the novel as a "two-part pastoral" (Alexandra's story and the romance of "The White Mulberry Tree"),[12] but doubtless she meant simply to indicate the rural subject of her book. For her novel eschews the return to childhood and self-analysis of pastoral writing; her focus is on the struggle of the earliest pioneer settlers of the prairie and on the embodiment of their most heroic gestures in the stalwart figure of Alexandra Bergson. That we respond to Alexandra as an epic heroine there can be little question. She is introduced to us in the first chapter as "a tall, strong girl" who "walked rapidly and resolutely, as if she knew exactly where she was going and what she was going to do next" (p. 6).[13] Her character and her role are defined early in the novel when her dying father turns over the responsibility of the farm and the family to his daughter rather than to his two grown sons. Alexandra is not only strong in body (at one point she is described as "Amazonian"), but also her father recognizes in her a strength of will and dependability which are wanting in his sons. That initial image of Alexandra taking up the heavy burden of a man's life does not change during the course of the novel; eventually Alexandra becomes the most successful landowner on the Divide, and in effect the leader of the Swedish pioneer community.

Epic focuses on the struggle of a people against a hostile force —here it is the "Genius" of the land, a force unfriendly to man, "like a horse that no one knows how to break to harness, that runs wild and kicks things to pieces" (p. 22). Those with some imagination sense that "the land wanted to be let alone, to preserve its own fierce strength, its peculiar, savage kind of beauty, its uninterrupted mournfulness" (p. 15). But from the beginning Alexandra is resolute in her determination to prevail over the wild country. She promises her father on his death bed that she will never lose the land, and she not only suffers through the harshness of its seasons, but through three long years of drouth and failure. Many families give up and move away, but Alexandra endures and ultimately triumphs, for those years were "the last struggle of a wild soil against the encroaching plowshare" (p. 47). Because Alexandra's vision is to do something big, the landscape and the heroine begin to merge in identification and purpose. Riding across the prairie she reflects on how beautiful, rich, and strong the land seems: "Her eyes drank in the breadth of it, until her tears blinded her. Then the Genius of the Divide, the great, free spirit which breathes across it, must have bent lower than it ever bent to a human will before" (p. 65). Later that same day she resolves to stay on in spite of the drouth and her brothers' wish to move down by the river, realizing that her own destiny is one with that of the land.

While Alexandra as a woman is a particularized character, her struggle to prevail over the landscape and prepare the way for generations to come is representative of the race of early pioneers who settled the American prairie. Our attention is frequently directed in the epic manner to the activities of a whole people. In the prefatory poem, "Prairie Spring," the labors of the pioneers are described in the "miles of fresh-plowed soil," and in "The growing wheat, the growing weeds, / The toiling horses, the tired men." In the first chapter of the novel, despite its particular concerns, we are made aware from the continual reference to people in the background of the typicality of the scene and of the concerns that the people hold in common: "The farm people were making preparations to start for home. The women were checking over their groceries and pinning their big red shawls about their heads. The men were buying tobacco and candy with what money they had left, were showing each other new boots and gloves and blue flannel shirts" (p. 13). When Part II begins we see the fruit of their labors not just in the Bergson farm, but throughout the countryside:

> From the Norwegian graveyard one looks out over a vast checkerboard, marked off in squares of wheat and corn; light and dark, dark and light. Telephone wires hum along the white roads, which always run at right angles. From the graveyard gate one can count a dozen gayly painted farmhouses; the gilded weather-vanes on the big red barns wink at each other across the green and brown and yellow fields. The light steel windmills tremble throughout their frames and tug at their moorings. [P. 75]

We are reminded of the movements of a whole people in those conventional set pieces (the French church fair, the grain harvesting, the great confirmation service, the mourning of the people for Amédée Chevalier), which expand the novel's focus to include those joys and sorrows which are communal. A visually striking epic sequence (the single image multipled) describes the cavalcade of forty French boys riding across the plains to meet the bishop; it is charged with the extremes of fundamental human emotions, the ecstatic zeal of high animal spirits tempered by the somber fact of a young friend's death. But always in the foreground remains the figure of Alexandra whose valor and foresight embody the essence of the heroic spirit.

As epic heroine Alexandra's character never changes—her strength of purpose, her dependability and kindness, are constant throughout. We are told that "her mind was slow, truthful, steadfast" (p. 61) and that she was without cleverness, perhaps like the heroic figures of the "Frithjof Saga," an old Swedish legend she has in part committed to memory. She is a woman who feels deeply (she is not without tears in her eyes at moments of crisis), but not one who can show or express her feelings very freely. Moreover, she is always able to control her emotions and proceed with the business of everyday life. When old Ivar finds her alone in the graveyard in the rain she reassures him immediately that everything is all right: " '*Tyst*! Ivar. There's nothing to be worried about. I'm sorry if I've scared you all' " (p. 280). But consequently

Alexandra is essentially a flat, one-dimensional character. While she suffers through many disappointments and losses (most agonizing is the death of Emil and Marie), there is never any question as to how she will respond; her character is constant and predictable. It is to Alexandra that everyone else turns with his or her troubles: she protects the old people like Crazy Ivar and Mrs. Lee from the indifference of youth; she advises her family and neighbors in their struggles to tame the wild land; she gives guidance and love to the younger people around her—the Swedish working girls from the old country, Emil and Marie, and her brothers' children. Her strength and compassion are such that she instinctively forgives Frank Shabata, who has destroyed almost everything she has loved. In the courtroom "her heart had grieved for him" (p. 285) and at the novel's close she goes to Lincoln to see what she can do to lighten his punishment.

Alexandra wears a man's coat, but ultimately it is the maternal protection of a strong woman that she offers to those around her; and it is this quality—that of a larger-than-life mother figure—that is at the heart of the imaginative conception of her character. Alexandra is one-dimensional because as epic heroine she is idealized, and accordingly we can feel only a limited sense of identification with her. Her sorrows and her triumphs are those of someone stronger than we are. We hold her strength and virtue in high esteem and yet we cannot really share or emulate them. Rather our imaginative involvement is with that maternal protection she affords those around her.[14]

In a work of the epic imagination the artist does not necessarily appear within the story. It is in the pastoral mode (in a book like *My Ántonia*) that the artist assumes the role of both creator and central figure in his art because the urge to create in pastoral is born out of a desire to understand oneself and one's past experiences more fully. That need for understanding (an understanding which ideally will lead to more satisfying forms of experience in the present) is evaded in epic by the unquestioning acceptance of other men's values and by seeing internal conflict in the form of physical or cosmic moral struggle. In becoming the spokesman for the people the epic artist eliminates his own responses and assumes a sentimental, humble point of view, one which affirms the traditional values of human experience without question. There is no pervasive humor or irony in epic because a comic response involves a critical judgment, an opposition of values which would fracture the vision of social unity. The perspective which controls the narration of *O Pioneers!* is a humble one which threatens to lapse into the maudlin, but at the same time this sentimental perspective is the source of the novel's peculiar effectiveness, for it is this point of view which bathes the humble subjects of the book and the simple facts of their lives in an enduring warmth and affection. Such a viewpoint was the means by which Miss Cather was most fully able to transmit her deep sympathy for the figures of her personal past, her almost childlike love and admiration for their humble, faithful lives.

The artist may not dramatize himself overtly in an epic, but in the manner of narration and in some of the lesser characters he invariably projects something of his intimate involvement into the story. In *O Pioneers!* the figure who most closely approximates the artist is Carl Linstrum, Alexandra's childhood neighbor and faithful admirer. Linstrum is the weak, sensitive, artistic man, ill-suited to the life of a pioneer. We first see him when he is a boy of fifteen looking through a portfolio of chromo "studies" at the drug store, and later we learn that he does water colors and owns a magic lantern. In his failure to find a meaningful or satisfying life, he anticipates the dilemma of several of Willa Cather's disillusioned and peripatetic protagonists.[15] He leaves the Divide to become an engraver in the East, but he never settles anywhere for long. There is little romance in this novel associated with people and places far away (the one exception is the "old country" which is an extension emotionally of home) and when Carl visits Alexandra on his way through to Alaska he leaves no illusions about the artist's life: " 'We have no house, no place, no people of our own. We live in the streets, in the parks, in the theatres. We sit in restaurants and concert halls and look about at the hundreds of our own kind and shudder' " (p. 123). One cannot help but catch a glimpse here of Willa Cather herself—the writer living in eastern cities making annual pilgrimages to her home in Nebraska. The emotion out of which the novel has been created, and which is focused in Carl's point of view, stems from that desire to return "home" to the heartland of America and to those strong, heroic figures, the pioneers.

The emotional quest to be reunited with the strong parental figures of the past describes something of Carl's relationship to Alexandra. Slight and narrow-chested, he is physically the opposite of his old friend; moreover, he is five years younger than she is. His strongest memory of Alexandra focuses significantly on an image suggesting maternal purity, one which seems to lie at the imaginative center of the book:

> There he sat down and waited for the sun to rise. It was just there that he and Alexandra used to do their milking together, he on his side of the fence, she on hers. He could remember exactly how she looked when she came over the close-cropped grass, her skirts pinned up, her head bare, a bright tin pail in either hand, and the milky light of the early morning all about her. Even as a boy he used to feel, when he saw her coming with her free step, her upright head and calm shoulders, that she looked as if she had walked straight out of the morning itself. Since then, when he had happened to see the sun come up in the country or on the water, he had often remembered the young Swedish girl and her milking pails. [P. 126]

The final marriage between Carl and Alexandra has something of a wish fulfillment quality about it—the wish perhaps of being united with the eternal mother. For Alexandra it is the attraction a strong woman sometimes feels for a weak, biddable man. The only lover mightier than Alexandra herself is the man of her dreams, a figure identified with the harvests and the seasons who, toward the end of the novel, is revealed to be the personification of Death.[16]

In any work of art certain images stand out more than others and remain fixed in our memory—these images have clearly involved the imagination of the artist most deeply. In *O Pioneers!* the image of Alexandra Bergson taking up the heroic task of cultivating the stubborn soil is at the center of our response to the novel —that epic response being reinforced by the Whitman poem of the book's title, with its eulogy to those who have conquered the wild country. Our sense of Alexandra's heroic stature is greatly enhanced by a number of visual images, like Carl's memory of her at dawn, in which her figure is adorned with light and radiates calm strength. When her father is dying and makes her his chief heir, she comes to him, a tall figure with the light of a lamp behind her. When she is working on the farm, the braids of reddish-gold hair about her head burn in the sunlight (the image suggests a gleaming Germanic helmet) and the fiery ends of hair make her head look like a big sunflower. In the sunlight of Marie's garden she is described as "the Swedish woman so white and gold, kindly and amused, but armored in calm" (p. 135).

But almost equally as engaging as Alexandra is the image of the garden, the enclosed, safe place, which is most fully dramatized in Marie Shabata's orchard with its protective mulberry hedge. The expansion of the novel by developing the love story (Miss Cather clearly felt Alexandra's story was not dramatic enough) may seem a gratuitous and unconvincing digression from the central theme of Alexandra and the land. And yet the image of the garden is as integral a part of the novel's imaginative structure as the figure of its stalwart heroine because it is that desire for an enclosed retreat, with its guarantee of maternal protection, which draws the imagination in this novel to its epic heroine. Significantly, Miss Cather dedicated *O Pioneers!* to the memory of Sarah Orne Jewett, a writer whose work was similarly motivated by a search for a green, protected place—realized fictionally in *The Country of the Pointed Firs,* with its half-forgotten village of Dunnet Landing presided over by the maternal, sybillike figure of the herb-gatherer, Mrs. Todd. Much of our instinctive pleasure in reading *O Pioneers!* must derive from our sharing in that wish to find a sheltered place, a refuge carved out of a hostile terrain. Mrs. Bergson's house and garden in which she tries to retain the order and routine of her life in the old country is an image of such a refuge maintained against formidable odds. Her garden survives the long drouth because of the water she carries to the plants despite the prohibition of her sons. Part III of the novel, "Winter Memories," is conceived of almost entirely as a kind of refuge—as an image of physical refuge against the cold of winter, and as an emotional refuge for those women whose men are far away. In one sequence Alexandra takes old Mrs. Lee for an afternoon's visit with Marie Shabata; the fuchsias and geraniums in bloom on the window sill, the coffee and sweet cakes, the exchange of crochet patterns are all redolent of the cozy domesticity of women together. Although Emil is in Mexico and Carl in the Far North, the scene is imaginatively complete, as the refuge desired is a maternal and innocent one.

The story of the lovers is at first wholly romantic and idealized. The idyllic description of the orchard after the rain (with its ripe cherries, its fragrant wild roses, the waving fields of ripening grain outside the hedge) and the description of the young lovers themselves (Emil with his scythe and Marie with the sparkling light in her playful brown eyes) are suggestive of the conventions of medieval art—like scenes from a "book of hours" or the sad, poignant "lais" of Marie de France. But their love is illicit and when Marie's garden becomes a place of erotic fulfillment it is destroyed because the epic vision which prevails, with its apotheosis in the "mother country," is maternal and innocent. The marriage between Carl and Alexandra will fulfill an old friendship rather than sexual passion; that way Alexandra feels they will be "safe."

Earlier in the novel when Carl comes back to the Divide and views what Alexandra and his old neighbors have made out of the land, he says: " 'Isn't it queer: there are only two or three human stories, and they go on repeating themselves as fiercely as if they had never happened before' " (p. 119). The two stories woven together in *O Pioneers!* stretch back to Genesis. Alexandra's is the story of creation, the story of a human civilization being shaped out of a land as flat and formless as the sea. Emil and Marie's is the story of lovers cast from the earth's garden through sin. The timeless, ever-recurring nature of these stories is secured by literary allusion. Alexandra's heroic character and actions are enriched by her connection with the old Swedish legends. Emil and Marie's story acquires a universal pathos by its association with classical tales of lovers who die. When old Ivar comes to the despoiled orchard at dawn he sees two white butterflies fluttering over the dead bodies, like metamorphosed lovers in Ovid's tales. The staining of the white mulberries with the lovers' blood recalls specifically the story of Pyramus and Thisbe. While their romance is still innocent Marie tells Emil of her love for the trees in her orchard and of the old Bohemian belief in the power of the linden's virtue to purify the forest. The innocent, domestic love of Baucis and Philemon is perhaps remembered here, for those faithful lovers, wishing to die together, were changed into trees, an oak and a linden. And there is a suggestion of the Endymion story when Marie resolves in the moonlight that to dream of her love will henceforward be enough.[17] The two stories of the novel are brought together in a nexus of creation and destruction as Ivar repeats to himself Psalm 101 from the Bible, a song of "mercy and judgment" in which the psalmist promises to remember the faithful of the land and to destroy all wicked doers.

In terms of the novel's epic theme—and it is the epic note which prevails at the end—the death of the lovers is necessary to give Alexandra's story a tragic depth and to allow her old antagonist, nature, to reassert its power. Marie's garden represents that order of life that Alexandra has worked so arduously to create out of the uncultivated landscape. Alexandra thinks of her struggle on the Divide as ensuring a better life for her brother, her "boy"; she loves both Emil and Marie, and without looking ahead to the possible consequences she encourages their friendship, much as if they were still young children. Their death gives Alexandra's life a tragic quality because they represent essentially everything for which she has lived and fought. At the novel's close she consents to marry Carl and yet it is the land which still has possession of her. Carl agrees that they must come back to the Divide after they are married: " 'You belong to the land,' Carl murmured, 'as you have always said. Now more than ever' " (p. 307). Alexandra, looking out over the great plains under an autumn sunset, concedes that in their struggle with the land there has been only a truce, that it is she who will ultimately be the one possessed: " 'We come and go, but the land is always here. And the people who love it and understand it are the people who own it—for a little while' " (p. 308). However, there is a sober triumph in the novel's conclusion, for here the epic view of nature as universal foe gives way to a cyclical and reassuring vision of mutability, and here the author can express once more those feelings of love and admiration for her heroine and for her people:

> They went into the house together, leaving the Divide behind them, under the evening star. Fortunate country, that is one day to receive hearts like Alexandra's into its bosom, to give them out again in the yellow wheat, in the rustling corn, in the shining eyes of youth! [P. 309]

Notes

1. For information about Willa Cather's life see any of the following biographical works: Mildred R. Bennett, *The World of Willa Cather* (New York: Dodd, Mead and Co., 1951; revised with notes and an index and reissued as a Bison Book, Lincoln: University of Nebraska Press, 1961);

E. K. Brown, completed by Leon Edel, *Willa Cather: A Critical Biography* (New York: Alfred A. Knopf, 1953); Edith Lewis, *Willa Cather Living: A Personal Record* (New York: Alfred A. Knopf, 1953); Elizabeth Shepley Sergeant, *Willa Cather: A Memoir* (Philadelphia: J. B. Lippincott, 1953; reissued with a new foreword and an index as a Bison Book, Lincoln: University of Nebraska Press, 1963); James Woodress, *Willa Cather: Her Life and Art* (New York: Pegasus, 1970; reissued as a Bison Book, Lincoln: University of Nebraska Press, 1974).

2. *Willa Cather's Collected Short Fiction, 1892–1912,* edited by Virginia Faulkner, with an introduction by Mildred R. Bennett, rev. ed. (Lincoln: University of Nebraska Press, 1970), pp. 359–79. Hereafter cited as *CSF.* Page numbers will be given in the text for quotations from the novels but not for quotations from the short stories.

3. See the [Lincoln, Nebraska] *Courier,* November 2, 1895, p. 6; collected in *The Kingdom of Art: Willa Cather's First Principles and Critical Statements, 1893–1896,* selected and edited with two essays and a commentary by Bernice Slote (Lincoln: University of Nebraska Press, 1966), p. 232. Hereafter cited as *KA.*

4. "My First Novels," *Willa Cather on Writing* (New York: Alfred A. Knopf, 1949), pp. 91 ff.

5. *Alexander's Bridge* (1922 edition with preface; New York: Bantam Books, 1962), pp. v–viii. All quotations from the novel are also from this text.

6. C. S. Lewis, *A Preface to Paradise Lost* (New York: Oxford University Press, 1961).

7. Lewis, *Willa Cather Living,* p. 78.

8. Unpublished letter to Zoë Akins, March 1912 (Huntington Library, San Marino, California).

9. *CSF,* pp. 3–41.

10. In keeping with the epic and mythic design of the story is Bernice Slote's suggestion that the central characters incorporate elements of pagan deities from a tale in Virgil's *Georgics* (3. 393–96). Ruddy-faced Nils, carrying a flute, reminds us of Pan, who lures away Diana, the moon goddess, to be his love. Clara, the huntress at night, suggests Diana; and her father, who keeps a jolly tavern, suggests Bacchus. See *KA,* p. 101.

11. Of course no imaginative response is ever limited to one time or place; the epic imagination with its vision of a people united in purpose under a strong leader is always a possible response in art. For example, the struggles and hardships of large numbers of people during the 1930s Depression created the need for an epic voice; that need was fulfilled by such diverse works of the imagination as John Steinbeck's populist novel, *The Grapes of Wrath,* and Leni Riefenstahl's *Triumph of the Will,* a cinematic adulation of Hitler as the strong man and of National Socialism. A modern example of a literary epic would be Ezra Pound's *Cantos,* which constitutes an artist's quest through history and literature for the type of leader who is both a strong warrior and a cultural hero.

12. See Sergeant, *Willa Cather: A Memoir,* p. 11.

13. All quotations are from the Sentry edition of *O Pioneers!* (Boston: Houghton Mifflin, 1962).

14. The question of "identification" between the reader and a fictional character is always a thorny one, for it depends on the reader's particular nature. For the artist there is a degree of imaginative involvement possible with the epic protagonist because, like the artist, he is a figure set apart from other men and his values are those of individual creativity. But the epic hero lives in the world of action whereas the artist and (presumably) his readers are essentially reflective and passive. Any further identifications must therefore confuse art and life.

15. Josephine Lurie Jessup in *The Faith of Our Feminists* (New York: R. R. Smith, 1950) sees Willa Cather viewing the men of her novels "through the eyes of a kindly tutor or warm-hearted elder sister" (p. 54). To Mrs. Jessup this explains not only the strength of the Cather heroines but the sympathetic attitude toward the essentially emasculated heroes as well. Mrs. Jessup, however, ignores the fact of the central consciousness or point of view which in many of Willa Cather's novels is a masculine one. Characters like Alexandra and Ántonia are viewed through the eyes of men whose admiration and love for these women is not fully consummated. Mrs. Jessup's thesis leads her to make some unfortunate esthetic judgments. In her feminist ardor she says that Jim Burden of *My Ántonia* "contributes nothing to the action and his point of view as spectator could be spared" (p. 60). But this is to ask for a different book from the one Willa Cather has written, because in *My Ántonia* Jim Burden is the central figure and his consciousness defines the world of the novel.

16. In her reading of Willa Cather's novels Dorothy Van Ghent identifies the dream lover as a kind of vegetation and weather god whose divinity is the principle of the unconscious. See Dorothy Van Ghent, *Willa Cather,* University of Minnesota Pamphlets on American Writers (Minneapolis: University of Minnesota Press, 1964), pp. 16–18. Mrs. Van Ghent's suggestion here is very helpful, for at the novel's close death and the land are identified as one in a vision of cyclical mutability. Though Carl is to marry Alexandra, they both recognize that it is the land which truly possesses her. See also Sister Peter Damian Charles, P. O., "Love and Death in Willa Cather's *O Pioneers!,*" *CLA Journal* (December 1965): 140–50.

17. Since Willa Cather was a classicist at university, it is not unlikely that other Ovidian stories of lovers came to her mind as well as that of Pyramus and Thisbe.

CHAPTER TWO

Pastoral

The Pastoral Imagination

In pastoral the imagination counters the failures of the present by moving back into the past. In recovering lost time the artist may seek to recapture a world of childhood innocence, or he may attempt to resolve the conflicts in his past experiences which have prevented him from living meaningfully in the present. In either case the term pastoral here signifies not just a rural subject, but a mode of art based on memory. Pastoral, in keeping with its classical etymology, has been a term in literary criticism applied to works of art with a bucolic setting. William Empson, however, in *Some Versions of Pastoral* expanded the term to indicate the proletarian cause in works of literature that present the dialectic of class struggle. Moving in the opposite direction, I have taken as the common denominator in pastoral the idea of retreat from society, and have expanded the term on a psychological basis to denote the artist's withdrawal into himself and into the imaginative realm of memory.

In its simplest form a pastoral of innocence marks a retreat in time and place to an enclosed, green world, a retreat expressing man's dream of a simplified, harmonious existence from which the complexities of society and natural process (age, disease, and death) are eliminated.[1] Mythically, pastoral seeks to recover a "Golden Age" when existence was ideally ordered and there was no conscious separation of self from the rest of the world—no separation of subject and object, all things sharing an identity of order and purpose. Wordsworth gives powerful expression to the dream of pastoral innocence in "Tintern Abbey" when he discovers in nature a principle of unity that informs "all thinking things, all objects of all thought," and is the source and nurse of his moral being. The pastoral landscape is ultimately a place of innocent erotic fulfillment wherein the imagination is reunited to the world in a maternal embrace.

A pastoral of experience is more complex: while it embodies the adult's escapist desire to return to childhood, it also recognizes that the past was not the perfectly secure and ordered world that it appears to be in retrospect. A pastoral of experience inevitably moves toward that point of recognition where the past is revealed as a time of rejection and failure, a time of anxiety rather than perfect happiness. The outrage committed by the past on the present is writ large in Faulkner's novels, where the myth of a more perfect past—the ante-bellum South—is exposed as an illusion and a lie. In a pastoral of innocence the imagination evades crisis and awareness, but in a pastoral of experience the imagination is caught up in conflict again and brought to a point of recognition and acceptance.

Pastoral is constantly preoccupied with the arresting of time, for its passage moves the adult farther away from childhood and innocence. Images of time reflect the protagonist's deepest anxieties and his despair. The extent to which he is reconciled to the fact of mutability measures the degree of awareness and acceptance achieved. Sexual awakening marks the end of childhood, so that in a pastoral of innocence the imagination also attempts to exclude sexuality. In a pastoral of experience, however, it cannot be evaded because it is the failure of sexual initiation which ties the imagination to the past.

Because it is highly subjective, pastoral art is impressionistic in style. Nostalgia is most effectively evoked by a nondramatic, allusive style which charges the subject (and thereby reshapes it) with the artist's emotions: vague outline in painting, lyrical description in literature, the dissolve and soft lens of the camera. The style of pastoral art is also highly selective, for in recapturing the past the artist seeks to evoke certain emotions and exclude others. Although its application is general, Willa Cather's dictum for the unfurnished novel provides a fitting description of the pastoral style. In her essay "The Novel Démeublé," she asserts that high quality in art derives from what is suggested rather than from what is described in detail, from "whatever is felt upon the page without being specifically named there." Realistic detail only assumes an esthetic dimension for Miss Cather when it is subsumed within the "emotional penumbra of the characters themselves."[2] Because pastoral is a wholly subjective art, it can be realized only through a style which places value, not on the details themselves, but on the emotion which they inspire.

Early Stories and *April Twilights*

Willa Cather's imagination was varied in its responses from the outset. In her early pieces of fiction she explored the different imaginative modes through which her later writing moved in more clearly discernible phases. In "Eric Hermannson's Soul" we find the primitive emotions of epic, in "The Treasure of Far Island" the nostalgia of pastoral, and in "The Sculptor's Funeral" the bitter reflections of satire. In one very early story, "The Burglar's Christmas," we even find the theme of filial waywardness which was to become a preoccupation in some of her last writings. Many of the stories and novels represent a blending of modes: the emotions of epic and pastoral are inextricably intertwined in "The Bohemian Girl" and *O Pioneers!* But the mode to which Willa Cather repeatedly returned and which informs to some degree almost all of her fiction is the pastoral, because most of her art was grounded in memory and autobiographical in impulse.

The earliest stories, many of them scarcely more than sketches, are pastorals similar in feeling to Wordsworth's poems about poor beggars and cottage dwellers. Willa Cather's poor country folk are European immigrants on the American plains, but, like Wordsworth, she identifies imaginatively with the humbleness and loneliness of their lives. "Peter" (1892), "Lou, the Prophet" (1892), "The Clemency of the Court" (1893), and "On the Divide" (1896) are all tales motivated by the author's sympathy for the downtrodden social misfit. These tales are pastorals not because of their rural setting, but because they project psychologically the author's imaginative retreat from the world of her contemporaries. Like Wordsworth's old shepherd, Michael, or his Cumberland beggar, the characters in these stories are not the artist's equals in society, but reflect instead her image of self-worth and dramatize feelings of homesickness and failure. The sensitive Peter (an early version of Mr. Shimerda in *My Ántonia*), suffocated by material concerns and by homesickness for Prague, commits suicide; Lou, a homesick Dane, finds release in mystical visions and preaching until he eventually disappears from the countryside; Serge Povolitchky ("The Clemency of the Court") is a motherless Russian boy who dies in prison after murdering the man who killed his dog. Only Canute Canuteson, the gloomy Norwegian in "On the Divide," finally overcomes his despair and with a new bride looks forward to the future. These stories with their numerous cultural allusions seem like folk tales, but the classification is not accurate: no matter how crude or simple, they are the product of an individual imagination rather than a group.

Some of the earliest stories are very crude psychological tales which dramatize vividly the mechanisms of the artist's psyche. These tales may be loosely termed pastorals for, although they do not deal directly with either a rural landscape or childhood, they embody certain psychological preoccupations which are obsessive and which do have their origins in childhood. The crudest and most painful of these stories is "The Clemency of the Court,"[3] mentioned above. Here the author identifies imaginatively with the plight of a Russian boy who is brutalized by the prairie environment. His own mother being dead, he is told that the State is his mother and will look after him. But after killing his master in a moment of desperation, he is sentenced to life imprisonment and is slowly tortured to death in his cell. Serge is an innocent, and the sympathy we feel for him is that for a child searching for its mother, always a central imaginative preoccupation in Willa Cather's fiction and, broadly speaking, of pastoral art as a whole. (We might note here that Willa Cather's orphans are numerous, especially protagonists whose mothers are dead. They include Jim Burden, Don Hedger, Niel Herbert, Tom Outland, Myra Henshawe, Cécile Auclair, Lucy Gayheart, to mention only major figures. The orphan is more than a romantic convention in Willa Cather's fiction; it suggests a psychological state central to her art.)

In "The Elopement of Allen Poole" (1893)[4] we find a crude dramatizing of another psychological state—the inevitable frustration of erotic experience. The hero of this tale, set in the Virginia of Miss Cather's earliest childhood, plans to elope with his sweetheart, but he is shot by her relations and only when he is dead does he spend the night with her. Nelly comes to him through the woods "like a little Madonna of the hills," and as he is dying we are told that "she rocked herself over him as a mother does over a little baby that is in pain," like an image of the *Pietà.* The lover identified as a mother figure and the fulfillment of such love through death are persistent preoccupations of pastoral. "The Burglar's Christmas" (1896)[5] with its Kafkaesque night setting and dreamlike coincidence is a more sophisticated treatment of the mother-child relationship. A destitute young man is about to rob a wealthy house when he discovers that it is his parents' home. He is reunited with his loving mother in a scene of heightened erotic wish-fulfillment: "She leaned over and kissed him, as no woman had kissed him since he left her." The young man is filled with remorse at having deserted her years before, a theme to appear in Willa Cather's last books, but we leave him with "the assurance of safety in that warm bosom that rose and fell under his cheek."

Willa Cather's first book was a collection of poems entitled *April Twilights,* published in 1903.[6] Like so many of her early stories these poems are written in the pastoral mode, expressing despair with the present and nostalgia for the past. The feeling which pervades the whole collection, more pronounced in some poems than others, is that of youthful insecurity and self-doubt —the hesitation of a university graduate going out into the world. The past, both literary and personal, provides a temporal escape from the dilemma of the present, but at the same time its irrecoverable and anxiety-ridden aspects urge more keenly the necessity of going forward into the future. These conflicting emotions are suggested in the title of the collection: April is the spring and the time for setting forth, but twilight suggests death and the reverting back to winter. The poems weave together what T. S. Eliot would describe as "memory and desire" with no sure movement in either direction, since the past can never be recaptured and the future for the artist is overshadowed by a conviction of certain failure.

The poems divide into two kinds: literary and personal. Just as the author's first novel, *Alexander's Bridge,* is characterized by a literary quality, so most of the poems in *April Twilights* reflect their source of inspiration in poetic models. In form and manner many of the poems are conventional and imitative: one hears the melodious romanticism of Hugo, Musset, Verlaine, and their English counterparts in Tennyson, Kipling, and Stevenson. Even more frequently one hears echoed the elegiac sadness of A. E. Housman, whose collection of pastorals, *A Shropshire Lad,* was probably Willa Cather's greatest enthusiasm at the time she was writing the poetry in this collection. The poem "Lament for Marsyas" is modeled closely on Housman's elegy "To an Athlete Dying Young," and another poem, "In Media Vita" with its celebration of life undercut by the repeated phrase, "And the dead, under all," echoes several of Housman's lyrics about life's transience. The literary world of antiquity—Arcadia—provides a retreat in time and place for the poet, but she is aware that classical pastoral is also preoccupied with mutability: *et in Arcadia ego.* The invoking of Arcadia in several of the poems produces nostalgia for the golden age that has passed with its heroes and lovers. In "Winter at Delphi" the poet knows that life will be renewed in the spring but that "Apollo, the god, Apollo" will not return; and in "Arcadian Winter" the shepherd lads now have silver hair and the maids are no longer fair. The alternate theme in the collection—the artist's sense of failure in the present—is also explored in poems of formal, literary inspiration. Poems such as "The Encore," "Song," "Sleep, Minstrel, Sleep" and "The Poor Minstrel" evoke pity for the artist—his suffering for an unrequited love, his early death. The poet is identified as a troubadour or minstrel, and in a traditional "L'Envoi" we are told that only "Loneliness" remains faithful to the poet to the end.

The poems of greatest interest and literary value, not surprisingly, are those which derive from the author's personal past, fusing together the two themes of nostalgia and the artist's suffering. In its imagery and rhythm " 'Grandmither, Think Not I Forget' " gives moving expression to a complex set of feelings. On the one hand, there is the poet's love for her grandmother, which becomes nostalgia for childhood and the protection of the old woman who is dead. On the other, there is the poet's sense of guilt and unworthiness: she wonders that the grandmother could have "loved the lassie so" and accordingly castigates herself for not coming more often to visit her grandmother's "bed beneath the thyme." The poet's nostalgia and feelings of guilt are occasioned by her failure as a lover. Her rejection in love sends her thoughts back to the old woman who cared for her, and the poem concludes with a death wish: "So when I plant the rose an' rue above your grave for ye, / Ye'll know it's under rue an' rose that I would like to be." The death wish here is a sober variation on the pastoral dream of being reunited to the world in a maternal embrace. The emotions explored in the poem reappear in the novels (Claude Wheeler in *One of Ours,* rejected by his wife on their wedding night, thinks of his mother and poor Mahailey at their work) and find consummate expression in the short story "Old Mrs. Harris," a tragic tale about the same grandmother, written nearly thirty years later. In "The Namesake" similar feelings are evoked: although here the poet assumes a masculine identity and likens herself to an uncle "with hair like mine" who died as a youth in the Civil War, the affinity with the uncle is based on the idea that he was rejected in love and rests in a lonely grave far from home. The conflict of emotions in the whole collection is underscored in this poem. In the next-to-last stanza the poet says to the dead uncle, "I'd leave my girl to share / Your still bed of glory there," but in the last stanza reconsiders and promises to "be winner at the game / Enough for two who bore the name." The ambivalent feelings of an April twilight—the excitement of going forth to conquer, the self-doubt and desire to retreat into the past—are carefully delineated in the blank verse "Dedicatory." The poem is addressed to the poet's brothers, Roscoe and Douglass Cather, who with their older sister "lay and planned at moonrise, / On an island in a western river, / Of the conquest of the world together." Their dream of a summer morning odyssey, however, is undercut by the April night of the poem, for twilight is a time of memory; moreover, the "somewhere, sometime" of the poem's first line is childhood and the past.

To the contemporary sensibility the short poem "Prairie Dawn" is perhaps the most effective piece in the collection. In eight chiseled lines of blank verse the author has rendered the essence of an emotion; as in the other poems it is that confused feeling of setting forth at dawn and at the same time relapsing into homesickness.

A crimson fire that vanquishes the stars;
A pungent odor from the dusty sage;
A sudden stirring of the huddled herds;
A breaking of the distant table-lands
Through purple mists ascending, and the flare
Of water ditches silver in the light;
A swift, bright lance hurled low across the world;
A sudden sickness for the hills of home.

The technique of seven exact lines of description in apposition to a concluding statement of feeling is not unlike the Japanese haiku, which Ezra Pound later introduced into the mainstream of English and American poetry. It is interesting that in this early poem the West represents the epic challenge of going forward, the odyssey of conquering, while pastoral emotion, as in "The Namesake," is associated with Virginia—"the hills of home." In the 1923 and 1933 editions of *April Twilights* the new poems, which are all related to personal rather than literary experience, identify the pastoral landscape as Nebraska. Homesickness, which is a persistent emotion throughout Willa Cather's writing, is expressed in "Macon Prairie" as a love for pioneer ancestors, and in "Going Home" the emotion is dissipated only when the narrator crosses the Missouri on the train going west—"the sharp curves and winding left behind." The feeling of homesickness is probably strongest in the last poem added to the collection, "Poor Marty," a lament by a fellow servant on the death of the kitchenmaid. The old woman was fashioned after the Cather family servant, Marjorie Anderson, who was also the model for Mahailey in *One of Ours* and Mandy in "Old Mrs. Harris." The tensions of her daily round are recorded in the first section; in the second section remorse is evoked by the memory of the thoughtless summons sent to the old servant the morning she died. As in the first poem of the original collection, " 'Grandmither, Think Not I Forget,' " nostalgia is identified with pathos and remorse.

Willa Cather first approached the themes and special qualities of her pastoral novels in two short stories, "The Treasure of Far Island" (1902) and "The Enchanted Bluff" (1909). "The Treasure of Far Island"[7] is an essential story in the Cather canon, for it embodies in both emotion and dramatic incident the substance of the author's imaginative life which gave shape to the major novels.

In this tale a famous dramatist returns to his home in Nebraska to recapture something of his childhood. Margie, his old playmate, says to him that geniuses never grow up, and in her ironic and "adult" mood she calls him " 'a case of arrested development.' " They go out to "Far Island" together, the scene of their childhood play fantasies, and not only does Douglass experience a thrill that surpasses a first night in the theatre, but Margie herself becomes a completely natural and spontaneous woman again. Childhood is seen as the perfect state. The same idea is central to another story from this period, "Jack-A-Boy" (1901), wherein a child, like Wordsworth's "Lucy," dies and escapes the inevitable disillusionment of the passing years, while the artist is left to reflect on the child's "divinity" in contrast with his own sad mortality. "The Treasure of Far Island" is an important story; but pastoral art achieves its effect through suggestion and the story suffers esthetically from being overexplicit. For example, when Douglass and Margie dig up a treasure box they had buried years ago, Margie explains what is already an obvious piece of symbolism, saying: " 'Why, Douglass, . . . it was really our childhood that we buried here, never guessing what a precious thing we were putting under the ground.' " There follows an interesting analysis of loss of innocence. Douglass tells Margie that it was when he saw her show fear he first fell in love with her: " 'That night, after our boat had drifted away from us, when we had to wade down the river hand in hand . . . you cried in a different way from the way you sometimes cried when you hurt yourself, and I found that I loved you afraid better than I had ever loved you fearless, and in that moment we grew up, and shut the gates of Eden behind us, and our empire was at an end.' " This first awareness of desire through fear looks forward to *A Lost Lady,* in which Niel Herbert's affection for Marian Forrester is aroused by her vulnerability. For all its explicitness, "The Treasure of Far Island" ends with a brilliantly ambiguous love scene in which the former child playmates kiss in the sunset. The scene is effective because the emotion is genuinely felt but, at the same time, recognized by the protagonists to be a hopeless cliché, a romantic parody—"he knew that she had caught the spirit of the play." The tension of pastoral between desire (desire to recover childhood, desire to have Margie as a lover) and recognition of its impossible fulfillment is perfectly balanced, so that the romanticism in the last lines, evoking cities and romances of old, is wholly moving.

"The Enchanted Bluff"[8] is very close in subject matter and feeling to "The Treasure of Far Island," but this time Willa Cather avoided dramatizing the emotion and rendered it in its simplest, unfurnished manner—as a memory. The particular feeling she sought to capture was the romantic wonder of childhood. Through the eyes of a boy on a sandbank in a sluggish western river the untried world appears as a vista of splendid horizons. The story has no plot, but through description, allusion, and association creates a child's feeling for romance and adventure. The six boys watch the night sky fill with stars, and their thoughts are of Columbus taking his direction from the sky and Napoleon reading his fortune in the stars. The image of heroic voyage is extended when the moon comes up over the bluffs "like a galleon in full sail." The moon is red and also suggests the Aztec rite of human sacrifice, which in turn evokes the story of Coronado, the Spanish adventurer, and his quest for the seven cities of gold. Each of the boys then muses about the places in the world he would like to see. The dream and the excitement of that night's musing is focused in the image of the Mesa Encantada, the great rock in the New Mexican desert which beckons to be explored and conquered. Each of the boys vows that he will some day climb that rock.

The story ends in a fashion similar to *My Ántonia,* with the narrator twenty years later looking back from the disillusioned perspective of adult life. None of the boys has climbed the mesa: one boy has died, another is a successful stockbroker and goes about only where his red touring car will take him. But even though none of them has been to New Mexico the narrator finds that the children of his friends are now dreaming of that same adventure. The story is shaped by the fundamental paradox of pastoral art: from the adult perspective in the larger world the imagination seeks to recover the experience of childhood wonder, which once imbued the world with the romance of discovery. The boys are impatient to set forth; yet we are aware, because this is a memory, that they are living in the most perfect time of their life.[9]

When Willa Cather came to write her first novels, the theme of memory's potency was subordinate to the drama of struggle and conquest: Bartley Alexander, Alexandra Bergson, and Thea Kronborg are all singled out as competitors and victors, each in his own way. But the pastoral theme is nonetheless important in all three books, for memory and the experiences of childhood carry the seeds of defeat for each of the protagonists. Alexander's desire to recapture his youth, to become a boy beside a campfire again, brings about the collapse of his bridge and his own death. The value Alexandra Bergson places on turning the wild land into a pastoral garden for her brother and Marie Shabata brings about the defeat of her highest hopes as a pioneer. Memories of childhood, which are fraught with hardships and failure, illumine the special defeat of Thea Kronborg as a human being and her transformation into a successful but hardened artist. *The Song of the Lark* is in fact a particular form of pastoral—a *künstlerroman*—in which childhood memories form a decisive aspect of the artist's growth to maturity.

Pastoral, however, became the dominant mode of her fiction when Willa Cather wrote her classic novel *My Ántonia,* published in 1918. Life for the author was changing in this period; the past was becoming more attractive than the present. The first flush of creativity and success for Willa Cather was over; the excitement of discovering her power as a writer was giving way to a more sober and thoughtful practice of her craft.[10] In 1916 Isabelle McClung married the violinist Jan Hambourg. By this time Miss McClung's parents had died and the family mansion was sold, so that for Willa Cather the old friendship had changed in many ways. Olive Fremstad, the opera singer Cather admired and who inspired in part the portrait of Thea Kronborg, also married in 1916, and perhaps the author began to feel a certain emptiness in her own personal life at this time. Also, Elizabeth Sergeant tells us that Willa Cather was deeply affected by World War I: "the conflict loosed in 1914 . . . soon tore her apart." To the spectacle of devastation in Europe Willa Cather responded: " 'Our present is ruined—but we had a beautiful past.' " This elegiac note marks the special mood of *My Ántonia.* In this novel the hero is no longer a strong creative character, but a man whose personal life is wanting, who retreats into the fuller life of his memories. Although the novel's heroine is a strong creative character, her value and significance are illuminated by the thoughts and feelings of a man who is in effect a kind of failure and wanderer. With *My Ántonia* Willa

Cather shifted from the epic to the pastoral mode, no longer looking confidently to the future but celebrating the past.

My Ántonia: A Pastoral of Innocence

In every work of art there exists a fundamental tension between two irreconcilable motives, for art has its source and momentum in conflict that cannot be resolved. A straightforward example is *Huckleberry Finn,* where the vernacular style returns us nostalgically to childhood and at the same time establishes a naive viewpoint for satire—Mark Twain being torn between a sentimental and a vicious view of the past. Similarly, in *The Great Gatsby* the romantic vision of Gatsby is continuously undercut by the ironic viewpoint of the narrator, Nick Carraway. The style in these novels is double-edged, embodying the author's conflicting emotions. The nondramatic style of *My Ántonia* makes the idea of conflict seem of little relevance to the novel, but pastoral art turns on the paradox that what is being celebrated can never be experienced again, that its reality is only a memory. Implicit in pastoral is an undying tension between the desire to return to the past and the sober recognition that such a desire can never be fulfilled. Nostalgia is the emotion evinced by pastoral art, and it fuses together the pleasure of remembrance with the painful awareness of mutability. The imaginative tension in *My Ántonia* is perhaps best described as a creative opposition between the novel's content and its form. As the narrator, Jim Burden, tells his life story revolving around the Bohemian immigrant girl, Ántonia Shimerda, he attempts to shape a happy and secure world out of the past by romanticizing disturbing and unpleasant memories. Yet the novel's form, its chronology in five parts, each of which represents a change in time and place in Jim Burden's life, invalidates the narrator's emotional quest, for the passing of time continuously moves the narrator away from the happy point of childhood and brings (for the pastoral imagination) the tragic realization that the past can never be recaptured.

The brief introduction to *My Ántonia,*[12] in which the "author" and the narrator meet on a train traveling across the Midwest, establishes the imaginative tension sustained throughout the novel. As a legal counsel for one of the great western railways Jim Burden frequently has the opportunity of traveling back to the actual scenes of his childhood in Nebraska. In this same vein of retreat we have Willa Cather, the "author," turning over the task of storytelling to a male narrator, thereby effecting in a conventionally acceptable manner a transition to an imaginatively more complete self-identification as a boy. But the introduction also includes a number of details about the narrator's present life which undercut the romantic vision of his childhood and his progress toward success in the world.[13] Here we learn that although Jim spends much of his time traveling across the Midwest, his permanent home is in New York. We also learn that he is married, but his wife is unsympathetic to his quiet tastes and the marriage is sterile and meaningless for him. The brief character sketch of Mrs. Burden as a rich patroness surrounded by a group of mediocre poets and painters prepares us for that moment near the end of the novel when Ántonia, surrounded by her children, asks Jim how many he has. Similarly, the image of Jim restlessly traveling across the country is juxtaposed with the happiness and fixed security of Ántonia's Nebraska farm. Later, as we read Jim's account of his childhood and of his successful progress toward achieving his professional ambitions, we are always aware of the futility of that success in the present. As a temporal framework around the whole novel, the introductory sketch sets up the creative pastoral tension between the memory of past happiness and the experience of loss and estrangement in the present.

The body of the novel is divided into five parts (books) representing different periods in Jim's life. The pastoral dream of recovering an ideally ordered and timeless world is most closely realized in Book I, in which the narrator describes the first year that he spent on his grandfather's farm in the West and his acquaintance with Ántonia Shimerda. The events and anecdotes that make up this first long section of the novel are imbued with a sense of timelessness and spacelessness, of life once lived beyond the reach of temporal change or the boundaries of a specific place. When Jim Burden, ten years old, arrives in Nebraska and travels to his grandfather's farm by wagon, his first impression of the country is of a feeling of spacelessness:

> There seemed to be nothing to see; no fences, no creeks or trees, no hills or fields. If there was a road, I could not make it out in the faint

> starlight. There was nothing but land: not a country at all, but the material out of which countries are made. No, there was nothing but land—slightly undulating, I knew, because often our wheels ground against the brake as we went down into a hollow and lurched up again on the other side. I had the feeling that the world was left behind, that we had got over the edge of it, and were outside man's jurisdiction. [P. 7]

He remembers a similar feeling in his grandmother's garden, situated a quarter of a mile from the house:

> I wanted to walk straight on through the red grass and over the edge of the world, which could not be very far away. The light air about me told me that the world ended here: only the ground and sun and sky were left, and if one went a little farther there would be only sun and sky, and one would float off into them, like the tawny hawks which sailed over our heads making slow shadows on the grass. [P. 16]

Accompanying this sense of spacelessness is a tremendous sense of freedom that is always an integral part of the narrator's descriptions of the landscape. He says that "the road ran about like a wild thing, avoiding the deep draws, crossing them where they were wide and shallow" (p. 19), and reflects that the "sunflower-bordered roads always seem to me the roads to freedom" (p. 29). After killing a rattlesnake and winning Ántonia's praise, he exults in the feeling that "the great land had never looked . . . so big and free" (p. 48). In memory this sense of freedom becomes focused in his relationship with Ántonia, whose wild, impulsive, and generous nature is so much a part of the untamed landscape.

More strategic for the recovery of lost childhood is the narrator's elimination of time in this first part. Events and anecdotes are not related to each other in a sequential pattern of cause and effect, but take their direction from the changing seasons. The fact that Book I takes the narrator through one complete cycle of the seasons (Jim arrives in Nebraska in early fall and the section ends the following summer) places his experiences in the context of a cyclical rhythm that is ever-recurring, hence outside of chronological time. Description of landscape in this part continually refers back to a world that has known no historical time: the endless plain covered with tall grass, moving in the wind as if it were a shaggy hide under which galloped herds of wild buffalo (p. 16), the restless wind in the spring rising and sinking like a playful puppy (p. 120), the prairie in an autumn sunset like a bush burned with fire but not consumed (p. 40). Human marks are frail—sod houses and dirt roads; they are of little consequence as measured against the overwhelming landscape.

Time and place do enter in the immigrants' stories of the old country. Ántonia nostalgically recounts to Jim something of her life in Bohemia; Pavel and Peter tell the gruesome tale of the wolves and the wedding party in Russia; and throughout there are allusions to times and places far away in such details as the Christmas-tree ornaments sent by Otto Fuchs's mother from Austria and in Bohemian customs, such as keeping food warm in a feather ticking, making sourdough bread and poppy-seed cake. But in this part of the novel these vistas in time and space do not function realistically to make the reader more aware of change and loss; rather, they are charged with romantic suggestion of times and places full of wonder to a child, like the magic of fairy tales. When the narrator recalls his night visit with Ántonia to the Russians' hut (the night that the dying Pavel tells his story to Mr. Shimerda), his description of the landscape, with its red sunset, the bright stars, and the coyotes howling over the plains, gives the whole episode a romantic cast. This is heightened by the secretive nature of the Russians' story, and Jim thinks to himself it was "as if the wolves of the Ukraine had gathered that night long ago, and the wedding party been sacrificed, to give us a painful and peculiar pleasure" (p. 61). When Mrs. Shimerda gives the Burdens some dried mushrooms she brought from Bohemia, the emotion evoked in the narrator is again a romantic one: "I bit off a corner of one of the chips I held in my hand, and chewed it tentatively. I never forgot the strange taste; though it was many years before I knew that those little brown shavings, which the Shimerdas had brought so far and treasured so jealously, were dried mushrooms. They had been gathered, probably, in some deep Bohemian forest" (p. 79).

The romanticizing of time and place is part of an imaginative process at work throughout the novel which either eliminates unpleasant memories or converts them into romantic vignettes.[14] The feeling of "peculiar pleasure" that Pavel's horrific tale gives the narrator is an example. Throughout Book I the harshness of life on the prairie, the very struggle to survive, is softened by Jim's memory as he yearns for a simple mode of existence again.

The poverty of the Shimerda family, making their home at the beginning of winter in a leaky dugout, is offset in Jim's memory by his fascination with their cultural differences—their food and folk customs. The misery of this new life brings some of the immigrants an early death; however, we do not feel the bitter failure they have suffered, only the sense of awe and mystery that death has for a child. The night visit to the Russians' hut, including the sight of the dying man's emaciated body and the blood-spattered sheets, has the cast of an exciting adventure for the boy. A few months later Mr. Shimerda commits suicide; the old man's despair is reflected in Ántonia's grief, but Jim softens his death by imagining that Mr. Shimerda's spirit rests first at his grandfather's comfortable house and then will make its way back to the old country he loved. This transforming of disturbing, painful realities into nostalgic and beautiful memories is a process effected by the pastoral style. Note in the following paragraph how an image of violence and dispossession (the Indians are now gone) is transformed into a wholly esthetic reflection:

> Beyond the pond, on the slope that climbed to the cornfield, there was, faintly marked in the grass, a great circle where the Indians used to ride. Jake and Otto were sure that when they galloped round that ring the Indians tortured prisoners, bound to a stake in the centre; but grandfather thought they merely ran races or trained horses there. Whenever one looked at this slope against the setting sun, the circle showed like a pattern in the grass; and this morning, when the first light spray of snow lay over it, it came out with wonderful distinctness, like strokes of Chinese white on canvas. [P. 62]

Book I ends with the dream of all pastorals being voiced. Thinking of her father's death, Ántonia says: " 'I wish no winter ever come again.' " And in his optimistic manner Jim reassures her that "it will be summer a long while yet."

Mutability, however, is the *sine qua non* of pastoral art, and in the following three parts of the novel the narrator becomes aware of time's passage and feels the restrictions of place. The sense of freedom and romantic horizon disappears from the book: though

Jim is growing into manhood and moving out into the world, the world is becoming smaller and setting limitations on him. Book II, "The Hired Girls," takes place three years later when the Burdens have moved into the town of Black Hawk. In the first paragraph describing the town, the narrator refers to his "lost freedom" in leaving the farm (p. 145). As time passes he feels more and more repressed by the confines of the village and the frustrating mediocrity of its social life. In a despondent mood he reflects on the repression and lack of imagination in the small town:

> On starlight nights I used to pace up and down those long, cold streets, scowling at the little, sleeping houses on either side, with their storm-windows and covered back porches. They were flimsy shelters, most of them poorly built of light wood, with spindle porch-posts horribly mutilated by the turning-lathe. Yet for all their frailness, how much jealousy and envy and unhappiness some of them managed to contain! The life that went on in them seemed to me made up of evasions and negations; shifts to save cooking, to save washing and cleaning, devices to propitiate the tongue of gossip. This guarded mode of existence was like living under a tyranny. People's speech, their voices, their very glances, became furtive and repressed. Every individual taste, every natural appetite, was bridled by caution. The people asleep in those houses, I thought, tried to live like the mice in their own kitchens; to make no noise, to leave no trace, to slip over the surface of things in the dark. The growing piles of ashes and cinders in the back yards were the only evidence that the wasteful, consuming process of life went on at all. [Pp. 219–20]

But the specific conflict that arises for Jim in Book II is sexual. In pastoral the imagination attempts to exclude sexuality because it is both individual and temporal and leads away from the innocent unified vision of childhood. At first Jim succeeds in his evasion of adult awareness and responsibility. The Burdens live next to the Harlings, a family with five children, and after Ántonia comes to town to work as the Harlings' "hired girl" Jim reflects that he and the other children "were never happier, never felt more contented and secure" (p. 193). The best times for Jim occur when the men are absent—when grandfather is at church and Mr. Harling is away on business—leaving the carefree world of happy children presided over by the indulgent Mrs. Harling, the older daughter, Frances, and Ántonia. But Jim is fourteen now, and as narrator he reflects that boys and girls "have to grow up, whether they will or no." The narrator's feelings at this point are again focused in Ántonia; where previously her wild, impulsive nature spelled the unrestricted freedom of childhood, her generous instincts now involve Jim in the complexities of sexuality. A number of the immigrant girls have come to Black Hawk to work as domestics, and to Jim these spontaneous, fun-loving girls (the sensual, slow-moving Lena Lingard, the fast-tripping Tiny Soderball, the three Bohemian Marys of dubious fame) are far more attractive than the repressed and imitative town girls, who have been bred to the social niceties and who seem utterly lacking in vitality. However, the rough manners and irrepressible gaiety of Ántonia and her friends are frowned on by the strict decorum of the town and they are looked upon as distinctly second-class citizens. Jim's potential initiation into sex is thus complicated by social taboo as well as by his preference for remaining a child. The situation comes to a head during "the summer which was to change everything" when the Italian dancing pavilion is set up in Black Hawk. Ántonia loses her place at the Harlings because they disapprove of her dancing and keeping late hours, and she takes a position at the Wick Cutters'. At the same time Jim is forced to sneak off to the Saturday-night dances because of his grandfather's disapproval. There is no doubt that his feeling for the immigrant girls is sexual: he has a recurring erotic dream of Lena in the fields and he kisses Ántonia passionately after one of the Saturday dances. Jim's guilt (in pastoral, sex is always guilt-inducing and destructive) is partly assuaged by Ántonia's playing a motherly and protective role; she warns him against involvement with Lena and encourages him to study diligently at school. But his relationship with the immigrant girls, which becomes a sublimated erotic dalliance during the picnic along the bowery river bank, finally has devastating consequences. Suspicious of her employer's intentions, Ántonia arranges for Jim to sleep in her bed while the Cutters are away. Wick Cutter does in fact return one night to rape Ántonia, but finds himself in a fight with Jim instead. The experience for Jim is disgusting beyond measure; in part it refers him to his own inadmissible desires (one hates most where one sees one's self reflected), but it also taints Ántonia as a sexual being, and his definition of her as older sister or mother has been spoiled: "I hated her almost as much as I hated Cutter. She had let me in for all this disgustingness" (p. 250). With this sequence Book II abruptly ends.

In Book III, "Lena Lingard," Jim is living in Lincoln where he is studying classics at the university. The central emotion of the novel—the increasing sense of loss and alienation as one grows older—is brought to the fore again in the narrator's relationship with the immigrant girls. Significantly, Ántonia, whose image has been sullied by the Cutter affair, does not appear in this part; it is the "forbidden" Lena Lingard, now living in Lincoln as a dress-maker, who visits Jim and revives in him all his feelings about his childhood with Ántonia. But even before Lena appears Jim has begun an imaginative process whereby his past experiences are translated into esthetic forms. As Jim reads the classics with his tutor, Gaston Cleric, his train of thought goes back to his child-hood and to the people he had known in the past. He is concerned about these people not for themselves, but as aspects of *his* experience: "They were so much alive in me that I scarcely stopped to wonder whether they were alive anywhere else, or how" (p. 262). The full nature of his concern is revealed when, reading Virgil's *Georgics,* he joins the expression of nostalgia, "the best days are the first to flee," with the artist's statement of purpose, " 'I shall be the first, if I live, to bring the Muse into my country' " (pp. 263–64). In order to recapture and redeem the past Jim is transforming it into art. The result of the process is, of course, the novel itself—Jim's memoir which he hands over to the "author" in the introduction; but within the narrative there are several instances where an incomplete or disturbing experience becomes an esthetic one. For example, the erotic picnic with the hired girls along the river concludes not in love-making but in the image of the plow against the sun—one of the most powerful images in the novel, which significantly recurs to the narrator as he reads Latin. After Lena's first visit, which quickens his memory of the hired girls, he reflects that "if there were no girls like them in the world, there would be no poetry" (p. 270). Jim's ensuing courtship of Lena takes its signature from art: they attend the theatre together, and one of the plays, *Camille,* which concerns the love of an art student for a woman of the demimonde, reflects something of their own mis-matched affair. As another critic has suggested, the whole courtship in Lena's parlor, with the idle talk of fashion, the serving of tea, the nuisance pet dog, the intrusion of older lovers, has the quality of a comedy of manners.[15] But Jim's involvement with Lena becomes more than a diversion—he loses interest in his classes and reading—and rather than risk a distracting and possibly dangerous sexual experience, he follows his tutor to Boston to study at Harvard.

When Book IV, "The Pioneer Woman's Story," opens, two years have passed and Jim is back in Black Hawk for the summer vacation. In this part he tells us almost nothing of himself except that he will enter Harvard Law School in the fall; but his continuing preoccupation with time and change is reflected in the stories of the immigrant girls, who have been compromised and disillusioned with the passing years. Moving forward for a moment chronologically, the narrator tells us how Lena Lingard and Tiny Soderball both left Black Hawk and achieved material success in the world, but that neither of them were really fulfilled or made happy by it. Tiny made a fortune in the Klondike gold rush and eventually settled in San Francisco, but she never married and had a family. She had numerous exciting adventures in the Klondike, but "the thrill of them was quite gone. She said frankly that nothing interested her much now but making money," and Jim reflects that "she was like someone in whom the faculty of becoming interested is worn out" (pp. 301–302). Lena also does well financially and goes to live near Tiny in San Francisco. Though she has not married either, she is considered a success by the people of Black Hawk because she has profited at dressmaking. These stories remind us of the emptiness of the narrator's own "success."

In contrast to those girls who have spent their lives in pursuit of material security, Ántonia has followed the dictates of her emotions—the result of which is a child born out of wedlock. The narrator, who has not seen her since the time of the Wick Cutter affair, says: "I tried to shut Ántonia out of my mind. I was bitterly disappointed in her" (p. 298). As in the Wick Cutter episode, Ántonia's relationship with the volatile train conductor, Larry Donovan, is sexual, and Jim tries to blot it from his mind. But Ántonia has been abandoned and, after hearing her pathetic story from the Widow Steavens, Jim decides to visit her before going East again. He finds her working in the fields as he often did when they were children, and for a place to talk they "instinctively" walk over to the unplowed patch at the crossroad where Mr. Shimerda is buried. Jim has forgiven Ántonia, for in his eyes she now resumes her maternal role of older sister and guardian of precious memories from childhood. As they walk homeward across the field at sunset he wishes he "could be a little boy again, and that [his] way could end there" (p. 322). After parting from Ántonia and walking on alone, he almost believes "that a boy and girl ran along beside me, as our shadows used to do, laughing and whispering to each other in the grass" (p. 323).

The fifth and last part of the book, "Cuzak's Boys," takes place twenty years later when Jim, now a railway lawyer, finally stops off in Nebraska for a visit with Ántonia and her family. At the end of Book IV Jim promised Ántonia that he would visit her again, but Ántonia was part of his past and because his memory could fashion out of it a more perfect order, he avoided a confrontation with its realities. Jim says: "In the course of twenty crowded years one parts with many illusions. I did not wish to lose the early ones. Some memories are realities, and are better than anything that can ever happen to one again" (p. 328). But from the introduction we know that Jim's life is emotionally empty, so it is not surprising that when Lena Lingard gives him "a cheerful account of Ántonia" he decides to risk a visit at last. The implication is that memory is no longer enough, and that in going back to Ántonia he is actually trying to relive the past.

In this part the creative tensions in the novel are tautly balanced: the feeling of transience and alienation effected by the passing of twenty years runs directly counter to Jim's pressing urge to eliminate all reminders of time and change. In Book V the narrator unwittingly attempts nothing less than to become a boy again and rediscover the happy, timeless world he once knew with Ántonia as his older, protective companion. Here is Willa Cather's intuitive art at its surest and finest. As Jim nears Ántonia's farm in his buggy he is greeted by two of Ántonia's boys, reconnecting him to childhood. They are at the roadside mourning the loss of a pet dog, but turn their attention at once to the visitor and lead him up to the farmhouse. Before Ántonia appears Jim looks about and his eye picks up many of the same details he noticed on first awakening in his grandparents' home as a boy: cats sunning themselves, yellow pumpkins on the porch steps, a white kitchen and ducks and geese running across the path (Jim's grandmother moved about quickly as if she were shooing chickens). As in the beginning of the book it is early autumn, the season of fulfillment but also the waning of the year.[16] When Ántonia enters the kitchen, she is not unlike Jim's grandmother in appearance—a stalwart brown woman, spare and aging but vigorous. Jim's stooped grandmother is described as a "woman of unusual endurance," and Ántonia is similarly "battered but not diminished." One of Jim's earliest Nebraska memories is going out to his grandmother's garden a quarter of a mile from the house, and in parallel fashion he is taken almost at once to see the Cuzaks' new cave "a good way from the house," where fruits and vegetables are kept. The past is constantly evoked in the present, for Ántonia has named several of her children after childhood friends, such as Norwegian Anna, Nina Harling, her sister Yulka, and her brother Ambrosch.

Jim's persistent idealization of Ántonia as a mother figure is fully and legitimately realized now. Surrounded by her children who come running out of the fruit cave like "a veritable explosion of life," Ántonia's maternal nature assumes almost mythic dimension. Standing in the orchard with her hand on one of the trees she has carefully nurtured, she suggests both earth-mother and fertility goddess.[17] Jim reflects "that she was a rich mine of life, like the founders of early races" (p. 353). On the other hand, he feels more than ever like a boy again and Ántonia says to him appropriately: " 'You've kept so young.' " He in turn delights in Ántonia's young sons and chooses to sleep with them in the haymow rather than in the house. He says: "I felt like a boy in their company, and all manner of forgotten interests revived in me" (p. 345). He takes most interest in the mischievous Leo, who, like Jim, is intensely jealous of Ántonia's affection and whom Ántonia confesses she likes the best. In accord with Jim's deepest wishes Ántonia's husband is conveniently away the first day, and sitting under the grape arbor in Ántonia's orchard with its triple enclosure of wire, locust, and mulberry hedges, Jim finds a perfect pastoral haven and "deepest peace." Ántonia's husband, however, does not disrupt the harmony of Jim's visit, for he poses no masculine threat. He is described as a "crumpled little man" without much force, and

Jim soon calls him "Papa" with the rest. In Cuzak's relation to Ántonia there is no suggestion of sex: theirs is a friendship in which he is simply "the instrument of Ántonia's special mission" of procreation. The elimination of sexuality is thoroughgoing. The one sexual incident in Jim's life relating to Ántonia is rendered comic when one of the children tells Jim about the grotesque end to Wick Cutter's life. In similar comic fashion Jim is told that Ántonia's aggressive brother Ambrosch has been unmanned by a fat, rich wife who bosses him about.

When Jim leaves Ántonia's farm and goes back to Black Hawk his mood is temporarily broken: he finds so many things changed —friends dead or moved away, old trees cut down, strange children in the Harling yard—that he is confronted again with the fact of time's passage. But he does not remain in town for long; he goes out into the country to a place where the landscape has remained unchanged and where his romantic, esthetic eye can transform it once again into the thing of beauty and permanence that his imagination craves. Note especially in the following passage images of color and texture which give the scene an unchanging plastic beauty.

> I took a long walk north of the town, out into the pastures where the land was so rough that it had never been ploughed up, and the long red grass of early times still grew shaggy over the draws and hillocks. Out there I felt at home again. Overhead the sky was that indescribable blue of autumn; bright and shadowless, hard as enamel. To the south I could see the dun-shaded river bluffs that used to look so big to me, and all about stretched drying cornfields, of the pale-gold colour, I remembered so well. Russian thistles were blowing across the uplands and piling against the wire fences like barricades. Along the cattle-paths the plumes of goldenrod were already fading into sun-warmed velvet, grey with gold threads in it. I had escaped from the curious depression that hangs over little towns, and my mind was full of pleasant things; trips I meant to take with Cuzak boys. [Pp. 369–70]

In Ántonia's family he has found a connection with his own childhood again: "There were enough Cuzaks to play with for a long while yet. Even after the boys grew up, there would always be Cuzak himself!" (p. 370). As he looks at the old road he first traveled with Ántonia he philosophically complements his feelings of having come home again by envisioning life as a circle which invariably returns a man to his beginnings. The novel is a pastoral of innocence for it asserts that life's greatest values are to be found in childhood. Our response to this final emotion is ambiguous, and therein lies the greatness of the novel. Aware of the impossibility of returning to childhood and recovering innocence, we are nonetheless drawn, like Jim Burden, to Ántonia and her farm; but unlike Jim we can never quite evade the poignant realization that we have already gone beyond, and that Ántonia and her family lie in the precious but irrecoverable past.

A Lost Lady: A Pastoral of Experience

Willa Cather's fictional heroines fall into two distinct groups: strong, hard-working, maternal women and genteel, finely attractive ladies of leisure. The imaginative response to the former is wholly innocent: these women, best represented by Alexandra Bergson and Ántonia Shimerda, but also by Mrs. Wheeler and Mahailey in *One of Ours,* are strong creative beings who not only guarantee the survival of the race but also the survival of man's most fundamental and cherished values. The response to the latter group is erotic: Willa Cather's romantic heroines such as Marian Forrester, Myra Henshawe, and Doña Isabella in *Death Comes for the Archbishop* are spoiled, self-indulgent, sterile women, yet their vanity and gay artifice are always an irresistible mystery and excitement.[18] In a pastoral of innocence the imagination, moving away from a meaningless present and at the same time evading the painful realities of the past, turns to the strong, maternal figures in hope of recovering the ordered and secure world of childhood. But a pastoral of experience recreates the passage from childhood innocence to adult awareness with all its attendant anxieties and failures, and in lieu of irrecoverable innocence offers the compensatory values of understanding and acceptance. Because initiation into awareness is sexual on a deep level, the heroine in a pastoral of experience is a lady of love. If Jim Burden had sought to understand rather than romanticize his past, then the focus of his memory would have been on Lena Lingard rather than Ántonia. In *A Lost Lady* (1923)[19] Willa Cather once again looks at her past through the eyes of a sensitive boy growing up in the Midwest, but Niel Herbert's story turns around Marian Forrester, a beautiful woman with whom he is infatuated, and whose shallow character he gradually comes to see without illusion. The story of Marian Forrester's decline is the story of Niel Herbert's initiation into experience. *A Lost Lady* is a pastoral of experience because it brings its hero from childhood innocence to adult awareness and acceptance of life.

According to Edith Lewis, *A Lost Lady* for all its appearance of ease and control gave Willa Cather some difficulty in the writing. She began the first draft by following her narrative method in *My Ántonia* and telling the story in the first person—in Niel Herbert's voice. But the effect was not right and she started the novel again using the third person.[20] At a casual glance the difference may seem arbitrary, for the story is still largely filtered through Niel's eyes and his consciousness provides the controlling perspective. Yet on closer examination the difference in narrative method can be seen as crucial, for the use of the third person allows the introduction of an ironic perspective into the story simultaneously with the romantic view of its protagonist. In contrast to *My Ántonia* Willa Cather's artistic purpose in *A Lost Lady* was not simply to romanticize the past but to expose its failure to bequeath viable values to the present. The novel has a social purpose: Marian Forrester's disintegration is not just an individual story but a chronicle of a society's decline. The double perspective created by the third-person narrator—that is, Niel's viewpoint circumscribed by an omniscient narrator—allows the reader both illusion and recognition; through Niel we experience the attraction of Marian Forrester's style and charm, but at the same time the narrator gently urges us to recognize the essentially shallow nature of the heroine.[21] Niel Herbert eventually sees his lady without illusion, but not until the end of the book. To broaden her canvas Miss Cather gives us an overview which both exposes Niel's romanticism and illuminates the failure of the pioneer aristocracy to perpetuate itself. The ironic, third-person narration also admits a subtle interplay between degrees of sexual awareness and innocence; it is not possible to determine whether a double entendre is always intended by the author, but the sexual overtones inherent in the imagery of flowers, jewels, animals, and moonlight are given full value by the novel's subject—a woman of love and the initiation of an innocent boy.

The double viewpoint is established in the novel's opening chapter. A pastoral perspective is created by the first sentence which moves us back thirty or forty years to the time of the railroad aristocracy and to "one of those grey towns along the Burlington railroad, which are so much greyer today than they were then." But the past is not simply idealized: even then Sweet Water was a "grey town," and the pioneer aristocracy were not without personal acquisitive motives. The narrator wryly observes that there were two distinct social classes in the prairie states: "the homesteaders and hand-workers who were there to make a living, and the bankers and gentlemen ranchers who came from the Atlantic seaboard to invest money and to 'develop our great West,' as they used to tell us" (p. 10). The tone of the opening chapter contrasts sharply with the introduction to *My Ántonia* where only the present is seen in terms of failure; in *A Lost Lady* the past is also discredited. We are given a brief glimpse in this chapter of the attractive heroine as she used to welcome her guests, and also a description of the Forrester home; but even in this preview of the story there is a definite hint, in her calculated dishabille, of Mrs. Forrester's vanity beneath her charm, and we are told that stripped of its vines and shrubbery the imposing Forrester home, with its fussy, fragile pillars and narrow porches, "would probably have been ugly enough" (p. 11). As a pastoral *A Lost Lady* is a drama of place and time (of inevitable change), and the first chapter concludes with a direct statement of this impetus behind the tale: "Mrs. Forrester was twenty-five years younger than her husband, and she was his second wife. He married her in California and brought her to Sweet Water a bride . . . . He grew old there,—and even she, alas! grew older" (p. 13).

Having firmly grounded her tale in a mood of irony and disillusionment, Willa Cather then takes us back into an idyllic past, to "a summer morning long ago, when Mrs. Forrester was still a young woman, and Sweet Water was a town of which great things were expected" (p. 14). The viewpoint here is wholly that of Niel, a boy of twelve, for whom Marian Forrester, the beautiful wife of a railroad builder, is the epitome of romantic love. For Willa Cather flowers are often an index to feminine sexuality, and the rose, in keeping with its traditional symbology, denotes a loved woman. On the summer morning when Niel and a group of village boys inquire if they can fish in the Forrester marsh, Mrs. Forrester is standing in the parlor window, "arranging old-fashioned blush roses in a glass bowl." To Niel, of course, she is a wholly innocent love object and she is appropriately wearing white when she comes down through the sunlit grove to bring the boys freshly baked cookies. The idyllic perfection of this scene, with its exquisite summer landscape and frolicking boys, is marred by the intrusion of Ivy Peters, an older, mocking youth who later becomes an intimate of the aging heroine and an exploiter of the small town's meager resources. He is cruel and aggressive (he carries a gun) and the small boys fear him. Moreover, there is a repellent, phallic quality in the description of him: his skin is red and swollen, his eyes are without lashes like an unblinking snake, and he carries himself "with unnatural erectness, as if he had a steel rod down his back" (p. 20).[22] These sexual innuendos are increased when Peters captures a female woodpecker (its gender is emphasized), slits its eyes, and sends it reeling back into the trees. The incident not only dramatizes the ugliness of his nature, but foreshadows the danger of his presence for the heroine. Niel attempts to rescue the bird (as he will later attempt to save Mrs. Forrester), but his efforts are ineffectual; he falls from the tree, breaking his arm, and is carried up to the Forrester house by Peters to await a doctor. Here Mrs. Forrester, surrounded by her expensive furnishings and bathing his forehead with cologne, is apotheosized as Niel's romantic ideal. The feeling is heightened by the brief, contrasting description of Niel's own home—the "frail egg-shell house" at the edge of town where he lives with his widowed father and poor-relation housekeeper, a family to which clings "an air of failure and defeat" (p. 30).

At the beginning of chapter 3 Mrs. Forrester's perfection is still mythical: "she was an excitement that came and went with summer" (p. 31). Niel associates her romantically with picnics in the grove and dances on moonlight nights. But time is passing: Niel is now nineteen, Captain Forrester has retired because of an accident, and the future of Sweet Water is no longer so bright. When the Forresters announce that they will not go away for the winter, their dwindling social prominence is identified with the declining importance of the town. More significantly, Mrs. Forrester is no longer the spirit of summer. But Niel's infatuation blinds him to the gradual erosion of her character along with their fortune. Here the double perspective in the narration begins to point up the gap between Niel's romantic ideal and the reality of the heroine. When Niel visits the Forresters the first winter they remain in Sweet Water, the reader cannot help but notice several little details which suggest the heroine's boredom and shallowness: her need for sherry in the afternoons, her insatiable desire for compliments, her whimsical dependence on "good luck" in the future. Niel, however, is enchanted by her "light, effervescing vitality," her musical laughter, and the loveliness of her person adorned by long earrings of garnets and pearls, the latter jewel betokening purity and innocence. Through his eyes the reader shares the heightened sense of a woman's presence, feels "that something in [her] glance that made one's blood tingle" (p. 41); it is romantically fitting that when Niel leaves he notices the moon, emblem of chaste love, directly overhead.

Niel's failure to recognize Marian Forrester's true nature is increasingly evident in chapters 4 and 5, where his innocence by contrast gives Marian's affairs a secretly voluptuous and exciting aspect. The Forresters give a Christmas party to which Frank Ellinger, a virile bachelor from Denver, is invited. Ellinger is in fact Marian's lover, but Niel does not realize it. Nor does he recognize the irony in Marian's wearing diamonds, the jewel of constancy and steadfastness, all the while she is planning a rendezvous with her lover. That night after the party Marian takes off her jewels before she slips from the conjugal bedroom to meet Ellinger by the fireplace. The attraction the lovers feel for each other is beautifully imaged when Marian's velvet dress brushes Ellinger's trousers and throws sparks. Even more effective are the animal images used to denote their frank and essentially rapacious sensuality. Earlier in the novel something of Marian's desirability is hinted at in the comic vignette of her being chased by a bull. The description of Ellinger, with his beaked nose, his curly, muscular lips, and teeth that could bite an iron rod in two, suggests a similarly dangerous and exciting physicality: "His whole figure seemed very much alive under his clothes, with a restless, muscular energy that had something of the cruelty of wild animals in it" (p. 46). When they meet by the fireplace Marian warns him against her young rival, Constance Ogden, saying: " 'Ah, but kittens have claws, these days!' " (p. 59). Next day when they go out in the sleigh to gather cedar boughs, Ellinger's eyes are "wolfish" with desire and he tears off his glove with his teeth before taking her hand. Marian teases him with her eyes and her voice until they find a deep ravine hidden away in the hills. Later, when Marian waits for Ellinger to cut some cedar boughs, her whole body shivers at the sound of her lover's axe. But all this is a world still undisclosed to Niel; his persistent innocence is reflected in the fact that the rendezvous is witnessed not by Niel, but by one of the village boys, Adolph Blum.

Ellinger's presence at Christmas, however, leaves Niel unsettled, and during the long winter that follows he begins to notice Mrs. Forrester's growing restlessness. On winter evenings he is still enchanted by her presence, by "the quick recognition in her eyes" and "her many-coloured laugh"; but one afternoon after a confining snowstorm he finds her with a sharp smell of alcohol on her breath, bemoaning her isolation in Sweet Water. She confides to Niel her fears: " 'Oh, but it is bleak! . . . Suppose we should have to stay here all next winter, too, . . . and the next! What will become of me, Niel?' " (p. 77). Her self-preoccupation is imaged in the Captain's winter flowers, narcissus and hyacinths—flowers of self-love—which fill the house. Marian says she hates to see sparkling, animated eyes in anyone but herself. Niel represses these details which detract from his ideal lady; when, looking at the new moon, she alludes to Frank Ellinger, Niel immediately thinks: "It was as Captain Forrester's wife that she most interested [him], and it was in her relation to her husband that he most admired her" (p. 78). Niel, who lives "with monastic cleanliness and severity," cleaves to an innocent view of the Forresters: theirs is a sexless marriage and Niel in his mind evokes the Captain's authority to banish the threat of Marian's suitor. But Niel's self-reassurance is for the reader ironic; when he evokes Marian's loyalty to her husband, thinking it was "something that could never become worn or shabby; steel of Damascus," we recall her rendezvous with Ellinger in the hills. To appease his own doubts Niel decides that her fascination lay in "the magic of contradictions."

Ultimately, Niel is no longer able to evade the truth about Mrs. Forrester. In June the Captain is called away on urgent business and three days later Niel discovers that Frank Ellinger is in Sweet Water. In his evasive fashion Niel stays away from the Forrester home in the evening, for he suspects that Ellinger will be there. However at dawn he goes out to the marsh and gathers for Mrs. Forrester, still his romantic ideal, a bouquet of wild roses. The description of the summer dawn, prelude to Niel's fall from innocence, assumes a mythic dimension:

> The sky was burning with the soft pink and silver of a cloudless summer dawn. The heavy, bowed grasses splashed him to the knees. All over the marsh, snow-on-the-mountain, globed with dew, made cool sheets of silver, and the swamp milk-weed spread its flat, raspberry-coloured clusters. There was an almost religious purity about the fresh morning air, the tender sky, the grass and flowers with the sheen of early dew upon them. There was in all living things something limpid and joyous—like the wet, morning call of the birds, flying up through the unstained atmosphere. Out of the saffron east a thin, yellow, wine-like sunshine began to gild the fragrant meadows and the glistening tops of the grove. Niel wondered why he did not often come over like this, to see the day before men and their activities had spoiled it, while the morning was still unsullied, like a gift handed down from the heroic ages. [Pp. 84–85][23]

The morning is perfect until the moment when Niel places the roses on the bedroom window sill and hears the lovers laughing within. Then innocence is no longer possible—only anger and disgust. Fleeing the Forrester place Niel tells himself bitterly that the morning and all subsequent mornings were forever ruined: "In that instant between stooping to the window-sill and rising, he had lost one of the most beautiful things in his life. . . . This day saw the end of that admiration and loyalty that had been like a bloom on his existence. He could never recapture it" (p. 86). The bouquet of roses, the emblem of love devised to win a lady's favor, is thrown into the mud. Niel thinks of lilies, the flowers of innocence, and mutters to himself: " '*Lilies that fester smell far worse than weeds*' " (p. 87). The roses in Captain Forrester's garden (and later on his grave), like the diamonds he has given his wife, are henceforth exclusively ironic in reference.[24]

Captain Forrester returns from his business trip a poor man. Just as his wife has been appropriated by an unprincipled philanderer, so his wealth has been depleted by unscrupulous young businessmen. In the financial crisis he alone acted honorably, saving many smaller men, but in so doing he lost his own fortune. On his return to Sweet Water he suffers a stroke which symbolically completes the collapse of his power. Later we are told that adventurous pioneers like Captain Forrester could conquer new land but, weak in defense, they could not hold it (p. 106). Willa Cather's admiration for this courteous brotherhood of pioneer aristocrats, "who were unpractical to the point of magnificence," hardly needs to be pointed out; yet at the same time she recognized that their world could not endure into another generation—it was enclosed and sterile, the end of a cycle rather than the beginning. The Forresters have no heirs for their elegant life style—only a house full of narcissus echoing a toast to "Happy Days." The West is being taken over by shrewd young men like Ivy Peters, now a lawyer, who exploits what the earlier generation created. As the most prized ornament of a society that is rapidly crumbling, Marian Forrester is becoming a tarnished figure—even in Niel Herbert's eyes. When an old railroad friend visits the Forresters during the Captain's illness, Niel notices how Marian's vanity touches everything; only when Cyrus Dalzell compliments her appearance does she come out of her despondent mood and revive her charms. Niel is still susceptible to those charms but in a last visit with the Forresters before leaving to study in Boston it puzzles him that a woman who gave "the sense of tempered steel" could be of so little faith.

A Lost Lady is a perfectly symmetrical novel in two parts. The parallels between the two parts are thematic as well as structural: in Part II Niel goes through the same experience of romanticism and disillusionment that he did in Part I. The opening chapter in Part II (as in Part I) gives a realistic account of the Forresters and Sweet Water. Niel has been away for two years, and on the train back to Sweet Water Ivy Peters tells him with satisfaction that he has rented the Forrester marsh and drained it to grow wheat, and that Mrs. Forrester seeks consolation for hard times in French brandy. But when Niel goes out to visit the Forresters the next day he attempts to restore them to their romantic stature of his childhood. Of course he cannot help noticing that the Captain, sitting paralyzed in his rose garden, has grown heavier and weaker, but he finds Marian dressed in the white of innocence again, lying in a hammock in the glade where he had fallen and broken his arm as a boy. His immediate impulse is to protect her from the passing of time: "He stepped forward and caught her suspended figure, hammock and all, in his arms. How light and alive she was! like a bird caught in a net. If only he could rescue her and carry her off like this,—off the earth of sad, inevitable periods, away from age, weariness, adverse fortune!" (p. 110). His Keatsian wish is momentarily fulfilled when she puts her hand under his chin "as if he were still a boy." But the illusion is broken when she expresses her horror at her husband watching his sundial: " 'How can anybody like to see time visibly devoured? We are all used to seeing clocks go round, but why does he want to see that shadow creep on that stone?' " (p. 111). Niel reassures her that the Captain hasn't changed much.

Throughout the novel Marian Forrester's value as a love object is measured by descriptions of her physical beauty; like a lady in courtly love poetry her physical charms are enumerated—especially her pale skin, her musical laughter, and her eyes with their mocking spark. But they are also a measure of her disintegration. Niel inevitably notices that she is now looking older:

> In the brilliant sun of the afternoon one saw that her skin was no longer like white lilacs,—it had the ivory tint of gardenias that have just begun to fade. The coil of blue-black hair seemed more than ever too heavy for her head. There were lines,—something strained about the corners of her mouth that used not to be there. [P. 112]

But Niel does not want to admit she has changed and revels in the idea that "these changes could vanish in a moment, be utterly wiped out in a flash of personality, and one forgot everything about her except herself" (p. 112). The interplay between illusion and recognition is subtly modulated throughout the chapter. As they walk up to the house Mrs. Forrester tells Niel that he must hurry and become a successful man because money is a very important thing; but then they stop and look back at the grounds, which are described as "Elysian fields," and Mrs. Forrester puts a white hand on Niel's arm. Again she disturbs his romantic illusion by inquiring discreetly what kind of pleasure a young man could find in coming back to Sweet Water and to old people. His pleasure is both erotic and esthetic; this is underscored when, inside the house his gaze falls on a slave-girl figurine, scantily clad, which he remembered from that first time he was carried into the house. Innocent illusion, however, is finally dispelled when Mrs. Forrester asks Niel on departure to post a letter for her; it is addressed to Frank Ellinger.

The betrayal of Mrs. Forrester once again by the passing of time and a changing society is accelerated in Niel's eyes during the summer. Niel had planned to read in the Forresters' grove but that *locus amoenus* is marred by Ivy Peters's frequent presence there. One night of "glorious moonlight" Niel finds Marian dressed in white down by the bridge, but their romantic encounter is spoiled by Ivy Peters who comes along to make arrangements for cutting his wheat. Marian, moreover, does not mind Ivy's presence; she tells Niel that he has invested money for her and that he is helping her in her struggle " 'to get out of this hole' " (p. 126). Summer is no longer the idyllic season of Niel's boyhood: the weather is uncomfortably hot and dry, and finally breaks in a destructive rainstorm. During the flood Marian hears of Ellinger's marriage, and makes a desperate phone call to him from the office of Niel's uncle. When she enters the office at midnight, covered with mud and smelling of alcohol, her physical beauty is almost wholly gone: her eyes are "shrunk to hard points," her lips are blue, and there are poisonous-looking shadows under her eyes (p. 131). After this scene it is no longer possible for Niel to remain a romantic bystander; now he is on the inside, fully engaged in preserving Marian Forrester's facade of dignity and respectability before the public. Before she can completely expose and disgrace herself on the telephone, he cuts the wire.

In the logic of the novel's social allegory, Captain Forrester suffers another stroke shortly after his wife's desperate sally and self-exposure. The Forresters are now reduced to the level of the townspeople who, doing charitable services, "went in and out of Mrs. Forrester's kitchen as familiarly as they did out of one another's" (p. 138). The townswomen pry into all the rooms and cupboards and conclude that there is nothing special about the Forrester place after all; they figure that if Mrs. Forrester has a sale of effects after her husband is gone, each of her tablecloths could be made into two and her champagne glasses would make good sherbert dishes or mantel ornaments. In the meantime, Marian has become a drudge in the kitchen, degraded like her possessions. One of the women finds her drunk late at night, washing the kitchen floor: "All the bars were down."

That fall Niel decides to stay in Sweet Water with the Forresters and "see them through." He enjoys his vigils at the house, especially being alone with the solid old things that were part of his romantic dream as a child. But after Captain Forrester's death in December no shred of romantic illusion is possible for Niel. Despite the unnumbered favors that Niel's uncle had done for the Forresters, Marian callously puts her business affairs in Ivy Peters's hands. Niel is not merely disenchanted; he is bitter. Without Captain Forrester, Marian has become "flighty and perverse" (the image reminds us of the blinded woodpecker), consorting much of the time with Niel's inveterate enemy. Marian Forrester's degradation and the novel's social allegory are completed in the next-to-last chapter in which Marian gives a party for the young men of the town. The party reminds us of the earlier Christmas gathering, except now Ivy Peters plays host and Marian is reduced to doing most of the cooking. At the table Niel studies her face coldly, almost clinically, and instead of a courtly-love lady he sees an aging woman, "pinched and worn" with thin, rouged cheeks and eyes hollow with fatigue. The contrast with happier days is further heightened when Marian tells the crude village boys the romantic story of her rescue by Captain Forrester after she had fallen when climbing the mountains. Niel's final image of her on that awkward evening is of an old actress going through her part, but with only stagehands left to witness: "All those who had shared in fine undertakings and bright occasions were gone" (p. 167).

The last chapter begins with a eulogy to the generation of pioneers who, like Captain Forrester, are now gone. For Niel they are subconsciously identified with his childhood and his innocence, whereas Marian Forrester, in the company of Ivy Peters, is part of the world of experience. Before leaving Sweet Water for good he goes over to see Marian once more. An earlier scene repeats itself: standing by the honeysuckle with its earthy suggestion of female sexuality, Niel looks in the dining-room window to see Ivy Peters embracing Marian in the pantry. Once again he rushes away from the house, but reflects: "It took two doses to cure him. Well, he had had them!" (p. 170). Marian Forrester is now a "common woman" to him and he leaves Sweet Water "with weary contempt for her in his heart" (p. 169). Niel's initiation into experience, however, does not leave him an embittered misanthrope like Hawthorne's Young Goodman Brown. It is several years before Niel can think of her without regret, but eventually "he came to be very glad that he had known her, and that she had had a hand in breaking him in to life" (p. 171). Niel is afforded one last glimpse of his lost lady, living with another rich husband in Brazil, her rouge heavier, her hair darker, and he is glad to learn that she had " 'come up again' " and was cared for to the end.

Notes

1. I am indebted to the late Renato Poggioli for the term "pastoral of innocence." In his article "The Oaten Flute," *Harvard Library Bulletin* 11 (May 1957): 147–84, Poggioli distinguishes two kinds of pastoral: the pastoral of happiness in which the rustic landscape is a place of erotic fulfillment, and the pastoral of innocence, a domestic idyll which celebrates age rather than youth. A good example of the latter would be Sarah Orne Jewett's *The Country of the Pointed Firs.* To denote its opposite I use the term pastoral of experience (with its Blakean overtones) rather than pastoral of happiness, as the retreat into memory more often uncovers sexual nightmare than erotic bliss.

2. "The Novel Démeublé," *Willa Cather on Writing,* pp. 35–43.

3. *CSF,* pp. 515–22.

4. *CSF,* pp. 573–78.

5. *CSF,* pp. 557–66.

6. *April Twilights (1903),* edited with an introduction by Bernice Slote, rev. ed. (Lincoln: University of Nebraska Press, 1968).

7. *CSF,* pp. 265–82.

8. *CSF,* pp. 69–77.

9. The story contains the seeds of much later fiction: the image of the boys on a sandbank in the river occurs in *Alexander's Bridge* and *My Ántonia;* the New Mexican mesa looks forward to the Southwest landscape in *The Song of the Lark, The Professor's House, Death Comes for the Archbishop;* the Coronado theme recurs in *My Ántonia;* and in *A Lost Lady* there are two German boys exactly like the Fasslers who take catfish from the river to sell in town. "The Enchanted Bluff" clearly gives expression to a particularly rich and fertile memory.

10. Elizabeth Sergeant speculates whether the writing of *My Ántonia* was not for Willa Cather "a real turning point of literary maturity, when

encouragement or criticism from without became irrelevant?" See *Willa Cather: A Memoir,* p. 148.

11. Ibid., p. 121.

12. *My Ántonia* (Sentry edition; Boston: Houghton Mifflin, 1961). All references are to this text.

13. My reading assumes throughout that Jim Burden rather than Ántonia is the central character in the novel. Early critics, such as René Rapin and David Daiches, erroneously saw Ántonia as the sole focus of interest and because she disappears for long stretches at a time were forced to conclude that the book was structurally flawed. More recent critics, however, such as James E. Miller, Jr., in "*My Ántonia:* A Frontier Drama of Time," *American Quarterly* 10 (Winter 1958): 476–84, and Terence Martin, in "The Drama of Memory in *My Ántonia,*" *PMLA* 74 (March 1969): 304–11, have recognized that the novel takes its shape from the narrator's sensibility, that the focus of the book rests not on Ántonia but, as the title suggests, on the narrator's perception of her.

14. Blanche Gelfant in her incisive article "The Forgotten Reaping-Hook: Sex in *My Ántonia,*" *American Literature* 43 (March 1971): 60–82, shows this process at work, especially as regards sexuality in the novel. Professor Gelfant's study is definitive of its kind, but the criteria upon which her examination of sexual attitudes is based are sociological rather than esthetic. She measures Jim's responses by a social norm and thus sees his preoccupation with childhood in a negative light; but the imagination always flouts such norms and derives its very vitality from what is indeed "complex, subtle, aberrant" (Gelfant, p. 61). By considering *My Ántonia* as a pastoral we see it as part of "the kingdom of art," with its affinities to the work of other pastoral artists such as Wordsworth and Proust.

15. Gelfant, "The Forgotten Reaping-Hook," p. 69. Willa Cather no doubt had the Dumas play in mind when she created these scenes between Jim and Lena, but Flaubert, of whom she had long made a cult, had written similar scenes in *L'Éducation sentimentale,* where Frédéric Moreau's affair with Rosanette, a girl of the demimonde, complete with talk of fashions, intruding older lovers, and nuisance pets, is overshadowed by his ideal love for Madame Arnoux.

16. Autumn is the prevailing season in the novel: the greater part of Book I takes place in the fall when Jim first arrives in Nebraska and Book V takes place entirely in the autumn. It was a time of year which made Willa Cather homesick. In her letters on her first trip to Europe, *Willa Cather in Europe: Her Own Story of the First Journey,* with an introduction and incidental notes by George N. Kates (New York: Alfred A. Knopf, 1956), she writes in September from Arles that "the sycamore leaves are beginning to turn a little, and over her narrow streets in the evening there falls the chill of autumn, the strange homesick chill that always makes one want to be at home, where there are geraniums to be potted for winter and little children to be got ready for school" (p. 170). A more accurate text of these letters appears in *The World and the Parish: Willa Cather's Articles and Reviews, 1893–1902,* selected and edited with a commentary

by William M. Curtin (Lincoln: University of Nebraska Press, 1970), pp. 889–952, with "A Note on the Editing," pp. 965–70. Hereafter cited as *W&P.*

17. See John H. Randall III, *The Landscape and the Looking Glass: Willa Cather's Search for Value* (Boston: Houghton Mifflin, 1960) for an expanded discussion of the mythic elements in Willa Cather's fiction. Ántonia as an earth-goddess is treated specifically in the section entitled "The Fruition of the Soil: The Garden of the World," pp. 138–49. See also Evelyn Thomas Helmick, "Myth in the Works of Willa Cather," *Midcontinent American Studies Journal* 9 (Fall 1968): 63–69.

18. A third type appears in the later fiction (best represented by Victoria Templeton and Sapphira Colbert) which combines the characteristics of the two contrasting women in the earlier fiction. With its source of the author's complex feelings about her mother, this figure is attractive and spoiled in the tradition of Southern womanhood, but is, by provenience, maternal and punitive as well.

19. *A Lost Lady* (New York: Alfred A. Knopf, 1963). All references are to this text.

20. Lewis, *Willa Cather Living,* pp. 124–25.

21. Dorothy Van Ghent, in *Willa Cather,* captures the effect nicely when she describes the book as "a series of sharply focused vignettes that catch [Mrs. Forrester's] brilliance and also the disturbing shadow of something illicit in her nature" (p. 27).

22. The association of male sexuality with the snake and with evil and cruelty is a persistent equation throughout Willa Cather's novels. Jim Burden, with his evasive attitudes to sexuality, expresses extreme disgust for the old rattlesnake he kills: "his abominable muscularity, his loathsome, fluid motion, somehow made me sick" (p. 45). In *Death Comes for the Archbishop* the wicked Buck Scales, like Ivy Peters, is described as snakelike in appearance, and the Bishop's fear of an ancient evil predating civilization comes to him in the Indian cave ("Snake Root") where, legend holds, serpents are kept for religious ritual. In the early story "El Dorado: A Kansas Recessional," the corrupt land speculator is justly killed by a poisonous snake when he tries to retrieve some personal effects connected with a woman; in "The Profile" the protagonist's little sister, one of the women in his past brutalized by men, symbolically dies from a snake bite. There are numerous other examples: the repellent image in *Shadows on the Rock* of the immoral French great ladies drinking viper broth; Nancy, the slave girl, who says she has a greater fear than snakes—that is, of Martin Colbert who wants to rape her; "the old beauty," who expresses her physical aversion to her assailant by calling him a "leech."

23. Dawn in Willa Cather's fiction is often a time of innocence and purity of intention. In *O Pioneers!* Carl Linstrum remembers Alexandra, a figure of maternal purity and strength, coming across the fields at dawn with "the milky light of the early morning all about her." In *My Mortal Enemy* Myra Henshawe wants to die at dawn, for "that is always such a forgiving time"; and in the light of a summer dawn Quebec in *Shadows*

on the Rock looks "like a holy city in an old legend, shriven, sinless, washed in gold." In *Sapphira and the Slave Girl* Nancy feels, after a night of fear, that the dawn restores both virtue and safety to her world at Back Creek.

24. More than one critic has drawn a parallel between *A Lost Lady* and Flaubert's *Madame Bovary,* but the importance of Niel to the novel creates closer parallels with *L'Education sentimentale.* Frédéric Moreau and Niel Herbert, both semi-orphaned and half-hearted law students, are subject to the treacheries of sex and beauty in a woman they romantically idealize. Both of the idealized women are married to men of declining means, and appearances are hard to maintain. One of the earliest images that both men associate with their romantic ideals is an ivory-handled parasol, and for both men a bouquet of roses thrown in the mud expresses disenchantment. The latter image might easily represent a direct borrowing by Willa Cather from Flaubert.

CHAPTER THREE

Satire

The Critical Imagination in Willa Cather's Short Fiction

Epic and pastoral are imaginative modes which give expression to powerful, universal feelings, but there are many works of art in which our interest is directed principally toward an idea or a different form of consciousness rather than an emotion. In the experimental prose of Gertrude Stein, for example, fictional technique is used to explore levels of being and awareness, and in the plays of Bertolt Brecht our emotions are deliberately alienated in the interest of an idea around which a play has been conceived and constructed. One might loosely term these works of art as products of the critical imagination. Willa Cather, unlike the majority of her twentieth-century comtemporaries, distrusted ideas as a source and *raison d'être* of art. In her very earliest reviews and critical writings we find her stating repeatedly that a genuine work of art is never "clever"; that literature is not made out of ideas, but out of people and emotions—something quite apart from knowledge. In her fiction her most accomplished artists and critics have similar feelings: in *The Song of the Lark,* for example, Harsanyi, the pianist, recognizes that Thea Kronborg is not quick to learn, but he sees that she has the emotion and desire to be a great artist; Don Hedger in "Coming, Aphrodite!," a painter far ahead of his time, avoids fashionable cliques of artists where ideas about art are discussed; Charlotte Waterford in "Uncle Valentine," one of the most postive characters in Willa Cather's fiction, has "good taste" rather than intelligence about both art and living. This attitude extends to form in Willa Cather's fiction as well: her novels are always built around a feeling rather than an idea of form—something organic that retains the complexity of the living experience. One thinks of Jim Burden with his manuscript about Ántonia which " 'hasn't any form,' " which is just a memoir, or Godfrey St. Peter's finding the form for his histories in the visual impact of a series of mountain peaks. The author herself likened the form of *Shadows on the Rock* to "a series of pictures remembered rather than experienced" and to a fragment of an old song.[1] Although Willa Cather never became an intellectual novelist, ideas did play an increasingly important part in her fiction as she grew older. This is especially true of the novels dating from the mid-1920s, a time in her life when she grew to distrust some of her strongest emotions. In order to illuminate the unique qualities of *One of Ours* and *The Professor's House,* this chapter will focus on the intellectual and critical dimensions of Willa Cather's art. The importance of these elements in her fiction is apparent when we recognize that in *The Professor's House* the author sought to free herself from the grip of self-destructive emotions through the discipline of a traditional structure of thought.

As in a study of epic and pastoral elements in Willa Cather's fiction, one finds in her apprenticeship pieces several examples of the critical imagination as well—in short stories constructed around baldly stated ideas. Through their esthetic limitations one gains another kind of insight into the nature of her craft. Some of the early "idea" stories are of continuing interest because their central theme or idea later became an organic aspect of Willa Cather's art. "A Son of the Celestial" (1893)[2] is such a story, written out of the author's curiosity about the contrast between Western and Eastern cultures. The story concerns a once brilliant American scholar who has taken to drinking heavily and smoking opium with an old Chinese artisan in San Francisco. He discusses philosophy and literature with old Yung and is horrified by the lack of passion in Oriental people: " 'You are so old that you are born yellow and wrinkled and blind. You ought to have been buried centuries before Europe was civilized.' " The idea of civilization gradually depleting itself of energy always fascinated the author and frequently underlay the broad conflicts in her novels.[3] Jim Burden, for example, feels the pull toward the vitality of the

Nebraska farm country as well as toward the sophisticated but effete civilization of the East. In "A Son of the Celestial" the idea is given dramatic interest by the scholar's horror at seeing himself becoming like Yung. Another idea story is "The Count of Crow's Nest" (1896),[4] which picks up the image of a people (here it is the European aristocracy) depleting itself—the blood growing tired and the family dying out. An aging and impoverished count lives in a Chicago rooming house treasuring his memories of a civilized past, while his daughter, a common woman, makes a living as a fifth-rate singer. She wants to publish some old letters that her father has brought from Europe which, because of their scandalous nature, would sell very well. The author resolves the conflict between the new life and tradition by giving her sympathy to what is imaginative, rather than to what is either simply old or new. The central character in the story, Buchanan, aids the count in resisting his daughter's exploitation of the past. Two other interesting ideas emerge in this story though they are not as integral to the plot. Near the beginning the narrator reflects that one hates most intensely where one has failed oneself. This recognition of human motives and behavior anticipates a deeply personal theme underlying *The Professor's House.* Also, when Buchanan and the old count are talking about art, it is interesting to hear the old man give expression to what is essentially the author's theory of the unfurnished novel; he says " 'the domain of pure art is always the indefinite.' " The value of this esthetic can be fully appreciated by contrasting these early tales to the later writing, where everything is suggested rather than openly stated.

A great number of the early idea stories are distinct failures. " 'The Fear that Walks by Noonday' " (1894), "The Princess Baladina—Her Adventure" (1896), "The Westbound Train" (1899), "The Affair at Grover Station" (1900), "El Dorado: A Kansas Recessional" (1901) are all particularly flat, unimpressive pieces of writing. What is instructive to note is that in each case the story's failure seems to derive from a common flaw—the author's attempt to develop plot and a clever, surprise ending. The invariable result is a quality of contrivance. In "The Westbound Train" a woman's travel passes are confused with another's and for a while she begins to doubt her husband and the validity of their marriage; when the confusion has been cleared away, so has any interest in the story. "The Affair at Grover Station" is potentially more interesting because it employs a male narrator reflecting on a love triangle and subsequent murder, but the focus falls finally on the narrator's having seen his friend's ghost, so the reader again is betrayed by suspense and a contrived ending. "El Dorado: A Kansas Recessional" also is a potentially interesting story, this time because the author is using an elegiac setting, a deserted prairie town, for which she clearly has much imaginative feeling. But as in another story called "A Resurrection" (1897) set in a dying town, the author projects our interest toward a conclusion which fails to satisfy our aroused expectations. In "El Dorado" a land speculator, who duped everyone into starting the town, returns for some pictures and artifacts connected with a woman he loved, and is killed by a poisonous snake as he is retrieving his goods. An old colonel who had stayed on in town after it failed is thereby able to get back his invested money. In "A Resurrection," whose real imaginative subject is the unsung nobility of forgotten, small-town people (one is reminded of Gray's "Elegy"), the heroine finally receives a marriage proposal from the man she once loved and whose son she has been raising. The "happily-ever-after" ending belies both the realistic setting of a dying western town and the stoical conception of the heroine's character. In each of these stories there is a shift away from the original imaginative inspiration behind the story to develop an idea and to fulfill the more conventional demands of a short-story plot.

As Willa Cather's writing matured she turned less frequently to ideas as a source of inspiration for fiction. Eventually her best fiction was to be written out of an emotion and developed largely in terms of setting and character. But one form of idea story continued to interest her and that was the Jamesian ghost story. In "Eleanor's House" (1907)[5] a ghost never actually appears, but a man's second wife finds that she must exorcise the spirit of his dead first wife before they can live happily together. The first wife, Eleanor, represents an idealized romantic youth and her decease must be accepted by the husband as the inevitable passage from innocence into the sober world of experience and responsibility. In its characters and setting (Americans living in Normandy) and in its emphasis on the subtle interplay of consciousness and feeling, "Eleanor's House" is probably the most Jamesian story Willa Cather ever wrote, but like so many of her other stories built around an interesting idea, it suffers from overexplicitness. The central consciousness in the story, a girlhood friend of the first wife, understands too well her friend's situation and we are left with few questions to tease the imagination. The final twist of the friend becoming obsessed by Eleanor—her husband says to her " 'You look like a ghost' "—is just that, a twist, rather than the revelation of a powerful hidden emotion in the story. In "Consequences" (1915)[6] the ghost who haunts the hero in the form of an old man is very real. The old man prefigures everything that Kier Cavanaugh will become, and after several glimpses into the jaded, physically depleted world of his future, Kavanaugh chooses to commit suicide. The contrast between the ruddy-faced protangonist and the decayed old man who pursues him is quite effective, but unfortunately the emphasis in the story falls on a lengthy debate between the hero and an acquaintance as to whether or not all suicides are explicable, and in the context of a thesis being demonstrated Cavanaugh's story is considerably weakened.

A few stories Willa Cather published after leaving her post as managing editor of *McClure's Magazine* might be described as ideas or current interests worked up into fictional form; they betray that at this time the author still had to sell her work in order to make a living. In "Behind the Singer Tower" (1912)[7] six men, out for a boat ride on the North River, reflect on the nature of a powerful city, their thoughts inspired by a fire in a great New York hotel which has killed hundreds of important people. One of the men, a humanitarian engineer, asks the others to consider also the countless little men, the many workers who are destroyed every day so that the city's great machinery can operate (the average for window cleaners who drop to the pavement, we are told, is more than one per day). When one of the group tells of "Little Caesar," an Italian day laborer from Ischia who is needlessly killed in a construction accident, the story moves into direct social criticism. But it ends with a vision of evolutionary purpose behind the dynamic processes of the city: the men are left wondering what new "Idea" will be born into human history from their civilization on Manhattan Island. This ending looks forward to a similar theme in *One of Ours.* David Gerhardt, the violinist, wonders if there is some unforeseen purpose behind the devastation of the war: " 'I've sometimes wondered whether the young men of our time had to die to bring a new idea into the world . . . something Olympian' " (p. 409).[8] This was an idea, however, which the author never dramatized any further. "The Bookkeeper's Wife" (1916) and "Ardessa" (1918)[9] are two more stories drawn from her experiences in New York. They are both stories about office workers, people who count for little in the city's great scheme of things, but who nonetheless suffer from the ironic twists of fate. Except for their biographical nature (we are given a glimpse of that world in which Willa Cather herself worked for six years), these stories have little of lasting interest, for their ironies are of a wholly conventional and hypothetical kind.

The danger for the critical imagination is overintellectualization—the reduction of esthetic experience to an abstraction. Frequently, art of a critical and ironic nature represents the revenge of the intellect on emotions which the artist himself cannot control. But emotion rather than intellect is the immutable material out of which great art has always been fashioned. Consequently the most powerful form of critical art is satire, for not only does it promote the function of the critical consciousness, but also it gives expression to those emotions—indignation and outrage—which spur on critical judgment. In a satire the artist projects his sense of personal failure and self-disgust (those emotions he cannot handle) on to the world at large, and by pointing to social injustice and to irrationality in the behavior of others he mitigates his own sense of failure and inadequacy. For example, the righteous indignation of Swift at the presumptions of the human animal seems to have had its source in the writer's own emotional instability and a body wracked by disease and pain. Thus while a satirist's professed purposes are rational and corrective—he wants us to recognize and alter an unhealthy state of affairs—he is in fact giving vent to his deepest feelings, and by establishing a moral norm from which all human behavior is accordingly judged aberrant, he is effecting a personal revenge on the world through his art. The central motive in a satirical work of art is to impose one's individual sense of order on the world and, by inspiring hatred or ridicule, to revenge oneself on an unsatisfactory way of life. The emotions out of which critical or satirical art arise include cruelty on the one hand and self-pity on the other, sadomasochism being their psychological extremes.

Self-pity and cruelty are emotions which recur with significant frequency in Willa Cather's fiction and which point to a persistent dark side to the author's imagination. Consider the importance of such despairing, self-pitying protagonists as Claude Wheeler or Godfrey St. Peter, and the unmitigatable cruelty exhibited by Ivy Peters, Myra Henshawe, or Sapphira Colbert. In two very early stories the cruelty latent in the author's imagination finds startlingly direct expression. "The Strategy of the Were-Wolf Dog" (1896)[10] is in one sense an innocuous (and artistically unimpressive) tale written for children at Christmas. But at the same time it is almost Iagolike in its conception. The evil were-wolf dog, who is despised and in return hates everything and everyone, leads Santa's reindeers out on a lake where the ice breaks and they drown after much struggling to save themselves. The tale ends happily with the other animals helping to deliver the children's gifts on Christmas Eve, but the one strong image in the story is that of the remorseless were-wolf dog watching the reindeer drown. In "The Dance at Chevalier's" (1900)[11] the two rivals' love for Severine Chevalier pales beside the loser's desire for revenge. The latter warns Severine that he likes to kill the things he loves, and before he poisons his rival at the dance he says to himself, " 'Love is sweet, but sweeter is revenge.' "

The author's personal drama of self-pity, cruelty, and revenge is set forth in a rather light-hearted but revealing tale entitled "Tommy, the Unsentimental" (1896),[12] written when Willa Cather was about twenty-two. The author's frank, boyish nature with its suggestion of emotional complexity is probably nowhere else presented in such a direct and engaging manner. The plot of the story is not biographical, but one cannot help feeling there is considerable honesty and candor in the characterization of the protagonist and her feelings. The story tells about a tomboy in a small western town who saves her boyfriend from financial disaster and at the same time finds him a very suitable wife. The central character is Tommy Shirley, a rough, boyish young woman (not unlike Willa Cather in some respects), who has the figure of a half-grown lad. Tommy's best friends are her father's business associates, and she can hold her own with them, whether it is at whist, billiards, or making cocktails. However, it is in the relationship between Tommy and two other young people that we catch a glimpse of the complex psychological relationships among characters in the author's major novels, and that the drama of self-pity and revenge reveals itself. Quite out of keeping with her good sense and practicality, Tommy is fond of Jay Ellington Harper, an effeminate bank clerk from the East who, according to Tommy, is good for nothing but keeping his hair parted and wearing a white carnation in his buttonhole. But Tommy is also "sweet" on a girl she brings home from school in the East—Miss Jessica, a vaporous and delicate young woman given to sunshades. Eventually Harper's affection for Tommy changes to love for Miss Jessica and Tommy arranges for her two friends to marry, but not before her own confused emotions find temporary release in a scene of subtle revenge. In order to save Harper's bank from collapse Tommy and Miss Jessica must cycle twenty-five miles upgrade to the next town. The sun is like hot brass and Miss Jessica almost perishes from the heat; but Tommy drives her mercilessly on. Miss Jessica, watching Tommy in front of her, reflects "that Tommy was not only very unkind, but that she sat very badly on her wheel and looked aggressively masculine and professional when she bent her shoulders and pumped like that." Finally, Miss Jessica, reduced to tears, gives up, collapses by the wayside and Tommy, laughing to herself, pushes on thinking that, after all, it only evened the score. But after saving the bank Tommy is left alone, and there is a touch of pathos to the girl who is a forerunner of Cather's lonely artist figure. However, in the controlled and rather light manner of the tale the heroine bites her lip and then shrugs her shoulders at both the foolishness and loveableness of more ordinary people.

For Willa Cather the emotions of cruelty and self-pity were most strongly associated with the small Nebraska town in which she was raised, and they first emerge as the substance of satire in "The Sculptor's Funeral" (1905),[13] a story set in the West. Without doubt "The Sculptor's Funeral" is one of Willa Cather's best pieces of short fiction: detail is always suggestive rather than explicit and the essential elements of the story—the satire, the pathos—come together in exactly the right relationship. Perhaps this is because the author may have had a formal model for the story in the pastoral elegy, the classical lament of an artist on the occasion of a fellow artist's death. Whether consciously or not, Miss Cather has woven into her story many of the elements of pastoral elegy as practiced by the Greeks Bion and Moschus, and in English by Milton ("Lycidas"), Shelley ("Adonais"), and Matthew Arnold ("Thyrsis"). The artist's body is brought back by one of his students to be watched over by his kinsmen and former neighbors, but as in the traditional poem only the fellow artist truly mourns his loss. For while the professed purpose of a pastoral elegy is to sing a lament for the dead poet, its real motive is satiric—to rail against those forces which diminish an artist's life. In "The Sculptor's Funeral" it is the conformity and ugly materialism of midwestern society which come under attack. The unsympathetic mourners represent all those negative aspects of life from which the artist originally fled.

Point of view in the story is divided between Henry Steavens, the artist's student who accompanies the body west, and Jim Laird, a drunken lawyer from Sand City, who appreciates what Harvey Merrick, the dead artist, made of his life. Steavens's viewpoint distills for us the pathos of the artist's life: through his eyes we feel compassion for Harvey Merrick coming from such raw, ugly surroundings, and we are assured of his significant achievement in the larger world. Laird's viewpoint is the bitter, satirical one; with his "astonishing cataract of red beard that grew fiercely and thickly in all directions," he is almost a personification of choleric man. In his angry speeches he denounces the drab western town where money is the only measure of success, and thinly disguised knavery the accepted means of acquiring it. Ideals in such a town, though everywhere professed, are destructive to anyone who takes them seriously, for cunning is the only currency with real value. The palm of distinction placed on Merrick's coffin, like the traditional tribute of flowers in pastoral elegy, is without significance to the townspeople; they discuss instead the possibility of a will and agree that Mr. Merrick should have sent his son to a business college instead of a university in the East.

The bitter mood of the story is underscored in the details describing the townspeople and the dead artist's home. The shuffling, ill-defined group of men gathered at the train station speak in a rough country slang and move about "slimily as eels." The

Merrick home with its clover-green Brussels carpet, its plush upholstery and hand-painted china plaques, is the epitome of conventional bad taste. The coffin is taken into the typically unused parlor and set "under a hanging lamp ornamented with jingling glass prisms and before a 'Rogers group' of John Alden and Priscilla, wreathed with smilax." The satire of bad taste and crude manners in a small western town deepens into personal horror with the portrait of the artist's parents: the violent, terrifying mother whose outburst of grief soon gives way to abuse of the maid for forgetting the dressing for the chicken salad, and the shameful, broken father who looks at his wife "with a dull, frightened, appealing expression, as a spaniel looks at the whip." Steavens recognizes them to be "the real tragedy of his master's life." These parents are a caricature of the dominant mother and weak father, but they prefigure the essential nature of several couples in Willa Cather's fiction, perhaps most significantly the Templetons in "Old Mrs. Harris" and the Colberts in *Sapphira and the Slave Girl,* both modeled to some extent on the author's own parents.

One of Ours: Willa Cather's Waste-Land Novel

Criticism of materialistic and Philistine attitudes continues as an important motif in much of the short fiction following "The Sculptor's Funeral" and in the early novels. Willa Cather's indictment of mean-spirited and unimaginative people in small towns comes to the fore in the character of Scott Spinney in the story "The Joy of Nelly Deane," first published in 1911.[14] In *My Ántonia* these feelings surface when Jim Burden rebels against the confines of the village, particularly the frustrating mediocrity of its social life. But the first novel in which the critical imagination sets the tone for the whole book is *One of Ours,* Willa Cather's Pulitzer Prize–winning study of a Nebraska farm boy who makes an unhappy marriage and is killed in World War I.

When Willa Cather wrote *One of Ours* she was in part remembering her past in Nebraska as she had done in *My Ántonia.* The vast difference between the two books illustrates among other things the difference between pastoral and satire. In *My Ántonia* Jim Burden is intent on preserving the past as a happy, idyllic retreat, whereas in *One of Ours* the narrator is bent on exposing that world for its limitations and failures. The mood of bitterness in *One of Ours* is felt from the very beginning. The book opens with the Wheeler family getting up for breakfast, and the narrative is immediately bristling with the hero's bitter observations on his family and the mismanagement of the farm. The details in the opening scene bring into focus the conflict (sustained throughout the novel) between a sensitive and imaginative response to life and the mercenary and crudely materialistic ways of a small midwestern farm community. The scene also illumines the frequent shifting of emotions in satire from anger to self-pity. Claude Wheeler, the sensitive protagonist, had planned to drive to the circus in town that day and had washed the car for that purpose, but at the breakfast table his father tells him that instead he must take the wagon and mules to town with a load of cowhides. Shy and self-conscious, Claude is humiliated at the thought of going to Frankfort where he will be seen by everyone with the greasy, smelling hides. He reflects angrily to himself how often the wagon had been to town that summer without the hides, and that it was the carelessness of his father's rough hired men that had resulted in the deaths of the four steers whose skins were to be sold. Moreover, he thinks, the price such hides would bring now was not worth half the time spent preparing them. Claude knows his father, who likes to embarrass him, has put this task on him as a crude kind of practical joke; the hired men and his brother Ralph are also amused at his expense. Too proud to object and expose himself further, Claude submits to his father's will; his anger changes into self-pity. Throughout the book Claude is thus put upon by the crudity and thoughtlessness of others. Confused by conflicting loyalities to himself and to his family, he reluctantly conforms to the community's stereotype (he takes over the farm and marries a local girl), but all the while rebelling inwardly at the necessary betrayal of his own instinctive values.

Generally in a satirical novel the central character either embodies those negative aspects of human behavior against which the satire is launched, like Sinclair Lewis's Babbitt, or represents a sympathetic viewpoint, like Huck Finn's, by which society is measured. In *One of Ours* Claude Wheeler serves both functions. He engages our sympathy because his restlessness and youthful idealism are pitted against the crudely materialistic way of life in a small farm community. Not surprisingly, Claude's critical views had their source in the author's own personal antagonisms. Willa Cather stated publicly that Claude Wheeler was modeled after a young cousin who had been killed in World War I,[15] but in letters to Dorothy Canfield Fisher she confided that she had conceived of Claude as herself, and through him she was reliving vicariously the painful experiences of being a misfit in a small town and of being culturally ill at ease in the larger, sophisticated world.[16] Certainly there is the immediacy of direct experience in Claude's conflict with the narrow strictures of small-town life, and his observations constitute a powerful critical attack on the debased values of modern American life. But at the same time Willa Cather was recalling her youthful struggles from the sober vantage point of middle age and from that perspective she viewed her hero ironically as well. Thus while Claude Wheeler is a potent critic of American life, he is at the same time an unsuspecting victim of its perverse ideals. His criticism of American life is concrete and valid, but his conception of a better life is dangerously romantic and abstract. To his Bohemian friend Ernest Havel, who hopes some day to marry and own a farm of his own, Claude insists that there must be something more splendid to live for than such a conventional form of life. Havel counters that the simple, reliable pleasures are enough: "'You Americans are always looking for something outside yourselves to warm you up, and it is no way to do. In old countries, where not very much can happen to us, we know that,—and we learn to make the most of little things'" (p. 53). Havel's reflection in essence prefigures the course of the novel and the fate of its hero, who needs something as large and abstractly conceived as the war in Europe to warm him up to life. *One of Ours* as satire is double-edged in its attack: not only does it expose the gross realities of American life but also the perversity of its romantic ideals. The first three books of the novel take place in America; Claude looks at life around him harshly and critically. The satirical viewpoint, however, modulates into a bitterly ironical one in Books IV and V, when Claude goes to war. He escapes the frustrations of life at home and finds a purpose for living in the war, but now the critical viewpoint is focused on him rather than on the details of American life; for in his romanticizing of Europe and the war Claude is revealed as the victim of his society's highest ideals.

In the first three books of the novel, which are specifically satirical in content, characterization tends towards caricature. There is a touch of this in the conception of the awkward hero whose name is aptly mispronounced "clod." The other characters are viewed more strongly as satirical types—individuals dehumanized by their stereotypical mode of existence. Willa Cather was too emotionally involved with the persons of her past to render them entirely as caricatures; moreover, her artistic purpose was to expose the limitations of what is realistically familiar. But nonetheless most of them are seen with an emphasis on a certain trait, and collectively they represent a cross section of that society from which Claude seeks to escape. Since a satirist's weapon is either ridicule or outrage, our reponse to the secondary characters is either to laugh at them or to feel angry contempt for them. Claude's father and brothers make us feel the latter; they are the very antithesis of those creative and visionary pioneers which Willa Cather idealized in several of her other books. Their energies are expended on wholly selfish and unimaginative preoccupations. Mr. Wheeler has the stature of a pioneer figure in his physical bearing and his power over other men, but he is an unashamedly lazy man who, in renting out his huge tracts of land, exploits the labor of others, and whose jolly, easygoing ways disguise a latently cruel and authoritarian nature.[17] His laziness and sadistic sense of humor are both at work when he cuts down the cherry tree so that his wife can reach the fruit; the destruction of the tree not only outrages his wife's gentle sensibility, but sends Claude, at that time still a small boy, into uncontrollable paroxysms of anger and hate.[18] Claude's older brother, Bayliss, is a parody of the self-made man. Prudent, hard-working, and ambitious, he courts Gladys Farmer, the town's most attractive girl, and buys the town's most prestigious estate. But he is nonetheless self-pitying and lacking in any real vitality—his one enthusiasm is Prohibition. That such selfish and unimaginative men are heirs to what was once a heroic country is a point underscored several times in the novel. Claude reflects that the people had changed: "He could remember when all the farmers in this community were friendly toward each other; now they were continually having lawsuits. Their sons were either stingy and grasping, or extravagant and lazy, and they were always stirring up trouble" (p. 102). Claude's younger brother, Ralph, represents another force at work in modern society—its mechanization. Insensitive to the needs and feelings of his mother and Mahailey, the old servant, who are confused by machines, Ralph continually replaces the household appliances with newer, more complicated models and gadgets. The Wheelers are "careful" with money (they would never take a luxury seat on a train or buy expensive, good-looking furniture), yet Ralph is allowed to waste countless sums of money on all the latest machines and appliances. Significantly, of all the Wheelers Claude is the only one who actually works the land.

Although Claude's mother is sympathetically drawn, she is nevertheless used to expose the religious attitudes of a small midwestern town. Because she is so kindly and well-intentioned (Willa Cather was doing a portrait of a favorite aunt) she is duped by the hypocritical posturings of supposedly religious men. To help her church and its cause she entertains a preacher named Brother Weldon for several weeks at a time. Claude sees through his mincing, apologetic manner and recognizes him as one of those young men who go in the ministry "because they wanted to be pampered by kind, trusting women like his mother" (p. 50). Ironically, because of Brother Weldon, Claude is sent to Temple College, a denominational school, instead of the State University. The narrow piety and sterility of religion is further exemplified by the Chapins, the brother and sister with whom Claude boards while he is at college. Edward Chapin, studying to be a minister, is old and wasted looking at twenty-six; his only distinction is his remarkable stupidity "after years of reverential study." His sister Annabelle is a sentimental, foolish girl "who can make the finest things seem tame and flat merely by alluding to them" (pp. 32–33). The descriptions of these religious people is wholly in the vein of comic satire; even their names suggest Dickensian caricature—Brother "Well-Done," Chapin (chapped, chip, pin).

In direct contrast to Claude's family and the neighbors at home are the Erlichs, a cultured German family, who befriend Claude while he is in Lincoln at college. The Erlichs are used to point up by contrast the limitations of American culture. The first time Claude visits them he is immediately struck by their relaxed, gracious manners, their eagerness to discuss and analyze ideas, and their appreciation of history and the arts: "Here there was none of the poisonous reticence he had always associated with family gatherings, nor the awkwardness of people sitting with their hands in their lap, facing each other, each one guarding his secret or his suspicion, while he hunted for a safe subject to talk about" (p. 41). In the Erlich home the bookshelves are crowded; on the mantel stands a plaster bust of Byron and over the piano hangs an engraving of Napoleon. At first Claude assumed that the widow and her six sons were rich, but he learned afterward that on the contrary they were poor; but they "knew how to live . . . and spent their money on themselves, instead of on machines to do the work and machines to entertain people" (p. 43). The Erlichs open Claude's eyes to the shoddy values of standardized living in America. When he goes back to Frankfort to live on his father's farm, he condemns in his mind the American way of life:

> The farmer raised and took to market things with an intrinsic value; wheat and corn as good as could be grown anywhere in the world, hogs and cattle that were the best of their kind. In return he got manufactured articles of poor quality; showy furniture that went to pieces, carpets and draperies that faded, clothes that made a handsome man look like a clown. Most of his money was paid out for machinery,—and that, too, went to pieces. [P. 101]

In his picture of the Midwest Claude sees all the people like his brothers, "either stingy and grasping, or extravagant and lazy" (p. 102). Julius Erlich goes abroad to study for a doctor's degree and lives on less each year than Ralph wastes. But except for Gladys Farmer none of Claude's contemporaries in Frankfort have an unselfish, creative vision of life, nor even a trade or profession that would contribute something to the world.

Significantly, Claude realizes at the same time that he is no better than the fellows he condemns: "[He] was aware that his energy, instead of accomplishing something, was spent in resisting unalterable conditions, and in unavailing efforts to subdue his own nature" (p. 103). Here the author has touched on the root of satire in self-dissatisfaction. Throughout the novel Claude's critical rejection of the world around him has its countermeasure in his own self-condemnation. He sneers at the puniness of his brother Bayliss and at the physically wasted look of Edward Chapin, but Claude himself, with his red hair, freckles, and a square-shaped head, is "exactly the sort of looking boy he didn't want to be" (p.

17). Claude views his fellows at Temple College with contempt, but it is really his own lack of spirit in allowing his parents to decide his future that he despises. In his self-destructive mood he takes a perverse kind of pleasure in his misfortunes, like the smothering of the hogs in the snowstorm or his being dragged by runaway mules and cut up in a barb-wire fence. In the latter incident the physical humiliation of his swollen and infected face brings him to a real peak of self-loathing. Claude measures his own perverse nature by comparing himself to his two positive-thinking friends, Ernest Havel and Leonard Dawson. Dawson is the *type* of happy, conformity-minded youth who farms successfully, marries happily, and raises a family. Havel, the immigrant boy, while sensitive and intelligent, is "never uncertain," and accepts the way of life decreed for him by the society of his adoption.

In order to present Claude's point of view as concretely as possible Willa Cather adopted a radically different style of prose in *One of Ours.* Contrary to her esthetic dictum of selectivity (the novel démeublé), this is a novel of saturation or what James might have called a "loose, baggy monster." So that we will recognize the specific nature of that society against which Claude rebels, the author has given us a heavily detailed picture, in the manner of Sinclair Lewis, of life in the Midwest in the early part of this century. She cut out all "picture-making," as she described it,[19] for not only would descriptive, evocative scenes belie the immediacy and credibility of Claude's perspective, but pastoral landscapes would betray the novel's essentially critical feeling.

Because a satirical novel depends on exposing the limitations of a carefully observed reality, *One of Ours* with its wealth of realistic detail has dated in a way that Willa Cather's other novels have not. The novel creates the mood of a specific time and place and, while the author's overall critical intentions remain clear, certain nuances relating to clothing, gestures, and regional customs (e.g., a dress covered with bugles and jets, a "Christian Endeavour" jest, a vegetarian sanatorium) are lost with time. However, the form or structure of the novel has an inevitable and lasting dimension which can be illuminated by comparing it to a very significant piece of contemporary writing. *One of Ours* appeared the same year as T. S. Eliot's *The Waste Land,* and while there is obviously no influence of the one on the other (Miss Cather did not know Eliot personally), they are both records of social and personal failure transcended by the spiritual visions of another culture. The five-part structure of both works follows a similar thematic pattern: part one is an extended panorama of society's failures, while parts two and three view that failure in personal terms, particularly as sexual failure; part four is a short "death by water" sequence, followed in part five by a promise of spiritual rebirth. It may be that both works had a common model in the five-part symphony as practiced, say, by Beethoven.[20] This has been suggested in the case of *The Waste Land* and could possibly be true for Miss Cather's novel; certainly both writers used musical analogues in other works. A motif which they both employ is the Parsifal legend as reworked by Wagner; the latter pretended to derive the name from Fal-Parsi, or "pure fool," and it is interesting to know that Willa Cather had originally intended to entitle the last part of the novel "The Blameless Fool, by Pity Enlightened."[21] In both the novel and poem a guileless hero, who has been wounded sexually (the name Claude means lame), sets out on a quest for the holy grail to be cured; the hero's quest in both cases reflects the failure of his society to provide any living spiritual values. Although there is no direct relationship between the poem and novel, the "waste land" nonetheless is a suggestive metaphor for the novel's mood and direction.

Perhaps most importantly it draws our attention to the fact that Claude's failure must be viewed on one level in specifically sexual terms. In the novel's satiric scheme Enid Royce (the name, like Chapin, has a pinched, abbreviated sound) is a stereotype of the innocent, virginal American girl. While her purity and physical paleness are held up as ideals, the painful reality is that she is impersonal and unfeeling toward others. Ironically, it is her cool, detached quality which first attracts Claude to Enid. When he was at the university Claude had been especially interested in the martyrs—his term paper had been on Joan of Arc. The torments and dissatisfactions of his own life had kindled in him a sympathetic response; moreover, as he explains at one point to Ernest Havel, he felt the martyrs discovered that " 'something splendid about life' " (p. 52) he was looking for—something outside of themselves to live and die for that was better than anything they had known before. Enid first comes to him when he is ill from being cut in the barb-wire fence, when in his physical misery his mind "prowled about among dark legends of torture,—everything he had ever read about the Inquisition, the rack and the wheel" (p. 142). Enid's controlled, graceful presence is coolly refreshing and brings back the earlier image of her being chosen for the Sunday School *tableaux vivants* to play the blind girl of Pompeii and the martyr in "Christ and Diana," there being a pallor to her skin and a submissive, unchanging quality about her eyes which suggests something "early Christian." Claude accordingly believes that Enid can raise him from the depths of his despair and self-disgust. But he eventually discovers (when it is too late) that her saintliness is not creative and life-giving, but achieved entirely through negations. All of her interests—religion, Prohibition, vegetarian diet—have the curbing of physical pleasure as their main objective. The idyllic scenes which associate Enid in Claude's eyes with the femininity of whiteness and flowers (planting sweet peas in the spring, gathering water cress with Gladys Farmer, dressed in white as a bride and surrounded by "all the June roses in Frankfort") become cruelly ironic when Enid, wearing her white silk dressing gown, turns Claude away on their wedding night, and when she continues to wear white and keep a flower garden after they are married. Even her chickens are without a dark feather and there is a notable absence of roosters in the flock. Claude's desire for Enid is sexual (he dreams of himself naked talking to her from behind the bushes, and waking he steals one of her lace undergarments), but to Enid a man's embrace is distasteful. Her sexual repression finds its outlet in efficient, executive attempts to convert others to her sterile mode of life. Most appalling of all to Claude is Enid's evasion of any feeling by depersonalizing all relationships. She can attribute Claude's mood after their wedding night to her belief that *all* men are cross before breakfast. Her departure for the mission fields of China is the natural fulfillment of a life structured around such generalizations and abstractions.

When Claude is locked out of the stateroom on his wedding night, he solaces himself with thoughts of home: "His hurt was of a kind that made him turn with a sort of aching cowardice to the old, familiar things that were as sure as the sunrise . . . . When he closed his eyes he could see the light in his mother's window; and, lower down, the glow of Mahailey's lamp, where she sat nodding and mending his old shirts" (p. 196). Until he arrives in France in the last part of the novel the only positive experiences in Claude's life center around his mother and Mahailey and the other motherly women he has known, like Mrs. Erlich in Lincoln and Mrs. Voigt, the German restaurant proprietress on the Burlington line. When these older women are being described the satiric viewpoint is temporarily suspended. Mrs. Wheeler is indeed the type of kindly woman whose faith makes her easy prey for religious opportunities (her fervent piety is suggested in her name Evangeline), but the author portrays her with such love that we never respond to her on the dehumanized level of a type. The same is true of old Mahailey, who might have been a type of simple family servant; but her eccentricities are drawn in such detail and with such affection that if anything she becomes a larger-than-life figure, like Faulkner's Dilsey, whose primitive instincts are attuned to a kind of transcendental wisdom. Yet Mrs. Wheeler and Mahailey are not really spared in the author's critical examination of society. Mrs. Wheeler is a romantic (her person always suggests a spirit trying to free itself from the body) who encourages her favorite son in his quest for an ideal, unattainable world. In Claude's relationship with his mother we begin to view him ironically, for the romanticism they share anticipates the sentimental patriotism so utterly impugned in the last sections of the novel.

No part of Willa Cather's writing has been so heavily criticized as her description of war through the eyes of a combatant; Hemingway, in derision, suggested she got her battle scenes from *The Birth of a Nation.*[22] Hemingway's remark is perhaps more insightful than he intended. In Books IV and V Willa Cather shifted her critical focus from satirizing the details of American life to an ironic view of American idealism and one of its victims. For Claude Wheeler, Europe and the war has the romantic cast of a dream and when we look through his eyes his experiences do acquire something of the theatrical and stagey quality that Hemingway suggested. The author's stylistic intention was not to describe the war in a realistic manner, but to reflect the romantic aura that for so many men gathered around the experience.[23] The shift in style from a detailed realism to something approaching the phantasmagorical is evident from the beginning of Book IV when Claude's train loaded with troops reaches the sea. Here Claude finds a strange scene contrary to his expectations about ship building:

> This was like a dream. Nothing but green meadows, soft grey water, a floating haze of mist a little rosy from the sinking sun, spectre-like seagulls, flying slowly, with the red glow tinging their wings—and those four hulls lying in their braces, facing the sea, deliberating by the sea. [P. 268]

To Claude, who has begun to give the war a sense of romantic purpose, the ships "were like simple and great thoughts, like purposes forming slowly here in the silence beside an unruffled arm of the Atlantic." Claude's heightened, theatrical conception of the war is also reflected in the epic overtones with which the troops and the ships are described. Book IV opens with a picture of the troops done in the epic manner—the single image multiplied:

> A long train of crowded cars, the passengers all of the same sex, almost of the same age, all dressed and hatted alike . . . . In the cars, incessant stretching of cramped legs, shifting of shoulders, striking of matches, passing of cigarettes, groans of boredom; occasionally concerted laughter about nothing. Suddenly the train stops short. Clipped heads and tanned faces pop out at every window. [P. 267]

The description of wooden ships going out to sea "when great passions and great aspirations [stir] a country" has a classical epic ring; when the troop ships pass the Statue of Liberty we are told "the scene was ageless; youths were sailing away to die for an idea, a sentiment, for the mere sound of a phrase . . . and on their departure they were making vows to a bronze image in the sea" (p. 274). Claude's ship is the *Anchises* which recalls another epic journey (the *Aeneid*) in which youth came to the rescue of old age. The epic feeling as the ship sets forth realizes Claude's desire to be part of something greater than himself. Earlier in the novel, when he read in the newspaper about the siege of Paris, he felt "there was nothing on earth he would so gladly be as an atom in that wall of flesh and blood that rose and melted and rose again before the city which had meant so much through all the centuries" (p. 173).

For Claude and for many of his fellows the war provides an escape from an unhappy life at home: "Though their pasts were neither long or varied, most of them, like Claude Wheeler, felt a sense of relief at being rid of all they had ever been before and facing something absolutely new" (p. 278).[24] But the voyage on the *Anchises* becomes a voyage of death; influenza breaks out and for many of the boys flight from home ends in burial at sea. In the description of the hold "fetid with sickness and sweat and vomit" (p. 297), the author reminds us of the reality upon which Claude's dream is built. Claude reflects on his comrades lost at sea: "How long would their bodies toss . . . in that inhuman kingdom of darkness and unrest?" (p. 319). As in Eliot's waste-land poem, the images in this death-by-water sequence echo *The Tempest.* For Claude the voyage is really one of rebirth (a death of the old self and birth of the new), and though there are many dying about him, he continues to wake every morning "with that sense of freedom and going forward, as if the world were growing bigger each day and he were growing with it" (p. 311).

That Claude should romanticize Europe is hardly surprising when we remember that it has always been the locus of his imagination—an escape world from the sordid and petty details of everyday life. In Nebraska most of the people that held a special place in Claude's life were European in origin—Ernest Havel, the Yoeders, Mrs. Voigt, the Erlichs. They each called up for him a romantic vista of places far away, but even more importantly they represented, in contrast to modern American society, cultures ennobled by ancient customs and traditions. Claude's discovery of French civilization is the ultimate fulfillment of that romantic dream. He contemplates making his home in France some day after the war, for he cannot conceive of returning to the ugly materialism and transiency of life in America.

> There was no chance for the kind of life he wanted at home, where people were always buying and selling, building and pulling down. He had begun to believe that the Americans were a people of

> shallow emotions. . . . Life was so short that it meant nothing at all unless it were continually reinforced by something that endured; unless the shadows of individual existence came and went against a background that held together. [P. 406]

Claude's experience of France consists in large part of pastoral gardens and wooded retreats. He is billeted at the home of an elderly French couple where life is centered on the garden with its sanded courtyard, rose vines, and cherry tree. When Claude awakens at the Jouberts' home one morning he notices the sun shining through the green jalousies, hears the pigeons flying over the old locust tree outside his room, and thinks of Mahailey and breakfast on the farm, reflecting "it was good to lie again in a house that was cared for by women" (p. 350). The memory of Mahailey points up how different this morning scene in France is from the prickly opening scene of the novel. Claude finds another idealized French garden at the old convent which has been turned into a Red Cross barrack and is presided over by the Sister of Mercy, Mlle de Courcy.

Most interesting perhaps is the pleasure Claude finds in being in the woods with his friend, Lieutenant David Gerhardt. With the distasteful memory of Enid at the back of his mind, male companionship becomes a superior, more ideal form of human communion for Claude. The author gently makes us aware at this point that the failure of Claude's marriage was not wholly Enid's fault. Enid denied Claude sexual fulfillment, but paradoxically it was her asexual whiteness and promise of purity which drew him to her. At college he had courted briefly a girl of easy virtue named Peachy Millmore, but had withdrawn from the relationship because he had "a sharp disgust for sensuality" (p. 56). When he goes to war Claude continues to evade the reality of sex in human relationships. When Victor Morse, one of his cabin mates on board ship and an American who has also "made himself over," tells Claude about a woman in London who loves him, Claude would like to think that his friend's relations with this older woman are of a filial nature. During the first nights on shore in France the air in town is heavy with erotic adventure, but Claude stays on the sidelines, his only experience being that of a voyeur who follows a couple to their love-making at the door of a church. Sexual love, moreover, is subtly discredited in almost every instance: the one-armed soldier Claude follows to his rendezvous at the church turns out to be a psychopathic case, the French girl from Beaufort and her Bavarian lover end as suicides, and Victor Morse's relations with his London mistress are shadowed by the fact that he has venereal disease. For Claude the innocent male companionship with Gerhardt in the countryside, anticipated in a very American way by his retreat to the timber claim on his farm and his pastoral encounters with Ernest Havel, is the only satisfying relationship possible.

Claude's friendship with David Gerhardt is not, however, an entirely idyllic experience, for Gerhardt brings Claude face to face with his old sense of self-doubt and inferiority.[25] Gerhardt is an accomplished violinist, a man of considerable sophistication, and with Gerhardt and his friends Claude feels himself to be "a wooden thing amongst living people." As in the earlier part of the novel Claude is filled with self-disgust: "He felt that a man might have been made of him, but nobody had taken the trouble to do it; tongue-tied, foot-tied, hand-tied. If one were born into this world like a bear cub or a bull calf, one could only paw and upset things, break and destroy, all one's life" (p. 418). But now, instead of criticizing and rebelling against the world around him, Claude exults in his belief that he has found in France a way of life worth dying for: "Ideals were not archaic things, beautiful and impotent; they were the real sources of power among men. As long as that was true, and now he knew it was true—he had come all this way to find out—he had no quarrel with Destiny" (p. 420). French civilization, like Parsifal's holy grail or the voices from the East in *The Waste Land*, gives Claude something to believe in and his critical restlessness becomes creative vision.

But the author's view of her hero, while sympathetic, is nonetheless an ironic one (he is her "blameless fool, by pity enlightened") because the war and the ideals for which he died are without glory and without purpose. Gerhardt, the artist, speaks for the author when he says to Claude there is no meaning in the war. When Claude asks him why he entered the army when he could have been exempted, Gerhardt says: " 'Because in 1917 I was twenty-four years old, and able to bear arms. The war was put up to our generation. I don't know what for; the sins of our fathers, probably. Certainly not to make the world safe for Democracy, or any rhetoric of that sort' " (p. 409). But Claude never sees the war in this nihilistic light. For him and for so many boys of his kind the war is a "golden chance"; for the first time in his life Claude has an exhilarating feeling of purpose in his breast. His romanticism is never destroyed by the trenches full of rotting bodies or the comrades mutilated in action, although through these details the author makes us aware of her darker vision in the novel. Claude thinks instead that only the war could take a roughneck from a small town and give him "a life like a movie-film "; again we are reminded of Hemingway's remark. The authorial view is a bitterly ironic one—the title of the last book, "Bidding the Eagles of the West Fly On," is meant to be recognized for the jingoism it is—and Claude's vision is finally a false one; but at the same time we admit the truth in his conclusion that no battlefield could be "as ugly as this world would be if men like his brother Bayliss controlled it altogether" (p. 419). At the end of the novel we are poised between two such negative alternatives. Claude dies in battle for a vision of a better world which could never bear the test of reality; but the fact that we are, like Claude's mother, happy that he died at this point is surely the author's greatest indictment of all of human society. The novel concludes: "He died believing his own country better than it is, and France better than any country can ever be. . . . Perhaps it was as well to see that vision, and then to see no more" (p. 458).

The Professor's House: "Letting Go With the Heart"

The Professor's House has puzzled literary critics more than any of Willa Cather's other novels. The origin and nature of the Professor's despair, the symbolic importance of houses, the relation of Tom Outland's story to the Professor's are all aspects of the novel which have teased critics since its publication. Two radically different readings of the book have been given by E. K. Brown and Leon Edel, the authors of Willa Cather's official biography. Because their essays contain vital insights into the novel upon which other interpretations must build, I shall rehearse briefly their arguments before proposing my own reading of the book as a form of satire.

Brown's approach is that of the formal critic who is concerned with matters of theme and structure in the novel. He begins by suggesting that the essential theme of *The Professor's House* is Godfrey St. Peter's unconscious preparation for death and then shows that this theme can only be perceived by scrutinizing the author's symbolic treatment of houses. Because of his physical depletion St. Peter can no longer go forward into the future: he has no interest in the new house built for his wife because it is expensive and modern, and he finds the home his daughter is building distasteful because it represents an exploitation of the past. As he enters old age he clings to a creative and unified vision of the past, symbolized by his attic study where he wrote his books and by the cliff dwellings of the ancient Indians in the Southwest. For Brown this theme is fully revealed near the close when St. Peter identifies the old couch in his study as his coffin; this is the Professor's "Truth."[26]

Moving in the opposite direction, Edel examines the novel in the light of personal conflicts suggested by Willa Cather's biography. His central thesis is that *The Professor's House* embodies imaginatively the painful experience in the author's life when her friend Isabelle McClung married and she was bereft of both a confidante and a place in which to write. Edel draws particular attention to those details in the biography which relate directly to the novel: the fact that the place in the McClung mansion where Willa worked had been a sewing room with some dressmaker's dummies still standing there; the fact that Jan Hambourg, like the Professor's faintly offensive son-in-law, Louie Marsellus, was Jewish; the fact that Willa Cather, like the Professor, had recently won a prize and some money (the Pulitzer Prize for *One of Ours*) which relieved her of financial worries. But perhaps most important in explaining the novel's genesis, he quotes Edith Lewis's account of an invitation extended by the Hambourgs to Miss Cather to come and make her home with them at Ville d'Avray in France. As in the novel, the question of abode was centered on the study; Miss Cather found the room charming and the surroundings attractive, but she knew that she could never work there. She eventually left the Hambourgs and retreated to Aix-les-Bains where *The Professor's House* was apparently conceived and the writing begun.

From this material Edel constructs a reading of the novel and finds reasons for what he feels are its weaknesses. As extensions of the author, Godfrey St. Peter and Tom Outland are viewed as caught up in a drama of rejection and withdrawal. For Edel, the symbolism of the houses has its psychological source in the author's childhood insecurity and her need for maternal protection —the house being a symbol for the womb. Just as Willa Cather was deprived of her study and her friend's maternal protection when the latter married, so the Professor must give up his old study and is left further and further behind in the activities of the family. In a parallel sequence Tom Outland is rejected by the government (his mother country), and when he goes back to his beloved cliff dwellings he finds that they have been denuded of their precious contents by his companion, Roddy Blake.

Thus far Edel's "inquiry" is of considerable value because it relates the novel to the emotional crisis in which it was probably conceived (although an earlier story, "Her Boss," predating the Ville d'Avray experience, contains a similar situation and many of the same feelings). But Edel goes on to argue that the book fails as a work of art because we are not given substantial reasons for the Professor's behavior. Why in the midst of scholarly and financial success does St. Peter become so filled with despair? Why does he yield so passively to the idea of death? How will he go on living? In this deprecatory vein Edel concludes his study by suggesting that these questions remain unanswered because Miss Cather herself was never able to resolve the personal problems she was projecting into the novel, and that consequently she said thereafter that the world broke in two in the early 1920s and she fell out of tune with the times.[27]

The interpretations put forth by Brown and Edel contain essential insights into the novel, yet both of their readings render the novel as something less than the sum of its parts. In his masterly exposition of the novel's symbolic structure Brown explains away the book's darker, more troubling dimensions. An awareness of possible death does preoccupy the Professor, but surely it is a gross oversimplification of the novel's emotional texture to suggest that the Professor's despair is finally physical in origin. This interpretation not only invalidates the social criticism integral to the novel, but what is more important, ignores the nature and significance of the Professor's resolve to go forward once again in life. The limitations of Edel's approach are primarily esthetic. In a laboratorylike format he has made psychology his final criterion for an evaluation of the novel rather than literary criticism expanded by psychological insights. Edel insists that the novel fails as a fully realized work of art because Miss Cather has not given us substantial reasons (motives) for the Professor's behavior. But this is to demand a kind of writing Miss Cather did not practice; her fiction is descriptive and reflective, seldom analytical or psychological. Moreover, specific motives are hardly essential to great art; if so, what do we make of *Hamlet?* Surely it is precisely because the Professor's depression and despair are not literally accounted for (as that of Ishmael in *Moby Dick* or the narrator of *Walden* are not) that they assume the dimensions of a universal experience, a dark night of the soul rather than an individual case study.

What Edel entirely overlooks in *The Professor's House* is Willa Cather's deliberate shaping of the book. Brown has begun an appreciation of the novel's conscious artistry in his study of the house symbolism, but numerous other structural patterns exist which suggest a wider range of artistic and intellectual purposes than Edel would admit. In a published letter the author herself directs us to the complexity of the novel's form. She says that two experiments in form interested her; the device used by early French and Spanish novelists of "inserting the *Nouvelle* into the *Roman,*" and the arrangement of narrative in a form something akin to a musical sonata.[28] The three-part formal design of a sonata weaves together two contrasting moods or themes in an alternating rhythm.[29] In *The Professor's House* one of these moods derives from what Edel designates as a drama of rejection and withdrawal—the pastoral desire to retreat to a more ideal order of life in the past. But the main theme (which Edel overlooks) derives from the author's critical rather than pastoral imagination—from her repudiation of personal ambition and possessiveness, motives which by analogy she sees as corrupting all human affairs. For the novel is structured in an elaborate pattern of references around the theme of power and possessions, both in terms of human relationships and in terms of their sublimated analogue, material possessions. The critical consciousness controls the dramatic action in Book I, "The Family," with its tale of ambition and greed, while the Professor's pastoral urge to escape remains a subordinate emotional alternative. The countertheme takes over in Book II, "Tom Outland's Story," the *nouvelle* within the novel which recounts a boy's exalted adventure on a mesa in the Southwest. In Book III, however, entitled simply "The Professor," the urge to escape, dramatized now in the Professor's death wish, is overcome by his conscious critical resolve to go forward again in life. What is important is that this resolve is grounded in the selfless disciplines of religion and art because in their communal nature lies the only antidote to the dilemma of personal power and acquisitiveness. The fully conscious and deliberate structuring of the novel by the author is suggested in a remark Miss Cather made in a letter to Dorothy Canfield Fisher. On returning from Europe in the fall of 1925 Miss Cather wrote her friend that she had taken to bed in order to work out an idea before she started writing again.[30] This was the first time she ever referred to writing in terms of ideas rather than emotions and memories. Elizabeth Shepley Sergeant also gives us a helpful clue when she quotes Miss Cather's note in a copy of *The Professor's House* the author gave to Robert Frost: "This is really a story of 'letting go with the heart' but most reviewers seem to consider it an attempt to popularize a system of philosophy."[31]

In *The Professor's House*[32] Willa Cather translated a recognition of her own selfish motives into a critique of American society and its preoccupation with material wealth. The social malaise is dramatized in the story of Godfrey St. Peter whose happy, creative life as a historian is gradually eroded by an awareness of the ambition and greed that surround him and that threaten the values by which he has always lived. This grim realization finds its focus in his relationship to his own family. In the opening sequence the two forces in tension throughout the book are present: the ambitious movement forward of the St. Peter family to a more affluent and influential life (symbolized by their new house), and the Professor's sense of exhaustion and instinctive withdrawal into the idealism of the past and of his work. The Professor's reluctance to move forward with the times is dramatized by his refusal to give up his study in the old house. It is not a comfortable room—it is badly heated and encumbered with the dressmaker's supplies—

but it has always been his retreat from the bustle of the world and the place where his best work was done.[33] In the new home, so zealously planned and executed by his wife and family, there is a modern study with all the comforts, but the Professor knows he will never work there. The Professor's inner turmoil at the beginning is almost entirely a war of instincts (it seems to be an irrational force which holds him back from his family's activities), but over a period of a year—the novel's time span—he comes to recognize the nature of those forces whose conflict brings into question the values by which he has always lived and the fact of his continuing survival.

St. Peter's achievement of this awareness is a gradual process brought on by everyday incidents in the life of his family. The familial conflict centers around the fact that the Professor's elder daughter, Rosamond, and her promoter husband, Louie Marsellus, have converted the scientific discoveries of Rosamond's late fiancé, Tom Outland, into a considerable personal fortune. In contrast, the Professor's younger daughter and her husband have relatively few possessions. Slowly the Professor comes to recognize that the family's desire for wealth and status is being fulfilled at the expense of all the civilized values he has lived and fought for. Like St. Peter and his wife, the Marselluses also are building a new house—an elaborate Norwegian country manor which they call Outland. The Professor feels in this name the cruel irony of Outland's death and the insensitivity of his well-meaning son-in-law, who has turned inspiration and genius into a show of personal wealth. The money from the Outland engine becomes the source of bitter conflict between the Professor's daughters and he laments philosophically to his wife that " 'all is vanity' " (p. 49).

With the Professor's growing recognition of the discord around him bred out of greed comes an increased sense of being continuously tired and a desire to withdraw from the vain competitive struggles of the world. He starts the new term at the university exhausted by the very idea of going ahead with his lectures, of meeting a new crop of students, and particularly of resuming his perennial struggles with faculty and administration to maintain the integrity and the standards of the institution. More and more of his time is spent in his old study lying down on the box couch. The quarreling and unhappiness in his family increase when Rosamond begins to acquire expensive luxuries for herself—furs, jewels, and elegant furnishings for her new home. Rosamond displays the symbols of her affluence ostentatiously, and her sister, Kathleen, is miserable with jealousy. One day when the Professor visits his younger daughter just after Rosamond has been there wearing new furs, he finds Kathleen's skin "had taken on a greenish tinge" (p. 86). Alone in his study that night he has a vision of his family in their misery; his elder daughter's face becomes haughty and cruel, the younger daughter's green and swollen with envy. Is it for this, he asks himself, that Tom Outland's light in the laboratory burned so far into the night? By implication we must assume that he asks himself the same question about his own long and lonely years of labor over the histories. In both instances imagination has been translated into money and has produced only jealousy and unhappiness.

The trip to Chicago with his daughter to buy Spanish furniture —Rosamond's "orgy of acquisition"—leaves the Professor completely exhausted and sickened. It is not simply Rosamond's desire to acquire great stores of furnishings which causes him to despair, but the fact that she has become hardened and thoughtless because of her absorption in possessions. She even neglects to offer to pay her father's expenses in return for his advice. St. Peter begins in earnest his retreat to his study, referred to now as a "shadowy crypt." Louie in the meantime makes plans for a summer trip to Europe—a summer of shopping and entertaining influential people—but the Professor knows he cannot go with them: "St. Peter knew at that moment that he would never be one of this light-hearted expedition, and he hated himself for the ungracious drawing-back that he felt in the region of his diaphragm" (p. 159). He sees his wife and daughter as "changed and hardened," and in reaction he thinks of his study and desk as "a shelter one could hide behind" and "a hole one could creep into" (p. 161). When he eventually tells the family that he has decided not to go with them to Europe, Rosamond is piqued because it upsets Louie's plans for meeting important scholars and getting advice on buying things. After they leave, the Professor retreats further from the present, moving his bed and clothing back to the old house, where he spends the summer enjoying his French garden and editing Tom Outland's diary for publication. Reading Tom's account of the mesa and the discovery of the Pueblo Indian villages is in part an escape into a pastoral world of innocence and youth—though inevitably Tom's story ends in the same vision of greed and self-seeking as that which the Professor now experiences.

The final and most bitter recognition the Professor must suffer —that which heralds his complete surrender to the death instinct —is his awareness that without her inheritance he and his wife, Lillian, could not have been happy. The realization that his wife's love and their domestic happiness have been dependent on comfortable financial circumstances drains him of any remaining desire to continue his life. He wants to run away from everything he has cared for; in his retreat he becomes a little boy again, to whom all the years of maturity appear "accidental and ordered from the outside" (p. 264). Now as he lies on his couch in the old study, he thinks of it as his coffin and reflects that he no longer wishes his wife to lie beside him in death. With the letter in his pocket announcing the family's imminent return from Europe he falls asleep and allows the possibility of death to take over. Significantly, it is the spare and ascetic dressmaker, Augusta, who rescues him from death in the gas-filled room. When he has recovered he recognizes that in his temporary release from consciousness "he had let something go . . . something very precious" (p. 282) but its relinquishment allows him to survive. What he has let go of is the will to power through love, the instinct to possess and dominate that brings great joy in achievement, but that also breeds much misery and unhappiness. Augusta's act of saving the Professor is symbolic of the route he will now travel. Augusta's life is essentially a joyless one, for she has known none of the pleasures of marriage, family, and possessions. She has, however, transcended these desires and, though her life is limited to her work and to watching over the sick, she is the embodiment of calm and "proper action," a person with whom the Professor feels he can be "outward bound" again.

The preoccupation with power and possessions is so all-pervasive in the novel that secondary characters and incidents are viewed entirely in this light. We see only two of the Professor's colleagues from the university, but both exemplify the limitations of a world circumscribed by a striving after social status and material wealth. We are told that Langtry, the Professor's rival from the beginning of his career, is a poor teacher and cares little for the standards of scholarship at the university. Langtry, however, holds a chair equal in importance to the Professor's because his uncle, influential in state politics, is president of the board of regents, and because he himself is willing to comply with the demands of administrators eager to include technical and agricultural studies in the curriculum. The scientist Crane is ultimately defined in terms of his poverty—his dignity as a man entirely stripped away by his chronic illness and by his failure to convert the results of his research into money. Crane and St. Peter have always had a mutual sympathy for the integrity of each other's work, but it is St. Peter's son-in-law, Louie Marsellus, who converts the results of Crane's research with Tom Outland into money, and thereafter the Professor must wrestle with the moral problem of Crane's right to a share in the profits and with the depressing aspects of Crane's financial ruin. Even Augusta and her uncle, from whom the Professor rents his house, are viewed in terms of their concerns over money. Appelhoff's one dominant trait is that of miserliness—he is a kindly old man so long as it is not a question of money. The only thing that happens to Augusta in the novel is that she loses her savings in a bad investment. The latter incident also serves to emphasize Rosamond's essential selfishness; she refuses to help the rest of the family make good Augusta's loss.

In direct contrast to this spectacle of greed and status-seeking in modern civilization is the countertheme of Tom Outland's adventure on the mesa—"a turquoise set in dull silver." The purity and beauty of the mesa with its ancient Indian village is described with such affectionate detail that it becomes a curious kind of pastoral center in the novel—a world transcending place and time, fixed in "immortal repose." Tom's instincts (the promptings of his idealistic nature) urge him to share his discovery with others; but when he goes to Washington he finds that his fellow Americans are little interested in the cultural values of the past, that they are wholly caught up in their own petty lives of appearances and material possessions. The director of the Smithsonian Institution and his staff show an interest in Tom's discovery, but more important to them is a free trip to Europe and the possibility of winning decorations at the Exposition there. The one man genuinely interested in the Indian remains—a Frenchman at the embassy—is too poor to give any help. Tom returns to the Southwest disillusioned with American government and society, but more devastating is his discovery that his companion, Roddy Blake, has sold the pottery and other artifacts of the ancient city to a German antiquarian who has taken the treasures out through Mexico. Tom grieves over this irreparable loss and accuses Blake of betraying all the things they had worked for. Blake's answer is that all things come to money in the end.

Again we are shown the acquisition of wealth as the source of envy and disaffection. When Blake sold the Indian pieces "for a neat little pile" the people living nearby the mesa became jealous of his luck, and on his return Tom finds "a good deal of bad feeling" (p. 237) in the formerly friendly town. In an attempt to conciliate Tom and console him for the loss of the Indian objects, Blake gives him the bank book and explains that he has deposited the money in Tom's name. But Tom replies in disgust that he will never touch the money and therewith, to Tom's later regret, Blake leaves the mesa never to be seen by him again.

Blake, an unsuspecting victim of his society's false values, could view the artifacts only in terms of their monetary value, and had he not sold them to the German he expected to peddle them at wayside hotels, a dollar a bowl. But Tom had never once considered selling them for a personal profit; in going to Washington he had only intended to share his discovery with his country. Tom's response to the Indian artifacts is not only a response to the purity of their esthetic design, but to their traditional and communal nature as well: " 'I never thought of selling them, because they weren't mine to sell—nor yours! They belonged to this country, to the State, and to all the people. They belonged to boys like you and me, that have no other ancestors to inherit from' " (p. 242).

Much of the novel's conscious symbolic structure is indeed worked out in terms of buildings. In its esthetic and communal integrity the ancient Indian city and its artifacts stand in sharp contrast to the ugly individualized dwellings of contemporary American society. Contrasted to the careful craftsmanship exhibited in each unit of the Indian city are such shoddy buildings as the physics laboratory at the university where cheap materials and hasty execution have betrayed a good design. Perhaps most starkly contrasted with the Indian dwellings is the Norwegian manor house being built by the Marselluses, a dwelling scarcely indigenous to the country and built entirely as a show place. Another subtle network of images in the novel focuses on colors as they acquire symbolic meaning from jewels. Our attention is first drawn to this by the epigraph, " 'A turquoise set in silver, wasn't it? . . . Yes, a turquoise set in dull silver,' " a quotation from the novel, when at Christmas Rosamond wears her new necklace of emeralds set in gold and Louie recalls a simple bracelet that Tom Outland gave her. Louie insists that because both pieces are beautiful they are of equal value in adorning his wife, and yet an insidious comparison has been made between a crude, semiprecious stone and a costly string of precious gems. The emeralds, which even Mrs. St. Peter feels are "out of scale," are the occasion for more jealousy in the family and their green color recalls the "greenish tinge" to Kathleen's skin after her sister's visit earlier in the novel. When Tom Outland gave Rosamond and Kathleen the crude turquoises he pointed out that they were naturally a soft blue color when they came out of the mine, "before the jewellers have tampered with them and made them look green" (p. 120). Once given a commercial value the turquoises take on the color of envy and greed. In contrast the idyllic experiences and reveries of both the Professor and Tom Outland are filled with images of blue, the color of innocence and vision. All his life the Professor has been homesick for the "innocent" blue water of Lake Michigan; to his friends in Europe he would explain that his lake was " 'quite another blue' " from the Channel or the Mediterranean: " '*il est toujours plus naïf*' " (p. 31). When he withdraws from his family and the competitive world about him, it is to the blue water of his lake. The blue of Tom's turquoises is also compared to "the sea on halcyon days of summer," but for Tom blue is associated with vision, for it is the color of his mesa where, suspended in "an ocean of clear air," he learns to transcend personal desire. Afterward when troubles came he would remember "there was that summer, high and blue, a life in itself" (p. 253).

Alone on the mesa, "in a world above the world," Tom has a visionary experience of what true possession consists of. He had read of it in the Latin poets, who called it "filial piety." For Tom it is a kind of religious emotion deriving from the oldest paradox of the Christian faith—that one must lose one's life to gain it. Only when desire has ceased will fullness of life be granted. Tom writes in his journal: "Every morning, when the sun's rays first hit the mesa top, while the rest of the world was in shadow, I wakened with the feeling that I had found everything, instead of having lost everything" (p. 251).

In Book I the reader is permitted to overhear the Professor lecturing to his students. Answering a question as to the value of modern science, the Professor argues that the laboratory has given man a number of " 'ingenious toys' " and made him comfortable, but this only distracts him from the essential and timeless problems of human existence. Art and religion, he suggests, have given man the only real happiness he has known. In concluding he insists that they are essentially the same thing, that the familiar prayer might be changed a little to say, *Thy will be done in art, as it is in heaven.* As the novel moves forward, art and religion become increasingly the only viable alternatives to the spectacle of ambition and greed that surrounds the Professor; they are a lasting source of happiness because they transcend personal desire. Augusta's need to express the emotion of love finds its fullest and most satisfying form in the ritual of the Magnificat; Tom Outland's only pleasure in material objects is in the love he feels for the communal artifacts of the ancient Indians.

In the final book of the novel the Professor reflects that he has had two romances in his life: "one of the heart, which had filled his life for many years, and a second of the mind—of the imagination" (p. 258). The dichotomy suggested by this reflection, however, does not simply set the values of art against those of an active life. Rather, the life of the imagination (in its ideal form) transcends that of "the heart" by eliminating the personal urge to power without eliminating human sympathy. Again, the two characters in the novel whose lives are exemplary are Tom Outland and the dressmaker, Augusta. Their acts are selfless, completely unmotivated by personal ambitions, and yet neither has become cold and impersonal. Tom goes to war to fight for a humanitarian cause he believes in; Augusta watches over the sick and dying as an act of charity and true compassion. When the Professor awakes from his sleep of death with Augusta at his side, he realizes he would rather have her with him than anyone else he knows. Compared to his wife, Augusta is "the bloomless side of life," and yet it is the fact that there is still a "world full of Augustas" which assures him that he can survive.

The image of Augusta as "bloomless" is another instance of the novel's conscious and very subtle artistry. The image is not casual in reference; it brings to mind, by contrast, several other images that associate flowers with women and the ambitions of romantic love. Rosamond's beauty is linked to flowers not only by her name, but in the comparison of her red lips to "the duskiness of dark, heavy-scented roses" (p. 37). When Tom asks Rosamond to a dance, the Professor's roses are in bloom. The Professor's memories of his own youth in France and of his romantic sensibility focus on a bouquet of pink dahlias he bought one morning and handed to a pretty schoolgirl. Louie brings violets for Mrs. St. Peter on Christmas. With every reference to the beauty of flowers there is also a melancholy hint of disappointment and a feeling of betrayal.

With its complex formal and thematic structure, *The Professor's House* is as complete and self-explanatory as any work of art need be. The novel works on two distinct levels: the emotional level of frustration and despair, which is countered on a critical, self-conscious level by images of Christian transcendence of desire. Leon Edel's objection that St. Peter's despair is never accounted for seems less persuasive if we consider for a moment the earlier story "Her Boss," published in 1919,[34] which resembles the novel closely at many points. There we find a successful, middle-aged man, Paul Wanning, whose wife and two daughters are caught up in the world of social engagements and material trappings. Come summer the family disperses, one daughter going to Europe. The protagonist escapes bleak thoughts by recalling an old friendship with a man who still lives in the Wind River Mountains in the West, and by writing his autobiography which returns him in memory to his youth as a college student (in the novel these two motifs are comprehended in Tom Outland's story). Wanning's only true companions are the black servant, Sam, and his secretary, Annie Wooley; like Tom and Augusta, they are outside of his family and society and act from purely selfless motives. The significant difference between the story and the novel is that we know Wanning is dying from a diseased kidney, and this not only explains his low spirits but considerably lessens the reader's involvement with his plight, the emotion in the story being accounted for biologically. The Professor's despair, on the other hand, can only be understood imaginatively and thereby achieves through mystery a universality.

However, relating *The Professor's House* to the artist's experience is still likely to raise some troubling questions. If the novel had its origin in complex personal emotions, is it not then largely an indulgence in self-pity? Does this not undercut, perhaps even discredit, its critique of American values? The charge of self-pity may be true, but that could hardly matter to art. What is a satire in the end but an artist's revenge on the world to soften his own failures? What is a tragedy but self-pity on a cosmic scale? Willa Cather herself knew early that the motives of art were dark and troubled, and that the only relevant consideration is whether the emotion, be it hate, love, envy, or pride, is convincingly portrayed. On this ground *The Professor's House* is a sound and lasting work of art.

Notes

1. "On *Shadows on the Rock*" in *Willa Cather on Writing*, p. 15. There are other examples. According to Elizabeth Sargeant in *Willa Cather: A Memoir*, Miss Cather wanted the heroine of *My Ántonia* to be like a Sicilian apothecary jar—"a rare object in the middle of a table, which one may examine from all sides" (pp. 138–40). In a letter she likens the narrative of *Death Comes for the Archbishop* to two white mules moving slowly forward (Willa Cather to Norman Foerster, May 22, 1933, Love Library, University of Nebraska–Lincoln).

2. *CSF*, pp. 523–28.

3. This is one of the major themes studied by Randall in *The Landscape and the Looking Glass*. See also "The Kingdom of Art," the second introductory essay by Bernice Slote in *KA*, pp. 93–97.

4. *CSF*, pp. 449–71.

5. *CSF*, pp. 95–111.

6. *Uncle Valentine and Other Stories: Willa Cather's Uncollected Short Fiction, 1915–1929*, edited with an introduction by Bernice Slote (Lincoln: University of Nebraska Press, 1973), pp. 65–84. Hereafter cited as *UVS*.

7. *CSF*, pp. 43–54.

8. *One of Ours* (New York: Alfred A. Knopf, 1922). All references are to this text.

9. *UVS*, pp. 85–97 and 99–115.

10. *CSF*, pp. 441–48.
11. *CSF*, pp. 547–55.
12. *CSF*, pp. 473–80.
13. *CSF*, pp. 173–85.
14. *CSF*, pp. 55–68.
15. Bennett, *The World of Willa Cather*, pp. 14–15.
16. Willa Cather to Dorthy Canfield Fisher, March–April 1922 (Guy Bailey Memorial Library, University of Vermont).
17. Central to what is negative about Claude's father is his thoughtlessness toward the women in the household. In an early story, "The Profile," the protagonist is haunted by the memory of his mother and sisters being harshly treated by the rough men of the family. Extreme examples occur in *Death Comes for the Archbishop* where Buck Scales treats Magdelena with inhuman cruelty, even killing her baby, and in *Sapphira and the Slave Girl* where Martin Colbert repeatedly attempts to rape the terrified slave girl, Nancy.
18. This scene is perhaps an intentional variant on the story of "The Cherry Tree Carol" where Joseph, the injured cuckold, refuses to gather cherries for Mary, and the unborn Jesus, weeping inside Mary's womb, causes the cherry tree to bow down to the ground before Mary. For Willa Cather the cherry is the jewel of fruits with both erotic and highly precious values: one thinks of the cherry tree in Joe Vavrika's tavern garden ("The Bohemian Girl") and Nils squirting cherry juice on Clara's white dress; of Marie Shabata gathering cherries while Emil scythes down the weeds in her garden of love; and of Nancy, the slave girl, who is threatened by her pursuer when she is in a tree picking cherries.
19. Willa Cather's observation on "picture-making" is quoted by Mildred R. Bennett from an interview by Eva Mahoney, Omaha *Sunday World-Herald*, November 27, 1921. See *The World of Willa Cather*, pp. 15, 234.
20. Willa Cather apparently found the five-part structure a satisfying form—perhaps in the manner of a Shakespearean play—for *O Pioneers!* and *My Ántonia* also are written in five parts. In these books the major themes are developed in the first three parts; the fourth part is a death sequence (death of Emil and Marie, dissipation of friendship between Ántonia and Jim Burden, voyage of death on the *Anchises*), while in part five there is the experience of rebirth through revaluation.
21. Willa Cather to a Mr. Johns, November 17, 1922 (University of Virginia Library). In this letter the author compliments Mr. Johns on detecting the Parsifal theme in the novel, for she felt she had hidden it carefully. She had even changed the title of the novel's last section from "The Blameless Fool, by Pity Enlightened" to "Bidding the Eagles of the West Fly On." These confidences to her reader are instructive about her method of composition. By keeping a certain literary motif in mind without referring to it directly, she could extract its essential emotion without reducing the experience to simply a literary idea: "Whatever is felt upon

the page without being specifically named there—that, one might say, is created" ("The Novel Démeublé" in *Willa Cather on Writing,* p. 41).

22. Hemingway's observation is in Edmund Wilson's review of *One of Ours,* collected in Wilson's *The Shores of Light* (New York: Farrar, Straus and Giroux, 1952), p. 118. The review first appeared in *Vanity Fair,* October 1922.

23. I am indebted to John J. Murphy for the suggestion that Books IV and V of the novel are deliberately theatrical in style. This idea rescues *One of Ours* from the charge of contrivance and sentimentality.

24. For a study of the novel in terms of the psychological needs which glorify war see Stanley Cooperman's article "Willa Cather and the Bright Face of Death" in *Literature and Psychology* 13 (Summer 1963): 81–87, reprinted in *World War I and the American Novel* (Baltimore: Johns Hopkins Press, 1967), pp. 129–37.

25. In two letters to Dorothy Canfield Fisher written in the spring of 1922 (Guy Bailey Memorial Library, University of Vermont) Willa Cather says that the emotional relationship between Claude and David derived from her friendship with Dorothy, and that Claude's sense of being such a roughneck was exactly her own in Dorothy's company.

26. E. K. Brown's full study of *The Professor's House* appears in *Rhythm in the Novel* (Toronto: University of Toronto Press, 1951), pp. 71–78. For Leon Edel's writing on Willa Cather, aside from his work on her biography, see "Willa Cather's *The Professor's House:* An Inquiry into the Use of Psychology in Literary Criticism," *Literature and Psychology* 4 (February 1954): 66–79, reprinted in *Literary Biography* (Toronto: University of Toronto Press, 1957), pp. 61–80; and *Willa Cather and the Paradox of Success* (Washington: Library of Congress, 1960).

27. Miss Cather's comment on the world breaking in two occurs in the prefatory note to *Not Under Forty* (New York: Alfred A. Knopf, 1936), p. v.

28. "On *The Professor's House*" in *Willa Cather on Writing,* pp. 30–31.

29. For a detailed study of the musical patterning in the novel see Richard Giannone, *Music in Willa Cather's Fiction* (Lincoln: University of Nebraska Press, 1968), pp. 151–68.

30. Willa Cather to Dorothy Canfield Fisher, November 1923 (Guy Bailey Memorial Library, University of Vermont).

31. Sergeant, *Willa Cather: A Memoir,* p. 215.

32. *The Professor's House* (New York: Alfred A. Knopf, 1925). All references are to this text.

33. Among the dressmaker's supplies are two dummies which refer us interestingly to the two "forms" or types of women in Willa Cather's earlier fiction. The one is a maternal form—a headless, armless bust that looks ample and billowy, "as if you might lay your head upon its deep-breathing softness and rest safe forever"; the other is a sprightly figure in a wire skirt, like a lady of light behavior poised on tiptoe, waiting for a waltz to begin. The feeling of rejection and alienation that Edel describes

in the novel is imaged in the deceptive maternal bust which is very hard to the touch, "a dead, opaque, lumpy solidity, like chunks of putty, or tightly packed sawdust" (p. 18). The Professor, however, becomes quite irrational when Augusta comes to take them away. They recall "certain disappointments" and "cruel biological necessities" but he would never complain of their presence.

34. *UVS*, pp. 117–39.

PART II

Forms

CHAPTER FOUR

Willa Cather's Mortal Comedy

In the three books she wrote after *The Professor's House*—*My Mortal Enemy* (1926), *Death Comes for the Archbishop* (1927), and *Shadows on the Rock* (1931)—Willa Cather explored through Christian imagery and myth the full range of the moral universe, that is to say, the whole spectrum of man's capacities for good and evil. By titling this chapter "Willa Cather's Mortal Comedy" I have made a loose analogy between Cather and Dante in order to suggest a relationship that exists between these three Cather books. *My Mortal Enemy* is an inferno of hate, a study of evil both unseen and dramatically revealed; *Death Comes for the Archbishop* holds up for consideration a paradisal vision of life, one sanctified through discipline and love; and *Shadows on the Rock* describes a purgatorial quest through sin and suffering for a refuge from evil and from man's mortal nature. Willa Cather wrote these novels when she was in her early and middle fifties. Dante's *Inferno* opens with the lines: "*Nel mezzo del cammin di nostra vita / mi ritrovai per una selva oscura / che la diritta via era smarrita,*" which translates "In the middle of the journey of our life I came to myself within a dark wood where the straight way was lost." I believe, as I have suggested in the Introduction, that when Willa Cather wrote these novels she experienced and came to understand most fully the instincts for good and evil within herself. However, the analogy with Dante is not meant to specify a model or literary source Cather might have followed (if so, how to account for the different order: *Inferno, Paradiso, Purgatorio?*), but rather to illuminate something of the universal imaginative character and design of these books.

The various modes through which Willa Cather's earlier fiction developed are all present in these books. *My Mortal Enemy,* with its ironic study of human nature, and *Shadows on the Rock,* with its emphasis on cruelty, guilt, and suffering, are related to the imagination of satire, while *Death Comes for the Archbishop,* the story of two missionary priests, is an epic of church history. Moreover, all three books are in part pastorals, since in each of them the author's imagination moves back into the past, whether it be personal or cultural. But what is of special interest here, more than the blending of imaginative modes, are the specific literary forms in which these narratives are cast. In her discussions of *Death Comes for the Archbishop* and *Shadows on the Rock* we find the author describing more precisely than she had done before the formal models for her writing (the other instance is her discussion of form in *The Professor's House*); and in at least two of the books to be considered in this chapter it is the form which determines and illuminates the book's moral vision.

The exception is *My Mortal Enemy.* Willa Cather herself never commented on the form of the book, which makes it difficult to assign to it, with authority, certain moral values in the light of its form. Moreover, *My Mortal Enemy* resembles closely in theme and structure the earlier novel *A Lost Lady,* which increases the difficulty of describing its unique form. However, I think it can be said that *My Mortal Enemy* represents an intensification, or a further distillation, of those formal aspects of composition the author practiced in *A Lost Lady,* and I think these intensifications point to the book's special vision—that of evil lurking just below the surface of human affairs. The extreme brevity of *My Mortal Enemy* makes it the prime example of Willa Cather's "unfurnished novel," for in no other book did she pare her subject down to such a stark and essential form. Nor in any of her other books do allusions and veiled references count for so much. Despite its urbane and frequently witty surface, the book's theme is ambition, cruelty, and hatred; and that sense of evil operating in human affairs becomes stronger and more pervasive when it is felt but not named, when it remains secreted behind closed doors.

Because of its brevity *My Mortal Enemy* is more accurately

described as a novella, a short narrative with a single focus and theme. The focus is on Myra Henshawe almost exclusively, and through her characterization the author develops her theme of evil in human nature. Also important in the form is the book's two-part structure, designed around two parallel sequences of disillusionment. *A Lost Lady* is similarly structured, and the comparison is significant because Willa Cather's special sense of evil is always approached through the loss of innocence. The two parts of the novella, with their emphasis on innocence and experience, respectively, dramatize through heightened contrasts the book's moral vision.

The allusiveness and brevity of *My Mortal Enemy* may have their origins in biographical elements. In *The Professor's House* Willa Cather denounced human greed and lust for power by means of a satirical examination of society, but in *My Mortal Enemy,* with its theme of self-confrontation, she turned that denunciation inward. The strong-willed, tyrannical heroine of the novella seems to me at some points to resemble Willa Cather herself; or perhaps it is more accurate to say that the essence of the characterization of Myra Henshawe suggests that Willa Cather knew intimately what her heroine was experiencing. Beneath the smooth, classical prose surface of this book there may lie the author's attempt to see herself honestly and to reconcile herself to her own personal situation. And perhaps the recognition that one's own worst enemy is often oneself allowed the author to return to happier, creative spirits again.

Death Comes for the Archbishop, one of Willa Cather's finest books, is of special interest for both its mood and its literary form. Art can be said to have its origin and momentum in conflict, but there is a kind of art—for want of a better term I will use the Dante image and call it paradisal—in which struggle is subordinate to the artist's sense of achievement, even resolution. The old problems that engaged the artist so deeply are still there, but they are viewed with detachment, the artist having discovered perhaps that they are not so terribly important, after all. A mood of serenity arises out of this recognition; the artist has temporarily (sometimes lastingly) made his peace with the world. We are made very conscious in this kind of art that the work itself is an artifice and its values are wholly esthetic. The paradisal mood is not a separate imaginative mode in itself, but a quality of serenity and detachment which characterizes a work of art executed in any of the major imaginative modes. Shakespeare's *The Tempest,* a work of the critical imagination, is a good example: the old problems of order and justice and human love which preoccupy Shakespeare in his major dramas are again the substance of this play, but their urgency is significantly undercut by the image of Prospero playing out his final drama on a stage. The same feeling characterizes Beethoven's Ninth Symphony, a form of epic, where the tragic emotions of the earlier compositions give way to a hymn of joy—a "song of sympathy and gladness" wherein all men are plighted brothers. The earlier movements of the symphony are not so much statements of new themes as they are rehearsals for the culminating choral. The mood is felt, though considerably muted, in Keats's last pastoral ode, "To Autumn," which like the earlier "great" odes is a poem about mutability, but in which anguish is replaced by an acceptance and embracing of beauty which fades and dies. Similarly, in Faulkner's last novel, *The Reivers* (1962), another pastoral, the tragedies of the past become a comic and childish invention. Francois Truffaut's film, *L'Enfant sauvage* (1969), provides a particularly good example in relation to *Death Comes for the Archbishop.* Truffaut's early classic film, *Les 400 Coups* (1959), presents the plight of an unloved child from the angry perspective of rebellious youth; in *L'Enfant sauvage* the same theme adheres, but this time it is presented as an eighteenth-century documentary about a boy found living in a wild state in the forest, and from this detached, historical perspective his case is examined rationally and with quiet sympathy. Some artists always remain embattled; others stand back for a moment and see the drama of their individual lives as part of the human comedy.

Death Comes for the Archbishop represents fictionally Willa Cather's achievement of detachment and serenity. In *The Professor's House* she found in the communal disciplines of religion and art a formula for transcending selfish personal ambitions. In *Death Comes for the Archbishop* this formula is given substance and is verified by the two missionary priests whose lives are sanctified and made tranquil by the timeless disciplines of religion and religious art. Like Truffaut in *L'Enfant sauvage,* Willa Cather in *Death*

Comes for the Archbishop uses a historical perspective to achieve the requisite mood of detachment. As a kind of cultural pastoral (a return not to the author's personal past but to a communal one), *Death Comes for the Archbishop* gives expression to the feelings of loss and alienation that characterize many of Willa Cather's earliest novels: the Bishop and his Vicar are missionary priests from France who spend all their lives in a foreign land, never to be reunited with their families or homes. But here emotion is muted and ensconced in legend; the conflicts in the priests' lives are not personal so much as they are representative of the universal Christian experience. The author's quest for a protective maternal figure like Ántonia is here redirected and fulfilled in the spiritual quest for the Holy Mother, and nostalgia is replaced by penance and long suffering. The surrender of the personal quest to the universal one is reflected most of all in the novel's form, wherein all the formal conventions of narrative are subordinated to the design of a saint's legend.

However, in September of 1927 (that same month which saw the publication of *Death Comes for the Archbishop*) the equilibrium which Willa Cather had achieved in her life was disrupted when she and Edith Lewis were forced to leave the Bank Street apartment where they had lived for over fifteen years. They put their furnishings in storage and took rooms temporarily at a hotel; but it was almost five years before they were settled permanently again. Moreover, in March of 1928 the author's father died and in December her mother suffered a paralytic stroke, breaking up the family home to which Willa Cather had always returned. For the next three years she watched her mother grow gradually weaker, suffering all the indignities of a failing human body until her death in August 1931. The effect of these changes on the author is apparent in her next book, *Shadows on the Rock,* a novel obsessed with life's vicissitudes and the fact of man's mortality. In the unchanging patterns of life in seventeenth-century Quebec Willa Cather found a fictional refuge from her feelings of homelessness and from the threat of time's passage. But I think from examining this novel and also the long story "Old Mrs. Harris," written in this same period, that the illness and death of her parents loosed in the author complex feelings of guilt and personal anxiety about the past which are in turn manifested in the novel's preoccupation with cruelty, guilt, and suffering. In this respect *Shadows on the Rock* suggests to me the author's personal purgatory. Again the form—the historical novel—points to the book's moral vision, for implicit in the historical perspective is the fact of dissolution—man's corruption both physical and moral. The reading of the three novels which follows will have as one of its underlying principles of organization an examination of moral vision in the light of form (especially saint's legend and historical novel); nowhere else in her writing does Willa Cather allow her imagination to be guided so strongly by the use of specific literary forms.

My Mortal Enemy: A Two-Part Novella

In the early part of her story Myra Henshawe, looking up at the moon over the city, confides to the narrator, Nellie Birdseye, that she once swore never to meddle in romantic love again, because one may bring a couple together so that they rise above the world in ecstasy, but " 'very likely hell will come of it!' " (p. 31).[1] In this brief reflection Myra prophetically describes the course of her own life—her romantic ambitions, her last days of bitterness and regret. The two parts of this novella juxtapose a picture of Myra as an ambitious and worldly woman with a picture of her as an embittered recluse seeking religious absolution before death. *My Mortal Enemy,* I believe, is Willa Cather's vision of the hell one can make of one's life and of the misery it can bring to others.

My reading of the novel is perhaps best approached through the title. Some critics have assumed that Myra's death-bed denunciation refers exclusively to her husband; he is her "mortal enemy" because he not only seduced her away from her family and religion, but then betrayed her by encouraging the affections of other women. Certainly Nellie directs us at first to make this connection. After Myra has spoken her bitter words (" 'Why must I die like this, alone with my mortal enemy?' "), Nellie says: "I looked at him [Henshawe] in affright, but he did not move or shudder" (p. 95). Willa Cather always held a skeptical view of marriage, at least for exceptional people, so the assumption is an obvious one to make. Of one of the happiest unions in her fiction (the Cuzaks in *My Ántonia*) the narrator of the novel says: "I wondered whether the life that was right for one was ever right for two!" (p. 367). But another reading of Myra's last words, which gives a greater depth of meaning to the book, is that they are spoken against herself as well, that her enemy in the final reckoning is her own proud and possessive nature. Shortly before she dies Myra says to Nellie: " 'I was always a grasping, worldly woman; I was never satisfied' " (p. 88). As Nellie sits and reflects on Myra's last outburst, she connects it with the earlier speech and says to herself: "I began to understand a little what she meant, to sense how it was with her. Violent natures like hers sometimes turn against themselves . . . against themselves and all their idolatries" (p. 96). Myra hates her husband because he represents the failure of everything she strove for in life (her "idolatries"), but it is for her inability to forgive him, to accept the defeat of her worldly ambitions, that she stands self-condemned.

My Mortal Enemy moves towards a final Christian reckoning, but Part I is a completely secular view of the heroine and her earthly ambitions. The story opens with the return visit of Myra Henshawe to her home town, Parthia, Illinois. To the young narrator Myra is a figure out of romance, for her "runaway marriage" and relinquishment of a family fortune have become a local legend. Nellie is only fifteen and through her eyes we get a heightened sense of Myra's handsome person and her imperious style. Nellie, however, is more than a simple narrative device to give us a romantic view of the heroine; her timid, uncertain nature makes her vulnerable to Myra's masterful presence and caustic wit, with the result that from the beginning we are aware of a cruel, aggressive streak in the heroine. At times that force in Myra's personality darkens into something wholly evil.

When they first meet, Myra tyrannizes Nellie, who feels "hopelessly clumsy and stupid" in her presence. When Nellie enters the room, Myra, who has caught a glimpse of her victim in the mirror, waits imperiously for an introduction. Nellie observes that "she stood markedly and pointedly still, with her shoulders back and her head lifted, as if to remind me that it was my business to get to her as quickly as possible and present myself as best I could" (p. 5). Nellie wants very much for Myra to like her, but feels she doesn't have half a chance with her. She avoids looking into her interrogator's deep-set, flashing eyes, fixing her gaze on a necklace of amethysts she is wearing. Myra chides her for staring and Nellie is deeply humiliated; her cheeks burn with shame. Nellie is never sure whether Myra is making fun of her or laughing at the things they are discussing, for, as she observes, "her sarcasm was so quick, so fine at the point—it was like being touched by a metal so cold that one doesn't know whether one is burned or chilled" (p. 7). The image impresses on us indelibly a sadistic quality in the heroine's nature. The sense of Myra's power is further enhanced when her husband joins the party. He has a rugged military air about him suggesting personal bravery and fine deeds that befits his wife's romantic station, and yet there is also something soft about him—he wears a limp, drooping moustache and his eyes are "dark and soft . . . like half-moons," friendly and languid. Myra dominates him, even to the point of making decisions about his wardrobe. Not surprisingly, Nellie feels herself much more at ease with Oswald Henshawe than with his wife.

Myra's first secular domain is the world of romantic love, filled with intrigues, betrayals, and thralldom. Myra's love of luxuries —expensive clothes and jewelry—made her elopement twenty-five years earlier a magnificently romantic gesture; not only did she marry against her uncle's wishes (Oswald Henshawe was the son of her uncle's enemy), but she did so knowing that she would be cut off without a penny. Her romance with Oswald was aided and finally accomplished in grand style with the help of all her friends. Years later Nellie thinks of the old Driscoll place, now a convent, as a palace that has lain in a trance "ever since that winter night when Love went out of the gates and gave the dare to Fate" (p. 17). The image of Love fleeing on a winter night leaving only religious ritual in its place is reminiscent of Keats's "The Eve of St. Agnes," and it is precisely the religion of love in the manner evoked by Keats that defines Myra in the first half of the book. When Nellie first meets her she instinctively feels court must be paid to this brilliant and attractive woman, who mesmerizes with her mocking eyes and voice. Like Keats's "la belle dame," she enslaves her admirers as much with the promise of pain (she laughs at their weaknesses, finds humor in accidents and disasters) as with the promise of pleasure. At times this identification shades off into something tyrannical and evil; we are told later in the novel by Myra herself that her head " 'was no head for a woman at all, but would have graced one of the wickedest of the Roman emperors' " (p. 63).

The Henshawes invite Nellie and her aunt to spend the Christmas holidays with them in New York, and the narrator has an opportunity to observe Myra in the world of her own creation. When Myra meets her visitors at the train station she has in tow a submissive young man, Ewan Gray, whom she is advising in his courtship of a friend. As a high priestess of love, Myra, according to her husband, nearly always has a love affair on hand. Gray, like Henshawe, is "that perplexing combination of something hard and something soft": tall and handsome, he is nonetheless a passive, subjugated young man who, through "fine grey eyes, deep-set and melancholy," looks down at Myra "with a grateful, almost humble expression, holding his soft hat against his breast" (p. 21). After he has left, Myra says: " 'You can see; he's just the sort of boy that women pick up and run off into the jungle with' " (p. 23).[2] Nellie soon catches the special flavor of Myra's world, and as they approach the city on the ferry, the dome of the *World* building appears to Nellie through a blur of snow "like a ruddy autumn moon at twilight." Diana, the cold, imperial goddess of romantic love, is never far in Nellie's mind from association with Myra. That same afternoon as she looks about Madison Square she admires the Saint Gaudens' Diana, "of which Mrs. Henshawe had told me," and Myra, finding Nellie under the spell of the city's wintry activity, calls her " 'moon-struck.' " Winter in the city brings no desolation and Nellie thinks of it as a tamed polar bear "led on a leash by a beautiful lady" (p. 25), another image, like those surrounding Myra and her male admirers, suggesting the mastering power of a loved woman. That evening the moon association with the heroine is made again when Myra says, " 'See the moon coming out, Nellie—behind the tower. It wakens the guilt in me. No playing with love' " (p. 31). We are reminded several times in the novel of Oswald's "half-moon" eyes, which reflect perhaps the sole purpose of his existence.

The larger implications of Myra's romantic "ambitions" are not yet revealed to Nellie. Through her inexperienced eyes New York City, with its style and sophistication, acquires a romantic glow. Nellie is bedazzled by the pleasant activities that fill Myra's life: a carriage down Fifth Avenue, tea in Central Park, theatre or an opera in the evening. But it is the Henshawes' apartment itself, with its surface charm and rich, tasteful furnishings, which particularly thrills Nellie: "I loved it from the moment I entered it; such solidly built, high-ceiled rooms, with snug fire-places and wide doors and deep windows. The long, heavy velvet curtains and the velvet chairs were a wonderful plum-colour, like ripe purple fruit. The curtains were lined with that rich cream-colour that lies under the blue skin of ripe figs" (pp. 26–27). To this elegant little apartment in an old brownstone come the principal players in Myra's world of artifice and romance. Ewan Gray brings to Myra, his confidante, two bracelets of opals and some love poetry, appealing for her counsel and encouragement.[3] Myra completely controls the world she has fashioned; there is a suggestion that she has even written some of the poems with which Gray is courting her actress friend, Esther Sinclair. For Nellie the most perfect time at the Henshawes' apartment is on New Year's Eve when they give a party for their friends from the theatre and the musical world. Nellie is enthralled by the aristocratic actress Madame Modjeska, another of the novel's statuesque, commanding women. Although Nellie is an innocent, the ambience of reversed sexual roles emanating from this room full of masterful women and gentle men is part of the special magic the evening has for her. Myra's world, with its masters and slaves of love, has its apotheosis for Nellie when Modjeska's friend from the opera sings the "Casta Diva" aria from Bellini's *Norma.* The apartment is flooded with moonlight and the aria of the Druidical priestess who perjures herself for love and then dies in order to be revenged summons up for Nellie a "compelling, passionate, overmastering something" in Myra's person.[4]

Although Nellie is thoroughly enchanted by Myra's world, she glimpses from time to time a hard, malevolent side to Myra's character deriving, Nellie deems, from her "insane ambition" (p. 41). She catches something of it in the veiled sarcasm which Myra directs at her German "moneyed" friends, and is exposed to it temporarily when a matinee at the theatre is ruined for Myra by the presence of a friend who betrayed her husband in business. Myra has an insatiable desire for wealth and social prominence as well as romance, and when she is eclipsed socially by an acquaintance passing through the park in a handsome carriage, she laments to Nellie bitterly that " 'it's very nasty, being poor!' " (p. 41). That "something in her nature that one rarely saw, but nearly always felt" is fully revealed to Nellie when she calls at the Henshawes' apartment and overhears the couple quarreling bitterly. Throughout the novel Myra's voice is a gauge of her mood; Nellie notices that in speaking of close friends like the dying poetess, Anne Aylward, "her voice invested the name with a sort of grace" (p. 43). Now Myra's laughter is angry and her accusations are a "burst of rapid words that stung like cold water from a spray" (p. 49). For Nellie the world is suddenly stripped of all civilization: "This delightful room had seemed to me a place where light-heartedness and charming manners lived—housed there just as the purple curtains and the Kiva rugs and the gay water-colours were. And now everything was in ruins" (p. 51). What Nellie feels is fear, fear of something malignant and evil in what is human, and the images of Myra as cruel mistress, wicked emperor, cold moon goddess acquire their full value in depicting her violent, despotic nature. Nellie goes with the dispirited Henshawe to see Sarah Bernhardt play Hamlet (another image of reversed sexual roles), and over their lunch together she reflects again on his curious eyes "without any fire in them," and on the courage and force that slept in the man. Part I concludes with Myra leaving New York on the same train as Nellie and her aunt. She is in a mood of "high scorn" and icily berates Nellie's aunt for her complicity with Henshawe over a gift of cufflinks from one of his admirers. Nellie leaves with the conviction that she will never like Myra so well again.

In Part II the view of Myra Henshawe is completely changed. Having exposed her heroine through gentle Nellie to be a wicked, tyrannical woman, the author now adopts an attitude of great sympathy for her. In the ten years that have elapsed between Parts I and II both the narrator and the Henshawes have suffered a reversal of worldly fortunes. Nellie finds them living in the same shabby hotel as herself. The disastrous change for the Henshawes is mirrored in the ugliness and vulgar newness of the unidentified "West-coast city" as compared to the metropolitan elegance of New York. Of greater interest for its contrast with Part I is the scene of Nellie's and Myra's reunion. Although Myra still delights in challenging Nellie's sober attitudes, the narrator now lets the emphasis fall on the things they have in common. Myra chides Nellie for becoming a teacher, exclaiming in her old manner "'only the stupid and the phlegmatic should teach.'" Nellie pointedly asks in return if she too might not be allowed " 'a temporary eclipse.' " When Myra continues by insisting on journalism as preferable to teaching, Nellie calmly answers: " 'I know what I want to do, and I'll work my way out yet, if only you'll give me time' " (p. 64). Nellie is no longer intimidated by Myra; she can observe her without self-consciousness and offer her sympathy. The scene ends with Myra's misery over the noise made by the people in the apartment above. (In such details as this we get a glimpse of the author herself. Willa Cather hated noise overhead; at one time she even rented the apartment above her own to ensure quiet. Like Myra, she found healing power in light and silence, and, like Myra, loved flowers to distraction.)

Myra's story in Part II bears witness to the vision that informs *The Professor's House:* namely, that the quest for power and possessions must end in failure and that only in religion and art is there any source of permanent values. During the last months of her life Myra becomes wholly preoccupied with religious faith; she tells Nellie that although she broke away from the Catholic Church and ran away with a German free-thinker, she still believes in holy words and holy rites " 'here in heathendom.' " Especially strong is her conviction of being a sinner in great need of forgiveness. She thinks of the great sinners of the past who always went home to die in some religious house, and later she tells Nellie that if her uncle were alive she would go to him and ask his forgiveness, for she hurt him when she ran away and she realizes now how lonely he must have been. In the novel's Christian schemata Myra's uncle remains an unregenerate sinner. A man of corrupt worldly power, he dies neither in humility (the Church goes to him with funeral pomp), nor with forgiveness in his heart, as the mocking clause providing for Myra in his will attests. He leaves his fortune to the Church not out of charity, but out of a desire for revenge on his niece. As Myra takes stock of her life she realizes how much like her uncle she is: " 'as we grow old we become more and more the stuff our forebears put into us' " (p. 82); she also recognizes that her foe has always lurked in her own bosom. In a moment of angry self-denunciation she says to Nellie: " 'I am a greedy, selfish, worldly woman; I wanted success and a place in the world' " (p. 75).

In contrast to her unsated desire for worldly power and success, Myra finds that " '*in religion seeking is finding*' " (p. 94), that religious desire is itself fulfillment. Her quest now is for immortality: instead of expensive jewels she keeps a crucifix and candles beside her. We are reminded briefly of Myra's former worldly ambitions, specifically of her court of admirers such as Ewan Gray, when she hears that a friend's son has shot himself over "some sordid love affair." Her only gesture in recognition of that past life now is to have masses said for the repose of Madame Modjeska's soul. Myra finds her "unearthly purposes" reflected in art as well as religious ritual. Nellie reads to her from Heine, and in the poem about the old tear left from youth's sorrows, and in the verse about the poor-sinner's-flower, she hears the drama of her own life rehearsed—the pursuit of romantic love, the sorrow of the penitent. She says to Nellie: " 'How the great poets do shine on . . . . Into all the dark corners of the world. They have no night' " (p. 82). Shakespeare for Myra is also a measure of life's immortal round. There are three Shakespearean references in the novel and they each deepen organically the meaning of the story. The reference to *Hamlet* played by Bernhardt not only reflects confusion of sexual roles in the Henshawe menage, but the painful uncertainty of the narrator as well. On her sickbed Myra would remember and recite long passages from Shakespeare's history plays, which appropriately are chronicles of worldly ambition and power. But perhaps the most significant allusion to Shakespeare is Myra's comparison of the headland by the ocean to Gloucester's cliff in *King Lear.* Shakespeare's tragedy is about the struggles of the generations and the gaining of wisdom, or "sight," in old age. When she is nearing death Myra comes to a windswept cliff and like Lear in his last scene with Cordelia she too wishes to be forgiven. When she and Nellie find the promontory for the first time she expresses her wish to be there at dawn, for " 'that is always such a forgiving time' " (p. 73). In her mind the image of the first light in the sky touching the water is like a kiss of absolution from heaven to the earth.

Myra arranges it so that she dies alone on the headland, and Nellie likes to think that before she died she saw the dawn and was forgiven. But Myra's last words, " 'Why must I die like this, alone with my mortal enemy?,' " cast grave doubts on her redemption. Myra seeks to be absolved of her earthly sins, but her pride will not let her forgive her husband. She suggests to Nellie that he is hateful in her eyes because he is a living reproach to her—a reminder of her own destructive willfullness. " 'Perhaps I can't forgive him for the harm I did him. Perhaps that's it' " (p. 88). When Nellie suggests to Myra that she is unreasonably hard on Oswald, Myra, still proud and quick to resent, bids Nellie leave her alone. As her illness becomes worse, she is increasingly consumed by hatred and self-recrimination. When Oswald does anything for her she thanks him in a guarded, cringing tone of voice (the reverse of her former imperial manner), and Nellie overhears her say to him: " 'It's bitter enough that I should have to take service from you—you whom I have loved so well' " (p. 92). In her misery she had thought of the woman upstairs as an infernal snake sent to torment her; now she attributes the noise entirely to her husband. Myra is trapped at the end of her life in a hell of her own making. Surrounded by all the offices of religion, she desperately seeks to be forgiven; but at the same time she cannot stop hating her husband, the embodiment of her life's failures. The priest absolves Myra before she dies, but her last bitter denunciation comes after he has left, and Nellie sadly reflects: "I had never heard a human voice utter such a terrible judgment upon all one hopes for" (p. 95).

The story ends in an atmosphere of forgiveness which further heightens our sense of Myra's self-damnation. Before leaving for Alaska, Oswald Henshawe asks Nellie to remember Myra as she was ten years before; in an image which powerfully recalls the old Myra he reassures Nellie that he would rather have been clawed by "Molly Driscoll" than petted by any other woman. Throughout Part II Nellie has shown great sympathy for Myra, and when Oswald gives her Myra's necklace of amethysts, we remember the book's first scene and recognize the breadth of Nellie's compassion. But Nellie's last thoughts of Myra are of a soul in torment. Her jewels are a reminder of her earthly vanity, and whenever Nellie sees young love begin to flower she hears Myra's final terrible words, spoken "like a confession of the soul" (p. 105).

The novella form, with its single and concentrated focus, is the perfect vehicle for the obsessive theme of *My Mortal Enemy.* The oblique fascination Nellie initially feels for Myra Henshawe is channeled into an absorbing preoccupation by the strict limitations of the book's form. The story never strays through secondary characters or a subplot from the portrait of Myra, which is the book's complete subject. The division of the story into two parts by the passing of time and by the narrator's loss of innocence brings us, through sharp contrasts, to a heightened sense of Myra's evil nature and the agony of her self-betrayal. With its suave but incisive form and with its portrait of an attractive but self-destructive woman, Willa Cather's vision of hell in *My Mortal Enemy* is both seductive and harrowing.

Death Comes for the Archbishop: A Saint's Legend

With little doubt Willa Cather's most successful formal experiment is her use of the saint's legend in *Death Comes for the Archbishop.*[5] In a letter to the editor of *Commonweal* she explains that she had long wanted to do something that would be the equivalent in prose of the frescoes of a saint's life, a narrative which, like the nondramatic stories of the *Golden Legend,* would have none of the artificial elements of composition.[6] She also explains that for a dozen years, since her first visit to New Mexico and Arizona, the subject that always most interested her there was the story of the Catholic Church and the Spanish missionaries. In the saint's legend she found an esthetic form which provided her, a non-Catholic, with an approach to her subject. The saint's legend also provided her with a nondramatic form of narrative[7] which would allow full play to her considerable powers of descriptive writing. No longer restricted by the necessity of organizing narrative in terms of plot or by the need to realize character in terms of psychological cause and effect, she was free to develop her descriptive writing as a mode of reflection upon some of the esthetic and moral problems with which she was most concerned.

Death Comes for the Archbishop was written with an ease and flawlessness that few books ever achieve; yet in no other novel does Willa Cather so constantly draw the reader's attention to the book's form and to the particular style she has adopted. From the outset it becomes clear that the essence of the book lies in its form—that our appreciation of the lives of the two Jesuit missionaries depends upon an appreciation of the novel's style. Miss Cather's full statement of her artistic intentions provides a suggestive point of departure:

> My book was a conjunction of the general and the particular, like most works of the imagination. I had all my life wanted to do something in the style of legend, which is absolutely the reverse of dramatic treatment. Since I first saw the Puvis de Chavannes frescoes of the life of Saint Geneviève in my student days, I have wished that I could try something a little like that in prose; something without accent, with none of the artificial elements of composition. In the Golden Legend the martyrdoms of the saints are no more dwelt upon than are the trivial incidents of their lives; it is as though all human experiences, measured against one supreme spiritual experience, were of about the same importance. The essence of such writing is not to hold the note, not to use an incident for all there is in it—but to touch and pass on. I felt that such writing would be a kind of discipline in these days when the "situation" is made to count for so much in writing, when the general tendency is to force things up. In this kind of writing the mood is the thing—all the little figures and stories are mere improvisations that come out of it.[8]

Later in the same letter she refers to Holbein's *Dance of Death* as the source of the novel's title. Some useful studies have been made of these remarks,[9] but most of them have focused on the significance of the pictorial models she cites for the novel. While the unique plastic quality of *Death Comes for The Archbishop* certainly owes much to the inspiration that she felt in viewing the St. Geneviève frescoes and the woodcuts of Holbein, her actual reading in medieval hagiography must also have contributed much to the evolution of her narrative method. In recalling the period of the novel's composition, Edith Lewis refers only to the novel's literary background: "All her life she had been profoundly interested in Catholicism—especially in the Catholicism of the Middle Ages, of the time of Abelard and St. Bernard. She had read widely on the subject long before she came to write the *Archbishop.*"[10] Given Willa Cather's profound appreciation and sensitivity for other literatures, it is difficult to think that she did not transfer to her own writing both consciously and intuitively some of the methods and philosophical assumptions of her reading.

Probably the best account of the saint's legend as a literary form is to be found in Erich Auerbach's monumental study *Mimesis.*[11] In his chapter analyzing the *Chanson de Roland* and the *Chanson d'Alexis,* an eleventh-century saint's legend, Auerbach suggests that because the medieval view of world order and human events was so highly structured, so thoroughly explained, there was little concern in the art and literature of the period for causal relationships. Because divine order informed earthly activity and made all events self-explanatory, interest in telling a story centered not on why or how something happened, but on its religious value and significance. Consequently, in this literature of moral exemplification plot counts for little. A medieval narrative typically consists of a series of scenes, each complete in itself, but which do not lead from one to the next. Auerbach calls this the paratactic style—scenes placed side by side, having equal value, but with no propulsive force moving the narrative forward. He compares the effect of this style to a series of pictures, related to one another, but each contained within its own frame. The events portrayed in the life of a hero or saint are never developed into a continuous dramatic sequence, rather they are strung out in a series of loosely related "pictures," each of which captures a gesture from a decisive moment in the subject's life. Because in the saint's life all experiences are as one when compared to the supreme spiritual experience of death, the trivial and the sublime are brought together and given equal importance. The spiritual world view precludes degrees of understanding (perspective) and fundamental philosophical conflicts that might be called tragic; yet within this framework a great range of emotions and descriptive effects is possible.

The literary phenomenon described by Auerbach corresponds very closely to the world created by Willa Cather in writing about the lives of the two missionary priests. The world experienced by Bishop Latour and his vicar, Father Vaillant, is circumscribed by a divine order, as it was for the medieval saints. The priests view all the events in their lives in the light of their faith. Crossing the desert without any water, the Bishop thinks on the greater suffering of Christ. The passion of Jesus, he reflects, is "the only reality." The landscape and its phenomena assume a divine topography: a thunderstorm brings a vision of the Creation when the land is separated out from the swirling waters; the Canyon de Chelly resembles an Indian Garden of Eden; the great mesa on the desert brings to the Bishop's mind the Rock of Peter on which the Church is built; a flock of white angora goats brings to mind the Apocalypse. The two priests frequently interpret events in their lives as providential interventions, particularly Father Vaillant, who never sees them as the result of natural causes or accident. The Bishop reflects somewhat wryly on his discovery of the village of Hidden Water, after he has been lost in the desert for nearly two days, that Father Vaillant "would almost be able to tell the colour of the mantel Our Lady wore when She took the mare by the bridle . . . and led her out of the pathless sand-hills" (p. 29), but even he is disposed to think of it as providential. There is no plot in *Death Comes for the Archbishop,* no dramatic focus to the story of the two priests' lives, because all events are simply aspects of a divine drama, the course of which is already known. In this light the novel's form is mythic and completely self-contained—the archetypal story being that of Christ's teaching, suffering, and martyrdom. Events of little and great importance—the blessing of an old slave woman or the confrontation with Martínez—are treated as of equal importance when measured against the supreme vision of heaven.

Unlike Willa Cather's other novels, where temporal perspectives are a crucial element of structure, time is only incidental in the *Archbishop,* because the vision suffusing this narrative is atemporal. Although the events in the book are related in a loose chronological order (from the meeting of the cardinals in 1848 until the Archbishop's death in 1889), time is of little significance. It is not the temporal duration but the quality and design of the missionaries' lives that are important, and the ever-present vision to which they are a witness. The structure employed for this narrative "without accent" captures the equilibrium of life lived within the framework of this faith. After the prologue, the novel is divided into nine books, each roughly equal in length, which gives a regular rhythm, like the nine strokes of the Angelus, to the narrative.[12] In making the novel approximate a spatial composition with a symmetry of parts and absence of plot (the movement of plot being temporal), Miss Cather also uses time spatially—*kairos,* significant event, as opposed to *chronos*—in a series of leitmotifs which bind chronological time into a continuous present. The stories of the missionaries' childhood, their school days, their early missions in Ohio are never unfolded in linear sequence, but are referred to from time to time throughout the book. We are also given glimpses into the future—the best example being the very title of the novel, which makes us see all actions from the vast perspective of eternity. This elimination of chronological time as it is felt by the Bishop himself is described at the end of the novel: "He sat in the middle of his own consciousness; none of his former states of mind were lost or outgrown. They were all within reach of his hand, and all comprehensible" (p. 290). Time has become something almost tactile which the priest can reach for and hold in his hands. Past and future are thus woven together into a static, continuous present which is informed throughout by the vision of an eternal Present.

The book "moves," then, not in familiar chronological sequence but through the juxtaposition of episodes and narratives which are loosely associated with the ideals of saintliness, and which offer an edifying or emotional contrast to each other. In the first two chapters of Book I, for example, the sufferings of the Bishop in the desert are contrasted to the physical and spiritual consolations he receives in the village of Hidden Water; and again in the first two chapters of Book VII, the spiritual optimism associated with spring is contrasted to spiritual drouth, here fittingly associated with the "December Night" of the second chapter's title. The nondramatic structure of the book is reflected in the author's choice of the type of saint's legend which she wished to relate. Rather than selecting as her central characters any of the numerous missionaries who suffered martyrdom in New Spain, she eschewed a theme which necessitated the treatment of events leading up to a dramatic climax and chose instead a much more understated kind of saintly ideal.[13] Any action in the novel is almost always described "after the event"; what is important is not the event itself, but its effect. The actual process of building the cathedral at Santa Fé is never related, but its visual impact, the circumstances of its creation, and its continuing significance are referred to frequently. The actual performing of the religious ceremonies at Hidden Water is never described, yet the whole chapter centers upon their significance. The figure of Kit Carson is referred to at intervals throughout the book, but we never see him at any moment of conflict; in fact, we see him only twice in the whole book, but a mystique gathers around this historical adventurer through the references that punctuate the novel from time to time. He becomes a continuous presence as do other figures like Magdalena, the cruelly mistreated wife of Buck Scales; Jacinto, the Indian scout; and Mother Philomène, Father Vaillant's devout sister in France.

This multiple view of the characters and scenes does not increase their complexity so much as it holds them in suspension in an ever-present continuum. Recurring visual images increase the plastic quality of the narrative and heighten the unity of spiritual vision. Within each book the chapters are organized around events in such a way that, like their models in the frescoes and the *Golden Legend,* each depicts a series of visual gestures: the Bishop kneeling at the foot of a cruciform juniper tree; the Vicar riding over the desert on his white mule; the wrathful Baltazar hurling a pewter mug at his serving-boy. The static, plastic quality of the book is underscored by the individual chapter headings, which are nearly all taken from the central visual image of that chapter: "The Cruciform Tree," "The Wooden Parrot," "The White Mules," "Cathedral."[14] Yet the visual gestures do not coalesce into a moving dramatic whole. In a single chapter (the basic unit of composition) Willa Cather may bring her narrative to the point of a dramatic conflict—Bishop Latour faces the incorrigible Padre Martínez for a showdown, or he and the Vicar both fall into the hands of the degenerate murderer Buck Scales—but just as we become emotionally involved, she moves us on, and perhaps in another chapter refers obliquely to the final outcome of the situation. Action is seldom narrated directly, but is presented in stories told by characters within the novel or as legends rehearsed in their time-sanctified form.

One of Willa Cather's critics opens his study of the *Archbishop* with the following statement: "The importance of Willa Cather's *Death Comes for the Archbishop* is that it is one of the most elaborately contrived novels ever fashioned by an American, rivalling in artistic allusiveness Eliot's *Wasteland* [*sic*] and in technical complexity Faulkner's *Absalom, Absalom!*"[15] Indeed in *Death Comes for the Archbishop* Willa Cather makes us conscious of formal structure and style in an emphatic way. A constant awareness of form in art has the effect of making us emotionally detached in our esthetic response. To the degree that we are conscious of form, we become objective and involved on an intellectual or reflective plane. This is the spectator's experience in viewing many of the contemporary visual arts; the "hard-edge" abstractionists, for instance, construct their art exclusively around the conscious appreciation of formal design and color. In literature, writers in the twentieth century, having exhausted the easy emotional appeal of romanticism and realism, have turned to more reflective and intellectually disciplined forms of writing. An appreciation of writers like James Joyce, Virginia Woolf, and Faulkner demands a disciplined participation in a form of writing which constantly puts the reader to the test intellectually. The fracturing of chronological narrative sequence, the morass of mythical, historical, and literary allusions, the intricate shifts in viewpoint, the complex image patterns, all intrude on the reader's direct involvement in the so-called content of the fiction, all demand attention for themselves, combining to provoke a reflective, self-conscious attitude in the reader. Yet this alienating and retarding of the emotions makes them much stronger and more lasting in the end.

Beside Joyce and Faulkner, Willa Cather's formal experimentation may seem very uncomplicated, but the consciousness of form functions similarly in *Death Comes for the Archbishop,* though not in most of her other novels. While all her best writing is descriptive and reflective, the formal structure and style of her other novels never draws attention to itself. Though *My Ántonia,* for example, is carefully structured around a series of temporal and spatial perspectives which embody in themselves the whole pastoral experience, we are scarcely aware, as we read, of the structuring and style which elicit our nostalgic, reflective response. In *Death Comes for the Archbishop* we are never permitted to become involved in this same way, for though the manner is still descriptive and reflective, we are always conscious of a formal restriction placed on the content of the narrative. In particular, the lack of any real plot denies the reader the traditional kind of narrative involvement. Moreover, the juxtaposition of scenes which elicits a direct emotional response in the other novels has no dramatic consequence in this book. Instead we are more likely to appreciate the esthetic rightness of this juxtaposition, reflect on the sureness of the book's overall design. The emotion we do experience, rather than being the result of a personal identification with the protagonists, is of a higher order, for it arises from increased awareness of the values (both ascetic and esthetic) of saintliness.

For this reason, all aspects of the novel's form continually draw attention to the spiritual purpose of the two priests' lives. One of the most important stylistic devices used to create this effect occurs in the descriptive landscapes so prominent in *Death Comes for the Archbishop.* These landscapes are frequently given an extended allegorical significance which, although less schematized than the great medieval allegories, is nevertheless carefully and consistently executed.[16] A striking example occurs at the opening of Book I, chapter 1, where the New Mexican desert in which the Bishop is lost acquires the secondary meaning of a spiritual testing ground comparable to the wilderness in which Christ was tempted by Satan. The insistent imagery of triangular shapes—the "conical red hills" and the "smaller cones of juniper" which confuse the priest's sense of direction, making him close his eyes "to rest them from the intrusive omnipresence of the triangle"—begin to suggest the mystical number of the spirit and the Trinity itself, and they culminate in a tree shaped like a crucifix, an inverted triangle in fact: "a naked, twisted trunk, perhaps ten feet high, and at the top . . . parted into two lateral, flat-lying branches, with a little crest of green in the centre, just above the cleavage" (p. 18). Through the suggestive nature of the landscape, the pattern of Christ's life emerges as the pattern of the priest's. The cruciform tree and the Bishop's growing thirst remind him of Christ's Passion: "He reminded himself of that cry, wrung from his Saviour on the Cross, *'J'ai soif!'* "; and we are told that, like Christ, he too has been rejected by those he has come to save: "He was a Vicar Apostolic, lacking a Vicarate. He was thrust out; his flock would have none of him." Here, the close integration of landscape with its allegorical implications establishes the pattern of quiet saintliness which is the basis of the portrait of the two priests, and which it is all the more important for us to recognize since Miss Cather has chosen to describe a saintly life rather than a martyrdom.

The allegorical significance of the landscape is not insisted upon in an obvious, rigidly schematized way; Willa Cather's method is rather to isolate a particular feature of a landscape and concentrate upon it in such a way that it acquires a depth of meaning, an aura of significance in terms of the spiritual life. Similarly, medieval saints' legends are not highly developed allegories, but they assume allegorical significance through the primacy of the Christian archetype which provides them with a common structure. Their landscapes are generalized and symbolic rather than particular and realistic: the most popular settings include forest (symbolic landscape for the trials and complexities of this world), storms at sea (providential acts), and deserts (testing grounds, or settings for the ascetic life). Landscapes are rarely specified or differentiated in geographical terms since only their general relevance to the spiritual progress of the saint is important. Here, of course, Willa Cather differs from the medieval writers since she is at pains to specify the particular geographical landscapes in her book, but the effect of her concentrated descriptions is frequently to direct our attention to a more general spiritual meaning ("a conjunction of the general and particular"). That this is indeed her intention is emphasized by her habit of making the interpretation of the landscape explicit, though unobtrusively so, usually through the medium of one of the priests' meditations upon a scene. The extensive description of the mesa plain, for example (Book III, chapter 3), is carefully particularized in its strange and phenomenal appearance, but it is nevertheless dominated by a highly suggestive image: the great Rock on which the town of Ácoma is built, accessible only by a narrow staircase, and visible for miles over the plain. The original reason for building a town in such an inaccessible place, it is explained to the Bishop, was for safety: the Indians, hunted by their enemies, "had at last taken this leap away from the earth, and on that rock had found the hope of all suffering and tormented creatures—safety" (p. 97). At this point in the description, the Rock has already begun to acquire for the reader several Christian ideas which lift it far from the realm of mere geographical or sociological curiosity; we are reminded of the rock upon which the wise man builds his house, and of Peter, the Rock upon which Christ founded His Church, even before the Bishop makes the connection for us. The correspondence between concrete object and religious idea is a profound discovery for him, and one must conclude that the reader is intended to make the same discovery in other parts of the book:

> Already the Bishop had observed in Indian life a strange literalness, often shocking and disconcerting. The Ácomas, who must share the universal human yearning for something permanent, enduring, without shadow of change,—they had their idea in substance. They actually lived upon their Rock; were born upon it and died upon it. There was an element of exaggeration in anything so simple! [P. 98]

The image of the Rock does not remain a simple one, however; in the story of Friar Baltazar, an early priest of Ácoma who betrayed the Indians by forcing them to labor on a huge church, rectory, and garden which merely reflected his own worldly pride, Miss Cather contrasts the idea of the Rock as refuge, a true symbol of Christ's church, with the perversion of that idea by a minister of the church. The result of Baltazar's corruption is the negation of Christianity. The service which the Bishop celebrates in Ácoma depresses him: "He felt as if he were celebrating Mass at the bottom of the sea, for antediluvian creatures; for types of life so old, so hardened, so shut within their shells, that the sacrifice on Calvary could hardly reach back so far" (p. 100). The tragically perverted nature of the Rock has already been suggested by the flower which the Bishop notices growing at the foot of it: "a plant with big white blossoms like Easter lilies" which he recognizes as a species of deadly nightshade.

The antediluvian nature of the people still living on the Rock relates to another suggestive aspect of the moral landscape—the cave in the mountains used for secret Indian religious ceremonies. When Jacinto, the Indian guide, takes him there for refuge from a blizzard, the Bishop is immediately struck by a distaste for the place. The cave is connected with an indefinable quality of evil. The framework around the incident is fraught with fear of disease and death: Father Vaillant's dangerous illness (he has contracted black measles from the Indians) is the reason for the Bishop's journey; he spends the first night of the journey with Jacinto and his wife, whose baby's sickliness causes the Bishop to ponder on the extinction of the Pecos tribe. Even though the cave provides shelter from the snowstorm the Bishop himself falls into a physical state comparable to death, from which only Jacinto's fire and his own flask of whisky can revive him. The image of the snake within a cave has obvious connections with a concept of evil rooted in sexuality. However, the author avoids the limitations of this obvious analogy by directing us to the terrifying ancient quality of what is being experienced.[17] Jacinto leads the Bishop to a fissure in the stone floor where he hears a great underground river resounding through a cavern:

> The water was far, far below, perhaps as deep as the foot of the mountain, a flood moving in utter blackness under ribs of antediluvian rock. It was not a rushing noise, but the sound of a great flood moving with majesty and power.
>
> "It is terrible," he said at last, as he rose. [P. 130]

There is a sense of the Bishop's having passed through "the valley of the shadow" because when he reaches Father Vaillant the fever has broken.

Considered purely in terms of the visual pleasure they evoke in the reader, the landscape descriptions in the *Archbishop* are highly effective, but sensuous enjoyment is seldom the single effect being sought. Esthetic pleasure is usually employed in the service of an intellectual or religious idea, and the description of the Bishop's garden in Santa Fé (Book VII, chapter 1) begins with a typical double implication: "It was the month of Mary and the month of May." It is probably no accident that this description, with its intermingling of the natural elements in a celebration of growth and fertility, is strongly reminiscent of the conventional medieval seasonal headpiece, of which the opening to the *Canterbury Tales* is the best-known example. Just as the medieval headpieces function both sensuously and allegorically, so in this section of *Death Comes for the Archbishop* the natural description of the garden is carefully related to the description of Father Vaillant's May-time devotions to the Virgin while he was still a young curate in France.

The fertility of the Bishop's garden and his delight in caring for it accumulate further meanings: the garden suggests the whole of his "Great Diocese" (the title of Book VII), and its new-found order and fruitfulness are the product of the priests' hard work among the far-flung missions. Father Vaillant himself provides this interpretation when he compares the poor unlettered peasants to plants: " 'They are like seeds, full of germination but with no moisture. A mere contact is enough to make them a living part of the Church' " (p. 206). The two priests themselves have their allegorical representatives in the garden: Father Vaillant is connected with the flower of the tamarisk tree, which is associated with the poor Indians among whom he works, and the Bishop is connected with the rare lotus of contemplation, which he nourishes carefully in his garden pond.

Although Willa Cather's landscapes are allegorical in the suggestive rather than the rigidly schematized sense, the detailed consistency with which natural objects refer us by suggestion to spiritual counterparts is remarkable. Through the stylistic device of allegory our emotional and sensuous reactions are continually disciplined and channeled into an intellectual understanding of the character of saintliness, and the result is a level of appreciation which ultimately has increased impact—a sort of sensuous comprehension. The culmination of the garden landscape is the appearance of Magdalena surrounded by a flock of doves which "caught the light in such a way that they all became invisible at once, dissolved in light and disappeared as salt dissolves in water" (pp. 209–10). The suggestion of the Holy Spirit, at a moment of understated crisis in the relationship of the two priests, is inescapable, but we are never forced to make a simple constricting equation, so lightly does the author pass over the picture of the girl and the birds to concentrate immediately upon the girl herself, who is concrete proof of what the priests have been able to "grow in their garden."

As an art form, the saint's legend assumes a mode of proof rather than analysis. It rejects causality (since things are only divinely explicable) and omits levels of awareness and understanding. Its purpose is to *show* what happened, not to explain why. In *Death Comes for the Archbishop* Willa Cather's only concern is to describe the life of the priests, not to analyze their individual psychological motives. Their actions are viewed not in terms of psychology, but in terms of religious faith; consequently, characterization is very flat, creating a stronger impact visually than emotionally. This may not seem to be true of the two priests, Bishop Latour and Father Vaillant, for we are given glimpses (although not until the end) of their childhood and of the agonizing moments when they choose their life's work and when they part from each other. But from the beginning of the narrative these choices have been made, and having renounced all earthly ambitions they remain steadfast in their faith and unchanging in character. When we are first introduced to the Bishop riding over the hot desert, he is described to us only externally, but we are assured that his refined appearance accurately reflects his sensitive, gentle nature. In Father Vaillant we are given a portrait of diminutive stature and physical ugliness which, we are told, are made attractive by his generous and impulsive nature. No further attempt is made to analyze character—both its mystery and irrelevance are suggested when the Bishop reflects on how unexplainable his friend is: a man "greater than the sum of his qualities" (p. 228). The depth and the nature of their friendship is unfolded in the narrative, but their essential characters remain the same. In *Death Comes for the Archbishop* there is no dialectic of growing awareness shaping the book as in most of Miss Cather's novels—simply the fact of existence itself, inexplicable and inviolable.

The Bishop and his vicar are delineated in fine detail, so that we do not actually feel that they are stereotypes. However, this stylized presentation of character in fact resembles the method of characterization in medieval saints' legends (and of course in other forms of medieval literature). While one may not agree with D. W. Robertson that the concept of personality as we know it now, with its concentration upon the needs and desires of the individual, was entirely foreign to the Middle Ages,[18] it is nevertheless true that character is generally not presented in terms of psychological realism. Inner motivations and complexities are rarely developed; rather, characters act from motives of lust, greed, pride, or for other relatively straightforward reasons. This accounts for the consistent appearance of easily recognized stereotypes in all forms of medieval literature, and particularly in saints' legends, where the pagan tyrants are inevitably violent and irrational lechers, and the saints controlled, logical, and steadfastly virginal. The inward nature of these figures is certainly defined, but it is *moral,* not psychological nature, and the simple predominance of virtue or vice is usually reflected in the external features of their persons. Indeed, the medieval rhetoricians seem to have conceived of fictional characters largely as the stylistic amplifications of abstract ideas, that is, as the concrete images of moral or immoral qualities.[19] Thus, although not all their fictions are strictly allegorical in style, the allegorical mode of thought tends to dominate their concept of character.

In *Death Comes for the Archbishop,* the flatness of characterization—the quasi-allegorical nature of human beings regarded in the light of religious conviction—is most noticeable in the presentation of the lesser figures. A number of the portraits recall the style of medieval exempla, illustrating the Christian virtues and vices.[20]

Padre Martínez is the very personification of lust and Luciferan pride; he tells the Bishop, " 'We pay a filial respect to the person of the Holy Father, but Rome has no authority here' " (p. 147). Friar Baltazar suggests wrath, pride, and gluttony in equal proportions, and Padre Jesus de Baca, with his simple childlike faith, is the image of blind superstition. Padre Jesus' sight is actually obscured by a cataract on his right eye, and in adding this detail Willa Cather adopts the common medieval stylistic device, by which external appearance is made to reflect moral nature. Similarly the "grey, oily look of soft cheeses" (p. 145) which the Bishop notices on the face of Trinidad is not meant only to repulse us, but also to suggest a moral depravity which contrasts with the "fine intelligence" of the Bishop's countenance. Just as the more prominent features of the landscape in *Death Comes for the Archbishop* have their spiritual counterparts, so in the presentation of character external appearance is a guide to moral nature, and other complexities of human psychology are simply irrelevant.

Concrete description is not an end in itself in this style of writing since the ideal which underlies the book, and indeed all saints' legends, is the renunciation of the material world, and everything pertaining to it, for the greater life of the spirit. All the devices of hagiographical style are designed to serve this concept. The Bishop and his vicar are not given the opportunity to choose martyrdom, the ultimate renunciation of this world, but they do choose to relinquish the material comforts and amenities of earthly life in devoting themselves to serving God. In the prologue the old missionary tells the cardinals that the Bishop of New Mexico " 'will be called upon for every sacrifice' " (p. 10), and as we are introduced to Bishop Latour and Father Vaillant, we are made aware of the kind of earthly desires which they have sacrificed in becoming missionaries. Father Vaillant, physically frail, longs for a settled home in one mission, but following his bishop's guidance he moves continually to distant regions, suffering the physical and mental privations which his wandering life entails. A contemplative life enriched by esthetic pleasures lies at the heart of the Bishop's earthly desires, but like his vicar he has chosen to sacrifice a comfortable life in the cultivated ecclesiastical circles of Europe for the hardships of a bleak existence in the New Mexican desert.

Much of the strength of the spiritual ideal which informs the book is created by Willa Cather's use of contrasting portraits of priests who have followed their earthly, sensual ambitions. Some of these men are attractive and colorful in their own way, like the flamboyant Padre Martínez, but the negative aspects of Catholicism they represent are unmitigated by this attractiveness. We are not allowed to forget that they are ultimately perversions of the ideal so strongly embodied in the Bishop and Father Vaillant, nor that in terms of this ideal they are wretchedly misguided, from Padre Gallegos who "did not look quite like a professional gambler, but something smooth and twinkling in his countenance suggested an underhanded mode of life" (p. 84), to Padre Lucero, whose dying thoughts are of his gold. Their life styles, based on pleasure and materialism are drawn in sharp contrast to the inner, spiritual style of living developed by the Bishop and Father Vaillant. We are told that Father Vaillant "was scarcely acquisitive to the point of decency"; owning but his mule, Contento, "he was like the saints of the early Church, literally without personal possessions" (p. 227).

Willa Cather treats the theme of renunciation of earthly power somewhat differently from the traditional saint's legend by developing this theme in terms of art: an artist's act of creation may too easily become a desire for personal power, and art objects can be treated materialistically, as possessions. This extension of the basic saint's legend theme is examined primarily through the Bishop, who has a highly developed esthetic sense. It is introduced in the prologue, when the Spanish cardinal, de Allande, relates to his guests an anecdote of how his grandfather lost a valuable El Greco to a begging friar from New Spain who wanted it for his mission church. (The prologue, it should be noted, bears a striking resemblance in its detail—the elevation, the sunlight, the lavish dinner—to the Baltazar scene at Ácoma where a man of the Church is corrupted by worldly pride.) De Allande's main interest in the proposed new bishop is in whether he has " 'any intelligence in the matter of art' " and would be able to recognize and (presumably) return the El Greco if he came across it. The worldliness of de Allande and his two fellow cardinals is clearly meant as an underlying contrast to the Bishop. For the Bishop is indeed a man with "intelligence in the matters of art," as his characteristic reflection upon the artifacts he encounters in his travels indicates. His great pleasure in fine silver and good furniture suggests that even he is not immune to the temptations to which the worldlier ecclesiastics of history succumbed, becoming more famous as patrons of the arts than as men of the Church.

The theme of power and its relinquishment is developed in the novel through an examination of the nature of art, such that the ideal held up to us is a combination of the esthetic and the religious. Throughout the book we are made aware of numerous art objects upon which the Bishop, through whose consciousness they are always seen, reflects. These objects are not always religious, although most of them are, but they all have one thing in common: they are the products of long cultural traditions. They are in the widest sense the work of a people, and thus, though they may have been made by a single artist, they transcend the whole question of private possession and individual ambition. Consequently, whenever the Bishop contemplates one of these objects, he reflects upon the tradition which gave birth to it. In the little house of Benito in Hidden Water he examines the wooden figures of the saints on the shelf over the fireplace, and observes the fashion in which the Mexicans have adapted the saints of Europe to express their own needs and hopes: the figure of the Virgin wears "a black reboso over her head, like a Mexican woman of the poor" (p. 28), and St. Jacques has become Santiago, the patron saint of horses, in this land where horses are one of the most vital necessities. This cultural adaptation of an older tradition—the figure of the Virgin is compared to one in "the rigid mosaics of the Eastern Church"—is contrasted by the Bishop to "the factory-made plaster images in his mission churches in Ohio," where images are a mass-produced feature of the economy and therefore cease to be art. Again, when the Bishop first awakes to hear the sound of the Angelus bell which Father Vaillant has resurrected from an old church basement, its sound conveys to him a "sudden, pervasive sense of the East" and of the Holy Land, though he has never been there; later he traces this feeling to the fact that the Spanish taught their craft of silver-working to the Mexicans, and were themselves taught by the Moors, so that the bell is a product of the oldest Christian and pre-Christian traditions. Rarely is an individual artist mentioned in connection with the art objects in the book: the wooden parrot of old Padre Jesus de Baca was bought from an old Indian whose ancestors brought it "from the mother pueblo" where it had been carved from "one of those rare birds that in ancient times were carried up alive, all the long trail from the tropics" (p. 87).[21] The old Indian sold it to Padre Jesus only because he "was much indebted to him, and . . . was about to die without descendants." Even the little church of Laguna with its geometric decorations reminds us that art is the refinement of ages of custom, skill and feeling, rather than the product only of individual power: "It recalled to Father Latour the interior of a Persian chieftain's tent he had seen in a textile exhibit at Lyons. Whether this decoration had been done by Spanish missionaries or by Indian converts, he was unable to find out" (p. 90).

The traditional and communal origins of art are emphasized in nearly all the descriptions of art objects in the book, from the silver toilet set given the Bishop by Don Olivares, to the Indian blankets, "very old, and beautiful in design and colour," hanging on the walls of his study. This de-emphasis of the individual's part in the act of creation is central to the theme of renunciation of earthly desires, since it is precisely in the act of creation that the sensation of power is strongest. The Bishop's closest approach to a spiritual crisis is resolved through a contemplation of religious artifacts; this leads him to a renewed renunciation of temporal power. The incident occurs in his encounter with old Sada, a devout Mexican woman, who is a slave in a Protestant American family which does not permit her to attend mass or enter a church.The Bishop himself is suffering from a period of spiritual drouth when he finds her late at night huddled in the church door, and together they go to pray in the Lady Chapel. The scene focuses upon Sada's reaction to the religious images on the altar which she has not seen for nineteen years: "Old Sada fell on her knees and kissed the floor. She kissed the feet of the Holy Mother, the pedestal on which they stood, crying all the while" (p. 214). Through her reaction to the holy artifacts, the Bishop is able to re-experience religious ecstasy:

> He was able to feel, kneeling beside her, the preciousness of the things of the altar to her who was without possessions; the tapers, the image of the Virgin, the figures of the saints, the Cross that took away indignity from suffering and made pain and poverty a means of fellowship with Christ. [P. 217]

This experience of the "holy mysteries" through the religious images brings the Bishop to the supreme realization of what the renunciation of earthly power and ambition means:

> He received the miracle in her heart into his own, saw through her eyes, knew that his poverty was as bleak as hers. When the Kingdom of Heaven had first come into the world, into a cruel world of torture and slaves and masters, He who brought it had said, "*And whosoever is least among you, the same shall be first in the Kingdom of Heaven.*" This church was Sada's house, and he was a servant in it. [P. 218]

As the old woman leaves, the Bishop gives her a silver medal with the image of the Virgin on it, thinking, "Ah . . . for one who cannot read—or think—the Image, the physical form of Love!" (P. 219). This chapter extends the concept of the art object to include the communal nature not only of its origins, but also of its possession, in the sense that art has a quality which makes it the property of all humanity, rather than of a single individual. Every work of art ought to be "the physical form of Love."

After this point in the narrative, art objects are seen by the Bishop primarily in terms of their value as spiritual consolation and inspiration. The wooden figure of the Virgin in his own church in Santa Fé, with her elaborate wardrobe of dresses and jewelry made by the local women and silversmiths, becomes an image of divine consolation in the loneliness he feels after watching Father Vaillant depart for Colorado. He thinks of the Virgin as "*le rêve suprême de la chair*" and he associates her with an esthetic sensibility: "A life need not be cold, or devoid of grace in the worldly sense, if it were filled by Her who was all the graces" (p. 256). The care which the poor Mexicans lavish upon the wardrobe of the wooden statue is a translation of their love into art, just as "Raphael and Titian had made costumes for Her in their time, and the great masters had made music for Her, and the great architects had built cathedrals for Her" (p. 257). The little boots which the condemned Mexican boy makes for the statue of Santiago in his home town, as he awaits his execution, are also a kind of prayer for pity translated into art, and the Bishop's cathedral itself is an image of his need for consolation and redemption as he lies dying: "He felt safe under its shadow; like a boat come back to harbour, lying under its own sea-wall" (p. 273).

When Dona Isabella returns to New Orleans the Bishop purchases her sideboard and dining table, and enjoys the silver coffee service and candelabra which she gives him for remembrance. In this respect he is often contrasted with Father Vaillant, who has little eye for art and even less interest. The religious images he is most closely associated with are the colored illustrations and medallions which he gives to the Indians (and takes to Rome to have blessed in such vast quantities by the Pope), and his interest in objects like the Angelus bell is purely confined to their religious function. He has little patience with the Bishop's appreciation of the artistic tradition which lies behind the bell, and his response is typical: " 'I am no scholar, as you know,' said Father Vaillant rising. 'And this morning we have many practical affairs to occupy us' " (p. 45). A similar contrast between the two priests occurs when the Bishop takes Father Vaillant to visit the hill from which the rock for his cathedral is being quarried, and discloses to his friend his plans for the building. When he discusses the Romanesque tradition of which the cathedral is to be part, Father Vaillant's reaction is again a typical concern with practicalities rather than esthetics: "Father Vaillant sniffed and wiped his glasses. 'If you once begin thinking about architects and styles, Jean! And if you don't get American builders, whom will you get, pray?' " (p. 243). It matters little to him "whether [the cathedral] was Midi Romanesque or Ohio German in style" (p. 245) and his implied criticism—" 'I had no idea you were going in for fine building, when everything about us is so poor—and we ourselves are so poor' " (p. 244)—brings us to a concern with whether the Bishop is in fact creating an artifact for the same reasons that the Spanish cardinal desired his El Greco—selfish and worldly reasons—or whether his love of art is of a different order. The Bishop himself voices this concern:

> "I could hardly have hoped that God would gratify my personal taste, my vanity, if you will, in this way. I tell you, *Blanchet,* I would rather have found that hill of yellow rock than have come into a fortune to spend in charity. The Cathedral is near my heart, for many reasons. I hope you do not think me very worldly." [P. 245]

The answer to the question of motivation is never really in doubt, however, and the cathedral is the central, ideal artifact of the book, communal in origin through its relation to European architectural style and through the many hands involved in building it, and communally owned, in the sense that it belongs to the Mexican people. This point is made particularly in the description of the way the cathedral complements its setting. " 'Either a building is a part of a place, or it is not' ", the French architect tells the Bishop; " 'Once that kinship is there, time will only make it stronger' " (p. 272). That the cathedral was built to answer other than egotistic or worldly needs is suggested in the contrast between the "spiritual gold" of the rock from which the church is made and the material gold of the Colorado Rush which reduces men to such inhuman conditions in the remainder of Book VIII. A further contrast emphasizes the integrity of the Bishop's motivation: when he notes that " 'this hill is only about fifteen miles from Santa Fé; there is an upgrade, but it is gradual. Hauling the stone will be easier than I could have hoped for' " (p. 243), we recall the ill-fated church of Friar Baltazar on the Rock of Ácoma, for which "every stone in that structure, every handful of earth in those many thousand pounds of adobe, was carried up the trail on the backs of men and boys and women" (p. 101), and the huge beams of the roof were hauled by Indian labor from forty or fifty miles away.

The religious estheticism of the Bishop is contrasted to the worldly, acquisitive attitude to art of the Spanish cardinal in the prologue, and the cathedral embodies both material beauty and spiritual integrity. But the conflict between art as personal pleasure and art as selfless service to an ideal which the Bishop discerns in himself is perhaps less easily resolved in terms of the Faith than, for instance, Father Vaillant's conflicting desires for the settled life of a parish priest and the active life of a nomadic missionary. Father Vaillant resolves this conflict without a backward glance by devoting himself against his inclination to a life of travel among the rough mining towns of Colorado, but for the Bishop the struggle is a continuing one, no doubt because Willa Cather recognized the ambiguous nature and motives of art. The Bishop too is made to realize this, for he tells Father Vaillant that, in terms of the renunciation of worldly success, " 'You are a better man than I. You have been a great harvester of souls, without pride and without shame—and I am always a little cold—*un pédant,* as you used to say. If hereafter we have stars in our crowns, yours will be a constellation. Give me your blessing' " (pp. 261–62). The slight distinction drawn here between the Bishop and Father Vaillant makes us reflect again upon the nature of art—whether it is to be experienced largely in terms of pleasure, as a sublimated form of personal power, or in terms of its social function and moral significance. The Bishop's cathedral resolves the conflict; it is an art object which is not only communal in origin and function, but which is also created in the service of an ideal of which the basis is the negation of self in God.

From the outset Willa Cather has extended the basic theme of the saint's legend to include a consideration of the ideal nature of art, but this has not necessitated a break in the style which she originally chose for her narrative. Art and religion are seen to be analogous, since the individual's renunciation of power is vital to the integrity of both. Ultimately this theme is fully realized through the style and form she has chosen: just as the content of her narrative was communal in origin (she retells the story of Father Machebeuf recounted by the Reverend W. J. Howlett), so the style is the traditional form of hagiography, which demands the subordination of the individual to a spiritual and communal ideal. Willa Cather always thought of the arts as a vital source of pleasure. She was not, in the strictest sense, a religious writer, but religious art suggested to her the further possibility of the esthetic experience as a great source of enduring happiness.

Shadows on the Rock: A Historical Novel

Since they were first published, *Death Comes for the Archbishop* and *Shadows on the Rock*[22] have been grouped together as Willa Cather's historical novels. Set in the pioneer past of the Catholic church, they are generally viewed as reflecting the author's quest for some permanent human values in an age of ever-accelerating change. The similarities of the two books, however, go little beyond that general description; indeed, they differ widely in both style and emotional content. The vital distinction is a matter of literary form. *Death Comes for the Archbishop* is a saint's legend and its narrative conforms to the archetypal story of the Christian life. As a form of self-contained myth, the priests' story, though given a specific time and setting, is essentially atemporal, for time is measured in terms of significant action rather than chronology. The events in the priests' lives are not seen in terms of temporal causality, but in terms of the supreme vision of heaven which suffuses the narrative; the very title makes us see all action from the vast perspective of eternity. *Shadows on the Rock,* on the other hand, is more accurately a historical novel, because here the writing is directed to the evocation of life in a specific time and place —late seventeenth-century Quebec. In a published letter Miss Cather herself wrote that *Shadows on the Rock* "was more like an old song . . . than like a legend"; she describes the effect she sought to achieve as of something fragmented and incomplete, a feeling about life inherited from another age and molded by time and memory.[23] The title also directs our perspective: "shadows" suggests the ghosts or an aura from the past, something only experienced through memory or reflection, rather than the full-bodied presence of legend being relived.[24] Implicit in the historical perspective is a vision of mutability: man physically subject to disease, decay, and death and morally exposed to the evils and corruptions that hold sway in the affairs of men. In *Shadows on the Rock* Willa Cather is deeply preoccupied with man's mortal and corruptible nature; but at the same time human suffering is seen as providentially ordered because within the context of Catholic faith it provides man with a purgatorial passage leading from innate depravity to the promised redemption.

The special mood and concerns of *Shadows on the Rock* probably reflect some of the unhappy changes which took place in the author's life between 1927 and 1931: the loss of her Bank Street apartment in New York, the death of her father, and the prolonged illness of her mother, who had suffered a paralytic stroke. Edith Lewis singles out her mother's illness as particularly affecting the mood of her writing:

> The long illness of Mrs. Cather—it lasted two and a half years —had a profound effect on Willa Cather, and I think on her work as well. . . . In Willa Cather's long stays in Pasadena, where her mother was cared for in a sanatorium, she had to watch her continually growing weaker, more ailing, yet unable to die. It was one of those experiences that make a lasting change in the climate of one's mind.[25]

Accordingly, a sense of life's vicissitudes and man's mortality is felt throughout the pages of *Shadows on the Rock.* It seems to me, moreover, that the illness and death of her parents may have loosed in the author a deep sense of remorse over her often rebellious youthful behavior (explored in the long biographical story "Old Mrs. Harris"), which perhaps would explain this novel's recurrent view of man in the light of original sin. For Willa Cather the Quebec of her novel becomes a place of both refuge and atonement. In the story of the apothecary Euclide Auclair and his daughter Cécile, the author likely sought a haven of happy childhood memories as they focused on her father. For the author, as well as for the characters of the novel, Quebec is a retreat from the world at large; both take pleasure in "a feeling of being cut off from everything and living in a world of twilight and miracles" (p. 62).[26] But if the past is also the locus of personal guilt for Willa Cather, as I have suggested above, so seventeenth-century Quebec can only be legitimized as a refuge through emphasis on its penitential character. These, I would suggest, are the deepest themes and motives in the book—the quest for refuge, the vision of man's depravity—and their irreconcilable, backward-looking character give the novel its special evocative and melancholy quality.

Again in her published letter about *Shadows on the Rock* Willa Cather describes the composition of the book as "mainly anacoluthon," which refers technically to words and phrases not arranged in grammatical sequence. The stylistic effect being described is that of narrative without direction or movement forward. She also refers to *Shadows on the Rock* as a "series of pictures remembered rather than experienced." In both instances she singles out for attention a static quality in her narrative, a quality which perhaps she felt rendered best that sense of life's permanence in Quebec. The painterly quality for which Willa Cather's style is distinguished is strongly developed here: each chapter in the novel constitutes a self-contained, essentially plastic scene and almost every sequence of the book is set in a descriptive tableau which superbly evokes the colors and textures of the Quebec landscape. The best of these render the autumn season: "ledges of brown and lavender clouds lay above the river and the Île d'Orléans, and the red-gold autumn sunlight poured over the rock like a heavy southern wine" (p. 33). The city itself in this setting is compared to the work of a goldsmith: "In the Upper Town the grey slate roofs and steeples were framed and encrusted with gold. A slope of roof or a dormer window looked out from the twisted russet branches of an elm, just as old mirrors were framed in gilt garlands. A sharp gable rose out of a soft drift of tarnished foliage like a piece of agate set in fine goldsmith's work" (pp. 228–229). This highly visual, plastic element in Miss Cather's style points to the fundamental emotion in the novel—the desire to prevent change. Descriptive scenes momentarily arrest the movement forward in time which is basic to narrative; they embody the feelings of Cécile who dreads leaving Quebec and going back to the larger world of France.

This emotion—this desire to stop time—permeates the whole book, but it is most coherently realized in the concern for tradition. When the Auclairs come to Quebec with Count Frontenac they bring not only the apothecary's apparatus and supplies, but all the family household goods as well. "There was the same well-worn carpet, made at Lyon, the walnut dining-table, the two large armchairs and high-backed sofa . . . . The same candelabra and china shepherd boy sat on the mantel, the same colour prints of pastoral scenes hung on the walls . . . . As long as she lived, [Madame] tried to make the new life as much as possible like the old" (p. 23). When she becomes fatally ill, Madame Auclair carefully instructs Cécile in the French ways of making a home so that "a feeling about life that had come down to her through so many centuries" would be carried on. She wanted to die believing that "life would go on almost unchanged in this room" (p. 25). In earlier books Willa Cather's interest in customs was in the nature of cultural curiosity (as in *My Ántonia,* for instance), but here it centers on a feeling of security that tradition provides. Madame Auclair's last wishes are fully realized in her daughter's loyalty to French customs. Friends and clients who call at the apothecary's shop all remark on the fact that nothing has changed: " '*C'est tranquille, chez vous, comme toujours,*' " says Antoine Frichette (p. 139). Cécile fully appreciates the value of her mother's orderly way of life after her stay with the rude Harnois Family. In her kitchen she reflects: "These coppers, big and little, these brooms and clouts and brushes, were tools; and with them one made, not shoes or cabinet-work, but life itself. One made a climate within a climate; one made the days,—the complexion, the special flavour, the special happiness of each day as it passed; one made life" (p. 198).

The desire to prevent change is reflected not only in the details of the Auclairs' ménage, but in a number of other expressed preferences as well. The apothecary, in the face of considerable criticism, adheres to the medical practices of the previous century; "Change is not always progress," he argues. When Father Hector makes his winter visit to the Auclairs, he says of Cécile, " 'How I wish you could keep her from growing up, Euclide!' " (p. 148). Father Hector's wish is central to the emotional matrix of the novel, for Cécile is poised at the threshold of adolescence, but is not yet ready to accept either the emotional or physical realities of sexuality. One of her aunts sends her a blue silk dress from France—a dress for a young woman rather than a girl—but she lays it aside and puts on her jersey instead. Indeed, sexuality, the essence of existence in time, has been eliminated from this novel; the focal relationship is between father and daughter. The only passion described is Pierre Charron's frustrated love for the beautiful Montreal heiress Jeanne Le Ber, but she has immured herself in a penitential church cell for a life as a religious recluse. There are no married couples or complete families in the novel, just the Holy Family of the crèche, and even here the emphasis falls on the naive innocence of the Blessed Virgin and the gravity and age of her husband, Joseph. Willa Cather's descriptive style functions, then, not only to create scenes of rare beauty, but also, perhaps more urgently, to eliminate any reminders of time and sex from the novel.

In a letter to Dorothy Canfield Fisher, Willa Cather uses another metaphor from the plastic visual arts to describe *Shadows on the Rock,* this time comparing the process of its composition to working on a tapestry which one can pick up in leisure hours and put down without loss to the design.[27] The idea of a tapestry is suggestive not only of a static quality in *Shadows on the Rock,* but of a fundamental element of structure—an intricate design wrought through the comparison and contrast of figures and colors. As in a tapestry the characters and events of the novel are not related to each other through sequential dramatic action, but through juxtaposition in parallel and contrasting scenes. We begin to perceive this design more clearly when we recognize that many of the characters have been created as paired opposites. The most obvious contrasts can be seen in the religious figures: Laval and Saint-Vallier, Hector Saint-Cyr and Noel Chabanel, Mother Juschereau and Catherine de Saint-Augustin. Laval, the old Bishop of Quebec, has led a strictly ascetic life; we are told that his rooms in the Seminary are poor and small, that he had given his large land grants to the Seminary and his silver and linen to needy parishioners, that "he lived in naked poverty." As the leader of the Church he has been high-handed and tyrannical, but always with the good of the Church and his people his sole purpose. Saint-Vallier his successor, on the other hand, is a worldly prelate, fond of life's comforts and vanities. He has decorated his palace handsomely and takes great care with his personal appearance. His purposes, unlike those of Bishop Laval, are personal and inconsistent. One notices in his face something glittering and crafty, summed up when Frontenac says " 'Saint-Vallier belongs at the Court—where he came from' " (p. 250). Father Hector Saint-Cyr is a manly priest; the Indians respect him because he is "strong and fearless and handsome" (p. 147). But, curiously, Father Hector finds the most inspiring model for his calling in the martyred priest, Noel Chabanel, a man of "excessive sensibility" whom the Indians delight in tormenting. There is a similar contrast between Mother Juschereau, Superior of the convent, and her predecessor, Catherine de Saint-Augustin. Mother Juschereau is a hardy, sunny, practical woman of Canadian birth, who is enthusiastic about the Church "without being given to visions or ecstasies." Mother Catherine, on the other hand, had been "slight, nervous, sickly from childhood" and by age thirty-seven had "burned her life out in vigils, mortifications, visions, raptures" (p. 42). But these contrasts in character are not presented in a rigidly schematic fashion in the novel; rather, they are organic and subtly varied to form an unobtrusive and psychologically credible part of the total narrative design. Laval and Saint-Vallier are remarkable for their contrasting natures and yet both priests are arrogant and despotic, so that the contrast is not a simple one of types. Noel Chabanel's almost effeminate nature contrasts strongly with the outdoor hardihood of Father Hector, but both men are equally stoical in their dedication to the Church; both men had been professors of rhetoric and were fond of the "decencies" and "elegancies" of life.

Contrasts among other characters are not insisted on as strongly, perhaps, but they nevertheless form a significant part of the novel's color and texture. Cécile and little Jacques are playmates but they come from vastly different backgrounds. Cécile is from an honorable, tradition-minded family; her father is fastidious in caring for her and in making certain that she fulfills her mother's last wishes for her. Jacques Gaux is the child of a local prostitute who frequently leaves him to fend for himself in the streets. But both children have only one parent and both are meek and gentle. Jeanne Le Ber, the recluse, and Pierre Charron, the romantic *coureur de bois,* were also once playmates like Cécile and Jacques, but they are contrasted through the relationship that failed to be consummated between them. Euclide Auclair, a man of gentle, domestic instincts, stands in contrast to Pierre Charron, Father Hector, and Frontenac, who have all led very active, adventurous lives; but the apothecary loves these men because they have, as Cécile recognizes, "the qualities he did not have himself, but which he most admired in other men" (p. 266). A professional contrast is made between Euclide with his time-proven remedies and the king's physician, Fagon, who follows all the latest fashionable ideas of medicine—putting his faith particularly in bloodletting. There is also a contrast between Frontenac and the king, Louis XIV; both were once rivals for the favors of Madame de Montespan, later King Louis's mistress, but where Louis succeeded, Frontenac invariably failed because he was too forthright for seventeenth-century France and for the society of flatterers and schemers in the king's court.

Sharp contrasts among the characters give design to the narrative, but unlike those in *Death Comes for the Archbishop* these characterizations can never be separated from the time and place in which they are situated. The qualities which each character best exemplifies are not simply universal traits, but are rooted psychologically in the society and history of seventeenth-century France and Quebec. The portrait of Saint-Vallier, for instance, leans heavily on an understanding of the French court that has "spoiled" him. Similarly, the portrait of Blinker, the deformed and guilt-ridden wood-carrier, is intimately connected to the cruelties and atrocities of the French prison system in the seventeenth century. Religion and education are also personality forming. Laval's ascetic nature is related to the "severe" school he attended from the age of nine, and Pierre Charron insists that Jeanne Le Ber was warped by the discipline of her convent schooling: " 'If the venerable Bourgeoys had not got hold of that girl in her childhood and overstrained her with fasts and penances, she would be a happy mother today, not sleeping in a stone cell like a prisoner' " (p. 177). This psychological presentation of character is part of the novel's historical texture, for despite the plastic qualities in the book's style *Shadows on the Rock* is very much a story of time and place.

The tension between stasis and passing time is focused in Cécile's desire never to leave Quebec. Euclide Auclair brought his family to Quebec when he deemed it best to follow his protector, Count Frontenac, to the New World. Throughout the novel Auclair looks upon the relocation as only temporary, but for Cécile, who has only shadowy recollections of France, Quebec is home. The controlling emotion in the book as experienced by Cécile is a kind of homesickness, a clinging to what is known and secure in the face of threatened upheaval and departure. This emotion is dramatized poignantly in Cécile's visit with the Harnois family on the Île d'Orléans (their rough ménage contrasts sharply with the Auclairs' passion for cleanliness and order) and reaches an acute pitch at the end of Book V, "The Ships From France," when Cécile believes she must soon leave Quebec. One autumn afternoon she enters the cathedral and kneels to pray, but can only hide her face in tears. The contrast to Father Latour in his hour of need in the desert indicates the great difference between the emotion of the saint's legend and the historical novel.

Although so many elements in the style direct us to the static, unchanging character of life in Quebec, the seasonal structure dramatizes the inescapable awareness of time's passage. The novel's time span of a year suggests perhaps a cyclical rhythm to life on the Rock, but the accent falls on the dying of the year (the most moving descriptions are of Quebec in autumn), which is also the time that the ships set sail again for France. For Cécile, who dreads leaving Quebec, the passing of time brings her irrevocably closer to departure. Viewed thus, *Shadows on the Rock* is a form of pastoral, preoccupied with the arresting of time and haunted with a vision of impermanence and change.

The pervading awareness of mutability is reflected particularly in the preoccupation throughout the book with disease and death.

Auclair, as the apothecary, is sought out by the townspeople like Mother Juschereau, who has sprained her foot, and Bishop Laval, whose legs are swollen with varicose veins and ulcers. Many of the stories inserted into the larger narrative are accounts of physical accidents and deaths. Antoine Frichette tells the apothecary about his brother-in-law, Michel Proulx, who cut his leg open "from the ankle to the knee" working in the woods; the wound becomes infected (the leg goes black up to the thigh) and after many days of agonized suffering Proulx dies. Frichette himself ruptures his side working in the woods, and comes to the apothecary for a surgical truss. In the descriptions of numerous characters there is a focus on mutilations and imperfections of the body: Madame Renaude, the buttermaker, has a harelip with a bristling black moustache; Pommier, the shoemaker, has a dark red, fleshy face, seamed with unsightly purple veins; his mother has broken her hip so that one leg is permanently shorter than the other; Henry de Tonti, a *coureur de bois,* has only one arm and a hook for a hand; Blinker is cross-eyed and his face is misshapen from a decomposed jawbone. During the long winter, but especially on All Soul's Day, the thoughts of the people in Quebec go back to the churches and cemeteries in France where loved ones may be sick and dying, and many fear the news of suffering and bereavements that the summer ships may bring. The concern with illness and death occupies the foreground in the last long section of the novel, Book VI, "The Dying Count," where we look at the world for a time, not through the eyes of a child, but through the eyes of the aged Frontenac on his deathbed. The Count's death moves Auclair, predictably, to eulogize the old order which has passed away and which leaves nothing of noble promise in what is new.

Cécile's dread of returning to France is related in part to the prospect of her guardianship under the intelligent but "exacting" Aunt Clothilde, who is "much interested in the education of young girls." For Cécile the image of this aunt in her memory—a massive figure blocking the light—has almost a nightmare quality:

> The face of this aunt Cécile could never remember, though she could see her figure clearly,—standing against the light, she always seemed to be, a massive woman, short and heavy though not exactly fat,—square, rather, like a great piece of oak furniture . . . .

> Cécile could see her head, too, carried well back on a short neck, like a general or statesman sitting for his portrait; but the face was a blank, just as if the aunt were standing in a doorway with blinding sunlight behind her. [P. 12]

During the course of the novel both the apothecary and Frontenac recall childhood experiences of fear in which they are confronted by a figure that is similarly massive and faceless.

The tension in the novel between the desire to stop time and the fact of mutability is translated on a moral level as a drama of innocence and guilt. The prevailing mood of the novel is one of filial piety and innocent love, expressed in Cécile's devotion to her father and in her many solicitations for his well-being and comfort. That mood is at the same time heightened by Cécile's fear that their life together will end, that they will return to France and Aunt Clothilde. Cécile's fear is expressed in the evocation of France throughout the novel as a place of injustice and cruelty. Memories of France are riddled with grotesque tales of physical suffering and torture, like the story of old Bichet, the knife-grinder, who is tortured and hanged. The plight of this harmless old man is a paradigm of the gross injustices on which seventeenth-century French society was based:

> People died of starvation in the streets of Paris . . . . All the while the fantastic extravagances of the Court grew more outrageous. . . . The richest peers of the realm were ruining themselves on magnificent Court dresses and jewels. And, with so many new abuses, the old ones never grew less; torture and cruel punishments increased as the people became poorer and more desperate. The horrible mill at the Châtelet ground on day after day. [P. 32]

Other stories from France contain bizarre and grisly details, such as the making of poisonous bread from human bones during the siege, the great ladies of France drinking a broth made from vipers, and a little girl being torn to pieces by the carp in King Louis's pond. The latter vignette dramatizes perhaps something of Cécile's fear of returning to France and the security she feels by contrast in Quebec.

Before writing *Shadows on the Rock* Willa Cather had steeped herself in, among other books, the *Mémoires* of the duc de Saint-

Simon, who recorded first hand the events and gossip at the court of Louis XIV; his vision of man's base, self-seeking nature and essential depravity permeates *Shadows on the Rock* as a grim truth that cannot be evaded. The novel's glimpses of cruelty and abysmal depths of evil are placed alongside stories of extraordinary feats of penance and self-denial, forming on a moral level a purgatorial structure in the book.[28] The story of Blinker, who was once a torturer in the king's prison, connects the tales of cruelty in France with those of penance in Canada. After torturing a washerwoman, who is later hanged on the grounds that she has killed her son, Blinker contracts a loathsome disease which brings about the painful decomposition of his lower jawbone. In his misery the faces of those people he put to torture begin to haunt him. His spiritual agony is increased almost beyond endurance when the son of the laundress returns to the city; then Blinker "could never get the big washerwoman's screams out of his ears." He flees to Quebec, hoping to leave his memories behind, but the faces and voices of others who may have been innocent continue to rise up before him. The apothecary reasons with Blinker that his physical suffering was a manifestation of God's mercy because it taught him compassion. Blinker's face, however, recalls to Auclair the "terrible weather-worn stone faces on the churches at home,—figures of the tormented in scenes of the Last Judgment" (pp. 162–63).

The Rock of Quebec provides for Blinker a sanctuary from the evils of the larger world of men, but outside the city lies an equally cruel and terrifying world—"the never-ending, merciless forest." Blinker has such a horror of the forest and the Indians that he will not even go to the nearby woods to gather firewood. The description of that primeval world outside the city recalls something of the classical descriptions of hell:

> That was the dead, sealed world of the vegetable kingdom, an uncharted continent choked with interlocking trees, living, dead, half-dead, their roots in bogs and swamps, strangling each other in a slow agony that had lasted for centuries. The forest was suffocation, annihilation; there European man was quickly swallowed up in silence, distance, mould, black mud, and the stinging swarms of insect life that bred in it. The only avenue of escape was along the river. [Pp. 6–7]

The forest is also the place where European men are cruelly tortured by the Indians. One thinks here of part of the novel's epigraph: *"Tout y est sauvage, les fleurs aussi bien que les hommes."*

In the novel's moral and spiritual topography the world is a place of evil—of unlimited cruelty and suffering. Only the Rock of Quebec, described as a place of atonement for sin, is exempt from the universal damnation. The special holy and penitential nature of Quebec is suggested in descriptions of the landscape: the city in winter is likened to a "great white church, above the frozen river" (p. 136), and in a summer dawn the Rock stands "gleaming above the river like an altar with many candles, or like a holy city in an old legend, shriven, sinless, washed in gold" (p. 169). With its multileveled streets and terraces, Quebec is compared to a theatrical Nativity scene, suggesting both a place of innocent refuge and new beginnings; but more frequently it is defined as a place to do penance. Bishop Laval has told his parishioners that nowhere else in the world are the people so devoted to the Holy Family as in Canada, and Cécile connects this piety in her mind with the martyrdoms of the Canadian priests: "To be thrown into the Rhone or the Moselle, to be decapitated at Lyon,—what was that to the tortures the Jesuit missionaries endured at the hands of the Iroquois, in those savage, interminable forests?" (p. 102) The crimson afterglow of an autumn sunset makes Cécile think of the blood of the martyrs shed in the forest. The churches in Quebec are filled with sorrowing people on All Soul's Day: *"Priez pour les Morts, . . . Priez pour les tré-pas-sés,"* the cathedral bell seems to say. It is at Quebec that the soul of the poor sinner Marie, who lived in France, appears to Mother Catherine from purgatory and asks for prayers. Even little Jacques, seven years old, goes to the church seeming to feel the need of expiation.

Perhaps the most striking penitential figure in the novel is the beautiful heiress Jeanne Le Ber, who has immured herself in a chapel for life. Attractive, socially at ease, Jeanne chooses from an early age to deny herself all the pleasures of a comely life (she gives away to her schoolmates all the things her parents buy for her, and under her gay clothes she wears a haircloth shirt next to the skin). We do not fully understand the recluse's choice, but her sense of man's unfathomable depths of evil to be atoned for is made clear when Pierre overhears her in the chapel emit a groan at the altar " 'such as I have never heard; such despair—such resignation and despair!' " (p. 183). We think of Blinker when Pierre tells the apothecary that her face " 'was like a stone face; it had been through every sorrow.' "

The extreme and final form of penance is martyrdom and we are reminded from time to time throughout the narrative of the missionaries, Father Brébeuf, Father Lalemant, and Father Jogues, who have been tortured to death by the Indians. Father Hector's story of Noël Chabanel is the most vivid and horrific account of martyrdom in the book. Father Chabanel, who loved the decencies and refinements of a civilized life, bore one humiliation after another in the barbaric forests of Canada. Though a linguist, he could not learn the Huron tongue; moreover, he was repelled by the filth and indecency of the savages—the smoke and smells of the wigwam, the boiled dog flesh they gave him to eat. In turn, the Indians were contemptuous of him and on one occasion his converts fed him a portion of human flesh, then made sport of his retchings. Father Chabanel endured his sufferings because of a terrible conviction of guilt (manifest to him in a sense of God's withdrawal) and the need to do expiation. To curb his desire to return to France he made a vow of perpetual stability in the Huron missions. His death in an Iroquois raid was a release and absolution. In *Death Comes for the Archbishop* there are no martyrdoms and, save for the ludicrous crucifixion and scourging of Trinidad, no physical torture described; the saint's legend is pervaded throughout by the serenity of a timeless legend being retold with perfect esthetic harmony. But *Shadows on the Rock,* a historical novel, returns us to the world of time which for all Christians is a sinful world. With its vision of guilt, suffering, and penance, *Shadows on the Rock* is Willa Cather's *Purgatorio.*

Each of the three novels comprising Willa Cather's "mortal comedy" ends with the death of a central character: Myra Henshawe, the Archbishop, and Count Frontenac. The significance of religious values in these books becomes clearer if we consider for a moment the short story "Double Birthday" (1929),[29] written in the same period and preoccupied with many of the same themes, but set outside the framework of Catholic faith. Literally, the story is about a woman, Margaret Parmenter, who renews her friendship with two elderly bachelors, Albert Engelhardt and his uncle,

Doctor Engelhardt, on the occasion of their joint birthday. The friendship had waned over the years as the Engelhardt fortune declined, but Margaret finds to her delight that although the Engelhardts are no longer wealthy or influential, they have preserved something very agreeable from the past in their lives, and at the end she looks forward to enjoying their company once again. With its nostalgia for the past and optimistic program for the future, the story has a comfortable, even sentimental, surface which distracts the reader from the bleak vision of life underneath.

Two important motifs have been worked into the basic narrative framework: the uncle's memory of a young singer he once discovered, and the nephew's quest to keep life congenial amidst continually diminishing circumstances. The uncle's story—the great sadness in his life—reflects Willa Cather's preoccupation with disease and death at this time in her life. Doctor Engelhardt, who was a throat specialist, discovered a robust German girl, Marguerite Thiesinger, with a splendid voice. After first declining the Doctor's assistance and a brief, apparently abortive marriage, Marguerite finally allowed him to sponsor her for what promised to be a brilliant singing career. The Doctor thought of her as "a big peony just burst into bloom and full of sunshine"; but her appearance of glowing good health only made more terrible the discovery that she was dying of cancer. On the eve of a great career she was taken to a hospital for incurables, where the Doctor visited her every week for a year. On the day of her death he sat alone in the park and questioned in anguish the nature of existence:

> He dropped his face in his hands and cried like a woman. Youth, art, love, dreams, true-heartedness—why must they go out of the summer world into darkness? *Warum, warum?* He thought he had already suffered all that man could, but never had it come down on him like this.

Youth and vigor laid waste in the form of a beautiful and gifted girl dramatizes in a heightened fashion the author's preoccupation with death in this period.[30] Death here is not the completion of life, the final transcendence of earthly things that the Archbishop experienced at the end of a long, useful life, nor is it a purgatorial transition to a fuller life of the spirit; rather it is painful, ugly, and above all meaningless—a tragic measure of human existence rather than its romantic apotheosis. The Doctor lives the rest of his life with thoughts of what might have been.

His nephew, on the other hand, has allowed himself only happy memories from the past. To evade all the unpleasant aspects of growing old (the mutability theme connects the two strands of the story), he spends his leisure time among his old books and pictures and furnishings, for they are imbued with his youth: "At his piano, under his Degas drawing in black and red—three ballet girls at the bar—or seated at his beautiful inlaid writing table, he was still the elegant young man who sat there long ago." Margaret Parmenter says to Albert, " You've got a period shut up in here, the last ten years of one century, and the first ten of another. Sitting here, I don't believe in aeroplanes, or jazz, or Cubists.' " Yet in Albert's evasions and in the prospect of his future ("If one stopped to think of that, there was a shiver waiting round the corner") there is something disturbing and pathetic. One is perhaps reminded here of the author and her search for an unchanging world in the traditional forms of life in Quebec. Pleasure is promised for the three characters of the story in the renewal of their friendship, but that friendship of course will be fed on memories from the past. It is a "double birthday" in every sense, reviving both joy and sorrow, achievement and defeat. The accent, however, falls on the latter, for the vignette at the end, of the pianist who has renounced life, brings us a glimpse again of the old Doctor's struggle at the death of his singer.

But the three novels of Willa Cather's "mortal comedy" do not end with a tragic, meaningless view of human existence. Although Myra Henshawe possibly is damned at the end of her life, the fact of a personal and universal hell implies its contrary. Death for the Archbishop is a subliminal experience of fulfillment and release. For Frontenac it takes the form of a last, long, remorseful reflection on life's deceptions and failures; but the purgatorial nature of existence in this novel points to man's final redemption.

The tension in *Shadows on the Rock* between man's innocence and guilt is presented in the epilogue again in terms of stasis and temporal change. At first, time would seem to prevail: not only have fifteen years passed, but the final scene in the novel is of the once proud and handsome Bishop Saint-Vallier returning to Quebec a heavy, lame old man. Throughout the book it was Saint-

Vallier who had worldly ambitions—he built an opulent episcopal palace and brought many pieces of furniture and tapestries from France to furnish it—and accordingly his fortunes have suffered the effects of time. But unlike Saint-Vallier, who has been away for thirteen years, the apothecary has "scarcely changed at all"; indeed we are assured that "even his shop was still the same" (p. 272). We learn too in this final section that Cécile has married her aging hero, Pierre Charron, and now has four sons—" 'the Canadians of the future.' " This contrasts with the news from Versailles and the deaths of the old king's successors. Auclair now deems himself "indeed fortunate to spend his old age [in Quebec] where nothing changed; to watch his grandsons grow up in a country where the death of the King, the probable evils of a long regency, would never touch them" (p. 280). But the real force of the Epilogue derives from the picture of the broken Bishop placed alongside the unchanged apothecary; this final juxtaposition defines not only the book's central conflicts (stasis and mutability, innocence and guilt), but their realization through the style.

Notes

1. *My Mortal Enemy* (Vintage Books: New York: Random House, 1961). All references are to this text.

2. There is a special erotic quality to the characterization of handsome but weak men in Willa Cather's fiction. Willa Cather herself apparently was attracted to men of a gentle, dreamy nature, such as her friends William Ducker in Red Cloud and the composer Ethelbert Nevin in Pittsburgh; and at the age of fifteen she recorded that "lamb-like meekness" was the quality she most desired in a matrimonial mate (Bennett, *The World of Willa Cather,* p. 113). In addition to Oswald Henshawe and Ewan Gray, a list of the weak man as romantic figure would include Valentine Ramsay in "Uncle Valentine" and Henry Colbert in *Sapphira and the Slave Girl.* The latter interestingly merges into a more fatherly character. In heightened erotic form this figure appears as the young man being subjected to physical pain or confinement, like the slave to the Aztec queen in "Coming, Aphrodite!," El Greco's beautiful male saint in meditation (described in the prologue to *Death Comes for the Archbishop*), and Casper Flight, tied to a tree and being whipped, in *Sapphira and the Slave Girl.*

3. As in *The Professor's House,* jewels assume an important symbolic value as the story moves forward; they adorn a beautiful woman, but they also signify the corrupting power of wealth and possessions. When Nellie

first meets Myra her intimidation by the older woman centers around the string of carved amethysts Myra is wearing. Later Myra warns Ewan that opals bring bad luck, which is reckless when love already is so dangerous. The truth of this observation is borne out when Oswald is given topaz cufflinks by one of his admirers; the gift brings on Myra's jealousy, the passion of possession. At the end of the story Nellie is given the string of amethysts, which reminds her thereafter of Myra's lifelong struggle to dominate and possess.

4. For a fuller treatment of the significance of *Norma* in *My Mortal Enemy* see Giannone, *Music in Willa Cather's Fiction,* pp. 169–83.

5. *Death Comes for the Archbishop* (New York: Alfred A. Knopf, 1959). All references are to this text.

6. "On *Death Comes for the Archbishop*" in *Willa Cather on Writing,* pp. 3–13. The letter was written in November 1927.

7. "Narrative" was the term Willa Cather preferred when forced to classify the book. Ibid., pp. 12–13.

8. Ibid., pp. 9–10.

9. See, for example, Clinton Keeler, "Narrative Without Accent: Willa Cather and Puvis de Chavannes," *American Quarterly* 17 (Spring 1965): 119–26, and Curtis Whittington, Jr., "The Stream and the Broken Pottery: The Form of Willa Cather's *Death Comes for the Archbishop,*" *McNeese Review* 16 (Spring 1965): 16–24.

10. Lewis, *Willa Cather Living,* p. 147.

11. Erich Auerbach, *Mimesis,* trans. by Willard Trask (New York: Doubleday and Co., 1957). Most studies of the saints' legends have been done from sociological and historical viewpoints. The most comprehensive treatments of the saints' lives from a literary perspective is Theodor Wolpers, *Die Englische Heiligenlegende des Mittelalters* (Tubingen: Max Neimeyer Verlag, 1964), which develops many of Auerbach's views.

12. The correspondence between the novel's form and the pattern of the Angelus was first suggested by Robert L. Gale in "Cather's *Death Comes for the Archbishop,*" *Explicator* 21 (May 1963): item 75, although it does not account for the prologue.

13. Père Delehaye in *The Legends of the Saints,* trans. by V. M. Crawford (Notre Dame: University of Notre Dame Press, 1961), p. 97, in differentiating between the two main forms which the saint's legend takes, points out that the "narrative [of a saint who is not a martyr] is necessarily less dramatic and less interesting, but it more easily admits of developments."

14. The importance of the concrete image to the legend form is emphasized by T. Wolpers, who finds in the later medieval saints' legends a characteristic use of the *Andachtsbild,*" a type of imagery which attempts to make spiritual truths concrete, i.e., to emphasize that earthly forms are the manifestations of God's works. Wolpers, *Die Englische Heiligenlegende,* pp. 29–32.

15. D. H. Stewart, "Cather's Mortal Comedy," *Queen's Quarterly* 73 (Summer 1966): 244–59.

16. In *Death Comes for the Archbishop* allegory is a stylistic device rather than a structural principle, since Willa Cather obviously is not attempting to write a continuous allegory. Medieval saints' legends occasionally contain passages which are suggestive in the same way; for instance, the saint and the tyrant are frequently depicted as types of Christ and the Devil. For the medieval writers, allegory could apparently mean either a stylistic effect or a structural principle; as the former it is classified by the rhetoricians among the ornaments of style, along with other types of figurative language. See *Poetria Nova of Geoffrey of Vinsauf,* trans. by Margaret F. Nims (Toronto: Pontifical Institute of Medieval Studies, 1967), p. 49. Bernice Slote describes this effect in Willa Cather's writing as "broken allegory . . . a style of mingled allusiveness and symbolism over a groundwork of fixed, related metaphors" (*KA,* p. 35).

17. Willa Cather's sense of mortality connected with the cave is related to Chaucer's old man in *The Pardoner's Tale* who ceaselessly begs "mother earth" to take him in but is refused, and to Spenser's evil figure, Maleger, who revives at earth's touch.

18. D. W. Robertson, Jr., *Chaucer's London* (New York: Wiley, 1968), pp. 5–6.

19. See *Poetria Nova of Geoffrey of Vinsauf,* p. 65, where character description is listed under ornaments of style and divided into *effectio* (external appearance) and *notatio* (character delineation), and the example chosen is "man, the second Adam," seen as the image of sloth.

20. It is doubtful, however, if Willa Cather worked in the rigidly schematized manner which D. H. Stewart suggests is comparable to Dante's organization of the *Divine Comedy.* Miss Cather's style is always more allusive and organic, and the lesser figures in the book are composites of various sins rather than strictly representatives of one aspect. In recalling the composition of *Death Comes for the Archbishop,* Miss Cather expressed the wish that her book be considered part of the great tradition of English literature formed by Chaucer, Shakespeare, and the King James Bible (Willa Cather to E. K. Brown, October 7, 1946, Yale University Library). She goes on to justify Chaucer's place in this tradition by praising his unequaled humor and humanity; and her singling out of the medieval poet may indicate a possible Chaucerian influence on *Death Comes for the Archbishop.* See M. A. Stouck, "Chaucer's Pilgrims and Cather's Priests," *Colby Library Quarterly* 9 (June 1972): 531–37.

21. Aside: the blind superstition and childlike faith of Padre Jesus de Baca, with his treasured wooden parrot, may owe something to Flaubert's Félicité in "Un Coeur Simple."

22. *Shadows on the Rock* (New York: Alfred A. Knopf, 1961). All references are cited from this text.

23. "On *Shadows on the Rock*" in *Willa Cather on Writing,* pp. 14–15.

24. The historical perspective is underscored by the author's footnotes pointing to observable changes in twentieth-century Quebec.

25. Lewis, *Willa Cather Living,* pp. 156–57.

26. In a letter dated May 1, 1931, to Dorothy Canfield Fisher the

author refers to Quebec as her refuge in these difficult years–the only thing that does not change (Guy Bailey Memorial Library, University of Vermont).

27. Willa Cather to Dorothy Canfield Fisher, n.d. (Guy Bailey Memorial Library, University of Vermont).

28. Maxwell Geismar says that Cather has excluded any deep sense of evil from her two Catholic novels (*The Last of the Provincials* [Boston: Houghton Mifflin, 1947], p. 200), but surely the very opposite is true of *Shadows on the Rock.*

29. *UVS,* pp. 39–63.

30. Throughout her career Willa Cather seems to have shared Edgar Allan Poe's feeling that "the death of a beautiful woman is, unquestionably, the most poetical topic in the world" (Poe's "The Philosophy of Composition"). Katharine Gaylord, Alexandra Ebbling ("On the Gulls' Road"), Nelly Deane, Marie Shabata, Cressida Garnet, Marguerite Thiesinger, Lucy Gayheart, and Lesley Ferguesson, to name only major figures, all are women who die young. Interestingly, Uncle Albert in "Double Birthday" refers to Marguerite as his "lost Lenore."

PART III

Themes

CHAPTER FIVE

Willa Cather's Portrait of the Artist

Newspaper Articles and Early Stories

The themes in Willa Cather's fiction are many and varied; during a writing career which spanned more than fifty years she found materials for her art in subjects as diverse as the American pioneer experience, World War I, contemporary urban life, and the history of Catholic civilization. One theme, however, which persists throughout Willa Cather's fiction and which helps to bind the whole canon together into a continuous drama is the relationship between art and experience, or, to put it more directly, the dilemma of the artist caught between his commitment to art on one hand and to life on the other.

That art and life should be seen as contraries does not in theory hold. Art and life cannot after all be separated: from life experiences come the materials of art, and art in turn gives to human life a sense of purpose and design. But in practice the artist's pursuit of excellence in his work can place severe limitations on his personal life. Art is an achievement, and like excellence or success in any endeavor requires great concentration and dedication. The goal of art, moreover, is to transcend the human condition—to create something permanent, immutable, outside the world of time and chance—and the commitment required for artistic creativity often excludes the artist from a full participation in and enjoyment of life. Paradoxically, while the values of art are intelligence, order, insight, and sympathy, they are frequently achieved only if the artist denies them in his relations with others. Thus a great artist, exalted in the practice of his art, may well be selfish, aloof, and emotionally empty as a man. Art serves to enhance and enrich human life, but it requires that the artist sacrifice much in his own personal life to achieve its highest ends. Art and life become contraries through the demands they place on the artist.

We know from her early critical articles that even at the outset of her career Willa Cather was aware of the deep split between the claims of art and life. The newspaper articles were written when she was still in her early twenties, but she already seems to have recognized the difficulty for the artist of reconciling these two claims. In countless columns and reviews, whether her subject was painting, music, the stage, or literature, Willa Cather touched in some way on the nature of art and the artist. By temperament she was a romantic and her instinct accordingly was to view art as the highest form of human endeavor. Frequently she raised art to the level of the divine, an experience akin to religion through which man comes closer to God. In describing the great pleasure afforded by a certain actor, she says the enjoyment of his talent is "in watching a man give back what God put into him."[1] She shares in the public denouncement of Oscar Wilde as a criminal, but with the important reservation that the artist in him cannot be killed because "it is of God" and a "heavenly birthright . . . which makes [him] akin to the angels and to see the visions of paradise."[2] In one column she says it is the writer's task to translate God to man;[3] in another she compares the artist's calling to a religious commitment: "In the kingdom of art there is no God, but one God, and his service is so exacting that there are few men born of woman who are strong enough to take the vows."[4] Willa Cather also described the artist in heroic terms and repeatedly refers in her articles to the glory and victory attendant on a great work of art: "O yes, art is a great thing when it is great, it has the elements of power and conquest in it, it's like the Roman army, it subdues a world, a world that is proud to be conquered when it is by Rome."[5] These are the metaphors that Willa Cather would later use in *The Song of the Lark* to describe the ascendance and triumph of her artist heroine.

But Willa Cather recognized that there was a dark side to the artist's life as well. In a column on the actress Eleanora Duse she says that while the artist is one of God's "elect," loneliness "besets all mortals who are shut up alone with God." Referring to a letter published by Duse, Miss Cather writes: "There is something wonderfully beautiful in that letter, it is so full of the loveliness and lovelessness and desolation of art. Of the isolation . . . of all creative genius. . . . Solitude, like some evil destiny, darkens its cradle, and sits watching even upon its grave."[6] Frequently during her career Willa Cather felt that loneliness was the inevitable fate of the artist and that great art could be achieved only if the artist sacrificed all other forms of personal satisfaction to that one end. In writing about the forthcoming marriage of the opera singer Helena von Doenhoff she insists that marriage and artistic greatness are incompatible; she implies a comparison between Doenhoff as a pilgrim of the arts and Bunyan's Mr. Doubting, who turns back and is seen no more. In this same rigorous vein Cather argues that the artist who cares only for success eventually will find it "empty and unsatisfying"; and that in art "complete self-abnegation is the one step . . . between promise and fulfillment."[7] But on another occasion, describing the homesickness and concern that Réjane, the French comedienne, felt for her husband and children when she was on tour, Willa Cather writes that possibly Madame Réjane "knows that there are other things on earth than art, things higher and more sacred."[8] Cather also understood that artistic pursuits were sometimes "personal, intense, selfish"; and that some successful artists sustain wounds that glory cannot heal.[9]

From the beginning, then, we find Willa Cather very aware of the complexities surrounding the artist's commitment to his craft. An artist may be a conqueror and godlike in his ability to create higher forms of reality or truth, but he does so by denying himself companionship and community with his fellow man. The artist's dilemma—the necessity of choosing between the antithetical values of art and life—appears again and again in Willa Cather's writing; it is the subject of one of her earliest short stories, "Nanette, An Aside," and I see it as a submerged but powerful countertheme in the last four books. In earlier stories such as "The Marriage of Phaedra," " 'A Death in the Desert,' " or "The Namesake," and in *The Song of the Lark,* although the dialectic may be broken temporarily by a strongly negative view of art, there is a deep underlying conviction that the artist's commitment to his work is ultimately sacred and positive. But in the last books

(*Obscure Destinies, Lucy Gayheart, Sapphira and the Slave Girl, The Old Beauty and Others*) that instinctive faith, in my view, is gone and what gives those books their peculiar haunting power, in addition to much else, is their mood of doubt and uncertainty and the picture they suggest of Willa Cather in the last decade and a half of her life questioning the validity of both a life's choice and a lifetime's achievements. Willa Cather's vision of life perceived a duality in all human experience, and in much of her fiction she celebrates without contesting the double nature of both man and his world; but as an artist she also strove to find a way of reconciling the opposing claims of art and life which would allow her to be both an artist and a woman. The conflict of art versus life is perhaps the most profound subject for any work of art; not only does it insist on an examination of those values to which art and life lay separate claim, but it touches at the very quick of the artist's desire and need to create. This is the theme, whether it be explicit or concealed, which gives greatness to the art of Mann, Joyce, and Proust, and, as I hope to show, to the art of Willa Cather.

There is an artist figure—the violinist Peter Sadelack—in Willa Cather's first published story, but her first study of a professional artist appears in "Nanette: An Aside" (1897).[10] Here we find an opera singer, Traduttori, who has achieved world renown as an artist, but whose personal life is almost a void. We learn in a brief aside that she has a crippled daughter hidden away somewhere in a convent in Italy and that her husband is a gambler and an alcoholic. Traduttori sadly explains to her maid, Nanette, that when she chose her career as a singer " 'everything dear in life—every love, every human hope' " lay between her and greatness and that she " 'had to bury what lay between.' " Nanette is the only person who has remained faithful to her and has been her confidante. The tragic side of Traduttori's life is dramatically revealed when Nanette decides to leave the singer to marry an Italian waiter. Traduttori wishes Nanette a lasting happiness, but after the maid is gone she puts her head down and weeps bitterly for her own loneliness and misery. The irony of the artist's fate is underscored in the last sentence where Willa Cather writes: "And yet upon her brow shone the coronet that the nations had given her when they called her queen." The author reworked the story in "A Singer's Romance" (1900)[11] to emphasize again the cruel ironies the artist suffers in life. In this story the opera singer believes almost till the end that she, not her maid, is the one being courted by the Italian. When left alone at the end she seems to be even more wretched, for not only is she unloved, but aging as well, although the unsentimental last line of the story ("Then she ordered her breakfast—and a quart of champagne") suggests she has her consolations and that Willa Cather had learned a thing or two about divas in the three years between the stories.

In two other early stories art is connected with failure in one's personal life. Although the characters in these stories cannot, strictly speaking, be classified as artists, their lives are shaped by their concern with the arts. In "The Prodigies" (1897)[12] an ambitious mother dedicates her two children, a boy and a girl, to a life of singing classical music in concert; but the vigorous physical discipline requisite eventually takes its toll on the girl and the final implication is that it will soon kill her. Although on its simplest level the story is about the cruel treatment of children, the fact that the mother's inordinate ambition seizes on music for its realization suggests something sinister as well as exalted about the arts. In "The Professor's Commencement" (1902)[13] an old teacher being honored on his retirement looks back with regret on a life devoted to esthetics in an industrial town. The old teacher is not an artist, but a sense of failure in his life derives from a feeling that he has missed his true vocation—that dedication to art in uncongenial surroundings was an evasion of his real test as a man of the arts. In all these stories personal failure is in some way related to art.

The Troll Garden and Stories about Artists

Willa Cather's first published book of fiction was *The Troll Garden* (1905).[14] The seven stories in this volume are closely related to each other, as they are all concerned with art and the artistic temperament, a subject which from the beginning was as important to the author as her pioneer childhood in the West. Critics have suggested that in theme and arrangement the stories form an intricate design. E. K. Brown sees them as arranged in a pattern of contrasting stories.[15] Bernice Slote likens them to seven panels, a variation of the septenary, from which several combinations of figures are possible through association and contrast.[16] Whatever their internal relationships, each story comes back to a fundamental problem which teased the author's imagination for years—the relationship of art to life. I shall consider the stories individually, because each story, like the facet of a prism, exhibits the nature of art in a different light. The full complexity of the book's theme, however, emerges through the qualifications that one story imposes on the others.

In the first story, "Flavia and Her Artists," the practitioners and patrons of the arts are seen mostly in a negative light. The story focuses on Flavia Hamilton, who courts the favor and company of artists with a kind of hysterical desperation even though she has a congenial husband and three well-mannered children. Flavia and her somewhat decadent ménage are seen through the eyes of Imogen Willard, a serious student, who has been a friend of Flavia and her husband in the past. During Imogen's visit, M. Roux, a French writer who has recently been staying at the Hamilton home, cuts Flavia up in an article subtitled "The Advanced American Woman, . . . Aggressive, Superficial and Insincere." Flavia's husband, Arthur, destroys the article before his wife can read it, but at dinner, in front of the guests, he condemns M. Roux and his kind as a reprobate class of men who, while indispensable to civilization, are unreclaimed by it.[17] Flavia's guests are insulted and the next morning most of them depart, leaving Flavia devastated socially and furious with her husband. Arthur Hamilton's view of the artist as reprobate appears to be endorsed by the author. Ironically, Flavia accuses her husband of bad taste; but Flavia's passion for the arts is only a social ambition, while her husband's insight and self-sacrificing sympathy are genuine. In this story Willa Cather makes it clear that an artist to her is not by definition a sacred personage. Indeed, in cliques and fashionable gatherings artists are often insufferably vain and pretentious. Honesty and humility are more valuable qualities than good taste, and here they belong not to the artist but to a quiet man of business.[18]

But perhaps Willa Cather intended the word "artists" in the title of the story to be read ironically, for in the second story of the collection, "The Sculptor's Funeral,"[19] the artist is the very opposite kind of man from Flavia's friends. Instead of the freeloading, fashionable man of the hour, the sculptor is a lonely, suffering figure who engages our complete sympathy. The distinction between the genuine artist and the celebrity is an important one in Willa Cather's fiction because only the true artist is capable of possessing nobility and insight. Tension in "The Sculptor's Funeral" exists between the world of the artist and that of the ordinary man which is seen as both limited and corrupt. As the townspeople rehearse in their crude and callous fashion the details of Harvey Merrick's life, we feel grateful, as does Jim Laird, the drunken lawyer and Merrick's old friend, that for a time he escaped the bleak realities of his home town, with its ugly, tasteless physical surroundings, its greedy, conformity-minded inhabitants, and its painful memories of home life. There is no question in this story but that the escape provided by art is valid and meaningful; only art has the power of infusing the sordid experiences of life with something more noble and lasting. Although "Flavia and Her Artists" and "The Sculptor's Funeral" appear to be antithetical in their view of art, they are fundamentally similar in lauding that which is genuine. Flavia's artists appear shams beside Harvey Merrick; indeed, they are as cruel and thoughtless as the townspeople in Sand City. The genuine response resists the pressures of fashionable conformity, whether it be a clique of esthetes or a group of small-town businessmen and farmers. What also is interesting in these two stories is that the artist is not held up as the sole repository of human values. Arthur Hamilton and Jim Laird, neither of whom is an artist, have the keenest insights into their respective situations.

In "The Garden Lodge" Willa Cather explores an altogether different aspect of art. In the person of Caroline Noble the respective claims of the practical and the imaginative life are at war with each other. Caroline's parents were indigent artists, and the impoverished, unhappy circumstances of her childhood were the result of her parents' excessive and impractical devotion to music. Caroline's brother, similarly enchanted by the muses, "shot himself in a frenzy" at the age of twenty-six. Reacting to these experiences, Caroline has repressed all her imaginative feelings and becomes a practical, successful woman. The crisis in her soul comes after a great opera singer, d'Esquerré, has stayed at her garden lodge; he awakens in her something vital which she has suppressed all her life, but which now demands expression. His singing gives her a glimpse of that spiritual world of the imagination whose existence transforms and gives meaning to what is mundane and assured. But Caroline's unrest is short-lived; when her husband suggests replacing the romantic garden lodge with a new summerhouse she gives her consent with little hesitation. The artists in this story are particularly interesting for their contrasting natures. Caroline's father and brother, who have failed to achieve worldly success through their art, are vindictive and self-pitying, and yet for the father, at least, the magic of great music continues to give purpose to his life. D'Esquerré, on the other hand, who has known great success, is an empty shell and only when he feels the fervent appeal of his audience can he experience again desire for the ineffable something beyond. Willa Cather was haunted from the beginning, as we have seen in her newspaper reviews and in stories like "Nanette: An Aside," by the fact that artistic success does not guarantee happiness in the artist's personal life.

In " 'A Death in the Desert' " the story focuses directly on the artist's suffering. The central figure is Katharine Gaylord, a well-known singer who has become consumptive and has returned to her home in Wyoming to die. She recognizes her tragedy to be not simply her illness and approaching death, but also her unrequited love for the composer Adriance Hilgarde. Through her eyes we glimpse something of this man: on the surface Adriance is successful, dynamic, and flamboyantly happy, but when Katharine hears his most recent compositions she recognizes a tragic emotion which lies underneath. His tragic vision is that of human mortality, the fact that all of life's efforts must in the end be swallowed up by death. As she listens to his music, Katharine hears " 'the feet of the runners' " as they pass her by, an image of life hurrying on without her; also, an image of life as a dance of death. Katharine Gaylord is not presented to us directly but through the eyes of Adriance's brother, Everett; he loved her for many years, but she always overlooked him because of her passion for his brother. The feeling in this story is not so much that artists are cruel and indifferent to others around them (as Flavia's artists are), but that almost by definition the great ones are caught up in a quest which places them outside the daily round and the framework of values by which ordinary men are judged. Katharine on her death bed sees her whole life in retrospect as a self-destructive quest for punishment, pursued most dramatically in her fruitless love for Adriance. The desert of the title suggests a place of suffering and of tragic recognition.

In "The Marriage of Phaedra" Hugh Treffinger, the painter, is another tragic artist figure. The outline of his life is gradually reconstructed as his biographer, McMaster, gathers information for a book about him. From Treffinger's sister-in-law and from his widow, McMaster learns that the artist's marriage was not happy; he and his wife contended with each other for mastery (they are both described as strong and aggressive) and their marriage stalemated in hate. It is through the servant, James, that McMaster comes closest to the man himself, and it is James who confides that for Treffinger painting the Phaedra was a destructive passion: " 'It was the *Marriage* as killed 'im . . . and for the matter 'o that, it did like to 'av been the death of all of us.' " The *Marriage,* though unfinished, is considered Treffinger's highest achievement. It is a painting filled with guilt and the promise of suffering; the fatal attraction between Phaedra and her step-son is not pagan but Christian and medieval in conception; Phaedra is not a daughter of Minos but of the early church, "doomed to scourgings, and the wrangling of soul with flesh." McMaster can learn no more about the painting or the artist's suffering translated on to the canvas. There is in the story something incoherent, because the guilt of Phaedra in the *Marriage* painting does not seem to relate to the failure in the artist's own marriage. Perhaps Willa Cather's chief concern was to dramatize the loneliness and misery of the artist's existence; certainly McMaster finds no one in Treffinger's personal life who cared for either him or his work except the loyal servant, James; and there lies another irony, for James is too uneducated to understand his master. The artist's life, in fact, inspired only hate; the story ends with Treffinger's widow vengefully selling the unfinished painting to a dealer from Australia in order to finance her new marriage.

"A Wagner Matinee," like "The Sculptor's Funeral," holds a special place in the corpus of Willa Cather's short fiction because it brings together the world of the arts and the world of the pioneer. The story itself is a simple one: the narrator's aunt returns briefly to Boston after a lifetime of pioneering in the West, and at an afternoon concert she catches a glimpse of everything that she has missed in her life on the frontier. Music here is a disturbing force; it brings not just pleasure but regret and longing for a world unrealized. In the careful juxtaposing of salient detail such as the elegant concert hall with the tall, unpainted house on the empty plains, the aunt's tragedy is poignantly delineated. Because of the point of view from which it is told, the story acquires a further, complex dimension: his aunt's presence evokes in the narrator a disquieting nostalgia. The dreariest details of life on the Nebraska farm—the dishcloths drying before the kitchen door, his aunt's concern for "a certain weakling calf"—bring to his mind the sacrifices she made for him when he was a boy; he owes to her "most of the good that ever came [his] way" in his boyhood, and it is a debt that never can be repaid.

In "Paul's Case" art is again a disquieting element. For the strange youth in this story, music and the theatre provide an escape from everything that is stupid and ugly in his existence. Art becomes a substitute reality which eventually claims him, body and soul. Paul is a classic study or analysis, as the title suggests, of an estranged youth—probably homosexual, certainly neurotic. Before the portrait was drawn the "type" was carefully observed: the hysterical brilliance of the eyes, the theatrical gestures, the twitching lips, and the physical aversion to human touch. The imaginative poverty of Paul's middle-class life with his father and sister, a life consisting of Sunday School picnics, petty economies, and cooking smells, is made tolerable by his work as an usher at Carnegie Hall. But when he is expelled from high school for insolence and forced to quit his job at the concert hall, he ends his compromise with the world, steals some money from his employer, and runs off to New York for a few enchanted days of luxury in a hotel. When his whereabouts is finally discovered, rather than return to his father's house he throws himself in front of a train. The seductive nature of art and the artistic temperament as touched by madness are set forth here in the most direct manner of all the tales in the volume.

The Troll Garden continues to be a vital collection of stories exactly because Willa Cather refused to mold them into a single pattern. Although the stories are built around such essential juxtapositions in her writing as art and experience, East and West, the artist and the "common" man, these dichotomies are viewed from a different perspective in each story, so that the collection as a whole becomes a complex network of interrelated themes. Design in this book touches on many of the author's major themes—the quest for what is genuine and lasting, the moral opacity of material possessions, the artist as tragic figure—and thereby in its own way comprehends the whole corpus of her work.

The artist is the subject of three more stories that Willa Cather published shortly after *The Troll Garden.* In "The Namesake" (1907)[20] art is viewed affirmatively as a means of expressing identity with one's family and one's country. A sculptor, Lyon Hartwell, who lives in Paris, is the son of an expatriate American whose family regarded him as a renegade because he did not return to fight in the Civil War. The sculptor son eventually is obliged to return to America to look after the last living member of the family —a mentally infirm maiden aunt. Hartwell feels no connection with the ancestral home: " 'The somber rooms never spoke to me, the old furniture never seemed tinctured with race.' " The description of the overgrown garden, with its rank, unhealthy vegetation, emphasizes the deadness of the present for Hartwell. However, the portrait of a boy uncle who was killed in the Civil War creates a link with the past for Hartwell, and when he finds a trunk full of the dead soldier's personal effects, he feels he has established a mystical but vital connection with the boy which gives him American roots and an identity for the first time. He compares the experience of that night to the emotion an artist feels when he has achieved something like truth in his work: " 'the feeling of union with some great force, of purpose and security, of being glad that we have lived.' " Although he returns to Paris, Hartwell develops into a sculptor whose work typifies the American experience. He has done figures from the different phases of American history (the *Scout,* the *Pioneer,* the *Gold Seekers*), and when he tells his story he is ready to cast in bronze *The Color Sergeant,* a figure from the Civil War like his boy uncle. Through his art Hartwell gives expression to that transcendental experience in which he discovered not only his own family identity, but his identity as an American. The narrator at the beginning of the story says: "Lyon Hartwell, though born abroad, was simply, as everyone knew, 'from America.' He seemed, almost more than any other one living man, to mean all of it—from ocean to ocean."

In "The Profile" (1907),[21] a psychological study of a man who marries a disfigured woman, art serves as a means of escape from reality. The central character, Aaron Dunlap, is a painter whose sensitivity to women has made him especially skilled at doing women's portraits. Dunlap's sympathy for women is related to his rough childhood in the mountians of West Virginia, where he saw his mother and other women being brutalized by men. By going to Paris, where he becomes a painter, he escapes the ugly realities of his home, although we are told that the French city would make him "the expiator of his mountain race." However, he is not reminded again of life's cruelties until he is commissioned to paint the daughter of a wealthy California landowner. The girl bears a hideous scar on one side of her face, and when he leaves her house after the first sitting, Dunlap is filled with a sense of tragedy and old memories: "All that he had tried to forget seemed no longer dim and faraway—like the cruelties of vanished civilizations—but present and painfully near. He thought of his mother and grandmother, of his little sister, who had died from the bite of a copperhead snake, as if they were creatures yet unreleased from suffering." Dunlap falls in love with and marries Virginia (her name refers him to the past also), because he feels that somehow love might heal her. But Virginia proudly refuses to acknowledge her disfigurement; the portrait becomes an emblem of the lie that she lives, for it shows her only in profile. When Dunlap eventually refers to the scar, she leaves him. In the meantime he has fallen in love with his wife's young cousin and after her face is also scarred in a fire (probably caused by the jealous wife) he marries her. Although we are told by an old painter at the beginning that physical mutilations " 'have no proper place in art,' " the point is perhaps being contested implicitly throughout the story. Virginia's "profile" adheres to the conventional idea of beauty in art, but it also feeds the woman's vanity and self-delusion. Dunlap's desire to release womankind from physical suffering, however, is a mission which may be too great for the offices of art.

These stories have a Jamesian feeling for social nuance and for the formal appropriation of parallel, coincidence, and narrative detachment. But the material in both stories is Willa Cather's: "The Namesake" is similar to an early poem by the same title, and "The Profile" turns on the motif of mutilation and disfigurement which recurs in Cather's fiction, particularly in *Shadows on the Rock*. However, "The Willing Muse" (1907),[22] another tale about artists, is contrived and imitative of James. In this story an impractical and unworldly novelist marries a woman who is also a writer, but her ambition far exceeds his and he is eventually reduced to being her secretary and publicity agent. In the end he saves himself by leaving her and disappearing altogether. Willa Cather often viewed marriage as a destructive relationship, especially for the artist, as we have seen in "The Marriage of Phaedra," but the vampirelike quality of the woman in this story, whose strength increases as her husband weakens, makes her much closer to May Server in James's *The Sacred Fount* than any of the wives in Cather's fictional marriages.

The Song of the Lark: A *Künstlerroman*

Willa Cather's most positive view of art and the artist's life is found in *The Song of the Lark* (1915).[23] The images of the artist as a divine figure and a heroic conqueror which occur in her journalistic writings are given their full dramatic value in the story of Thea Kronborg who becomes a famous singer—a Wagnerian opera star resplendent in "shining armour." Perhaps as Willa Cather developed her own powers, her sense of the artist's creative and unique calling took precedence over her recognition of the artist's limitations. Moreover, although she had an external model for her story in the person of the opera singer Olive Fremstad, Willa Cather was telling the story of Thea Kronborg from an intimately personal viewpoint, incorporating her own memories and experiences into the story of the artist's life. Thus Thea Kronborg's struggle to become an artist is in a very real sense Willa Cather's as well. In her 1932 preface to the novel she wrote that what she cared about was to show how "commonplace occurrences fell together to liberate [the artist] from commonness," how "fortunate accidents" will always happen to someone of Thea's vitality and honesty. In the novel the artist strives diligently to achieve excellence and fame; but, more importantly, there is about her life from the beginning a romantic sense of destiny, a certain conviction that no matter what befalls her she will ultimately triumph and become a great artist. The value placed on struggle and achievement and the emphasis on the sense of destiny give the book its particularly positive aspect. But at the same time the author did not overlook the hard fact that success in art is purchased at a high price. Thus at the end of the novel, while Thea has indeed become a great opera singer, we are made to recognize that in her personal life she has become hardened and depleted by her work, perhaps also by her success. Although the prevailing mood of the novel is creative and positive, Willa Cather's *künstlerroman,* carefully considered, presents us, as do her other studies of artists, with a double vision of art.

Briefly, a *künstlerroman* is a novel about an artist's development in which initiation into experience is conceived entirely in terms of an artist's mastery of his craft. On the surface it is a success story, for in the very act of writing the artist implies that he has achieved his goal; and in recording his memories he selects those experiences which bear directly on his growth and success as an artist. Yet at the same time the actual substance of such memories is invariably hardship, struggle, and even failure because the artist remembers not the experiences which were complete in themselves, but those seeking the rectification of art. The optimistic assumption upon which the *künstlerroman* stands is that the coherence of art redeems life's failures, and that such negative experiences are both necessary and creative; but the incontrovertible truth of every such story is that art is achieved at the expense of life, that only through isolation and failure does the artist acquire the motive and perspective essential to his art. Consequently the *künstlerroman* is a psychologically complex art form, for an artist's dedication is at once a creative and potentially tragic commitment.

The modern classic fiction of this type is Joyce's *A Portrait of the Artist as a Young Man,* wherein self-discovery is achieved through the exploration of language, the actual medium of the artist's craft. *The Song of the Lark* differs from the conventional *künstlerroman* in its portrait of the artist as diva rather than writer. Otherwise it follows the familiar pattern: memories of childhood, the struggles of a sensitive adolescent against the misunderstanding and bourgeois attitudes of family and neighbors, departure from home, and the slow, difficult progress of self-discovery through art. Interestingly, Willa Cather's novel begins with a sequence which is not dissimilar in method and feeling to the opening of Joyce's *Portrait.* Willa Cather's young artist is already a child of ten, but her disconnected impressions of the world from a sickbed are like those of the infant Stephen Daedalus in their almost exclusive preoccupation with physical sensation. While Thea is being cared for by Doctor Archie, her attention focuses on the hot plaster on her chest, made of "something dark and sticky on a white cloth," and on the details of the parlor "in the red light from the isinglass sides of the hard-coal burner—the nickel trimmings on the stove itself, the pictures on the wall . . . the flowers on the Brussels carpet" (pp. 10–11). As her consciousness comes and goes, Thea feels as if she is separated from her body, perched on the piano or on the hanging lamp, watching as the doctor puts the hot plaster on her chest. A little later Thea is absorbed in the look and feel of translucent white grapes and by the prickle of her red flannel underwear. The disjointed, dreamlike effect of the scene reflects the quality of vivid but incomplete memories from earliest childhood. Like Joyce, Willa Cather telescoped into one brief sequence that whole inchoate yet vital impression of first life out of which each individual emerges.

But most important in this opening scene is the way "first" impressions are coupled with the romantic idea of the artist as a special being. Thea's illness alarms Doctor Archie because he feels she is no ordinary child. "There was something very different about her," he reflects, and in a moment of annoyance with the other members of the family he says to himself "she's worth the whole litter." When he contemplates the incongruity of her delicate chin in a hard Scandinavian face, he wonders if some fairy grandmother had given it to her as a kind of cryptic promise. From the beginning Doctor Archie has a strong sense of Thea's special destiny and he urges her to set her goals high and never to compromise herself with ties and commitments to the small town in which they live. All the important people in Thea's life have this heightened awareness of her potential. Thea's mother, shrewd and practical in all matters, knows that her daughter is different in a special way, and when Professor Wunsch, Thea's music teacher, tells Mrs. Kronborg her daughter has "talent" she instinctively realizes this means hard work, not recitals for the local ladies' groups. Thea's Aunt Tillie delights in telling the neighbors that some day Thea will make them all sit up and take notice. But it is Professor Wunsch who defines and gives direction to Thea's "promise." One morning he startles her most secret thoughts when he says that she will some day be a singer: " 'Nothing is far and nothing is near, if one desires' " (p. 95). Wunsch (his own name translates from German as "desire") has singled Thea out from his other pupils as the one child who has both imagination and will. Wunsch himself has failed, but when he leaves Moonstone and looks back at Thea's figure on the station platform he consoles himself with the thought that "she will run a long way; they cannot stop her!" (p. 121).

Thea's strong, intimate sense of special destiny is like a voice or spirit inside her which in moments of imaginative excitement finds a correspondent echo in the outer world. For example, when she lifts a seashell from Spanish Johnny's garden to her ear, she hears a voice calling her from afar. For Thea the summons from the world of art is like a call to heroic action. She is stirred by the "piece-picture" on the Kohlers' wall of Napoleon's retreat from Moscow. The story of the first telegraph message received across the Missouri River inspires in her a vision of human courage which Professor Wunsch later identifies with the desire in great art; he says, when talking to Thea about her future as a singer, that " 'there is only one big thing—desire. . . . It brought Columbus across the sea in a little boat, *und so weiter*' " (p. 95). Thea's vision of human courage soaring above the world like the eagles over the Laramie tableland culminates an excursion into the sand hills with Ray Kennedy and Spanish Johnny which has a kind of mythic shape and purpose. The whole sequence is like a ritual of initiation into the world of the imagination: the journey out to the desert (a flight into the world of freedom), the warning from the mentor (Wunsch) against commitment to the ordinary world, the amphitheatre in the richly-colored hills, the storytelling, the music and singing, the play-acting of the children, and the final vision of the indomitable human spirit coursing westward. This call toward creativity with its accompanying *frisson* of desire is like an epiphany which brings Thea closer to her inner voice and builds in her a conviction of unique destiny.

The fact that art takes root in experiences of failure is also part of the book's substance from the beginning. Although Part I,

"Friends of Childhood," is seemingly the most idyllic and happy section of the book, nostalgia and wonder only partly veil a number of life's ugly realities. As its title implies, this long section of the novel is taken up with stories about the colorful characters of Thea's childhood (Doctor Archie, Professor Wunsch, Ray Kennedy, Spanish Johnny, Aunt Tillie), each of whom plays a significant role in her development as an artist. These people, however, are not Thea's peers, and Professor Wunsch and Spanish Johnny are not really reputable citizens of Moonstone. Thea herself is shy and inarticulate at school; she has no friends her own age and invariably stirs up the enmity of the respectable town ladies. Instead, her friends are "Mexicans and sinners," as her inveterate enemy, Mrs. Livery Johnson, puts it—people in the town who failed to realize their dreams but who continue to dream through Thea.

Most attractive of these is Doctor Howard Archie, who is both kindly protector and romantic hero to Thea. He is young, physically handsome, elegant in dress—his suits are made by a Denver tailor, he carries an alligator bag—and he is an incurable romantic in disposition. But despite his success as a doctor and his evident superiority to his fellow townsmen, he is seldom at ease with people. He is distant and evasive, " 'respected' rather than popular in Moonstone" (p. 106). His vulnerability is exposed to the public in his loveless marriage; his wife is a sterile little creature obsessed with saving money and keeping dust out of her home. It is natural that Doctor Archie warns Thea never to marry. Professor Wunsch is also an attractive figure. A romantic like the doctor, he believes that all things are possible if one has desire; and he urges Thea to remember the line from the hymn "Earth has no sorrow that Heaven cannot heal." But Wunsch's life is also without love; a wandering Orpheus, he lost his Eurydice years ago in Germany and has spent a dissipated existence moving aimlessly from town to town in the American Midwest. The romantic imagery which identifies him as an aged Orpheus figure is especially suggestive because not only is he a failed lover, but an artist *manqué* as well. Spanish Johnny gives Thea's world an exotic aspect. He is handsome, musical, fun-loving, but he is also a Mexican displaced in the progress-oriented American community and, like Professor Wunsch, he is an alcoholic who drinks to escape the reality of his situation. His art—his music—is also his undoing: when he plays his guitar and sings people listen to him, and in his excitement at communicating he drinks until he is overcome and then runs away from Moonstone. The emblem of his guilt and misery is his wife whose patience and resignation, Thea feels, are the saddest thing in the world. Aunt Tillie holds a special place in Thea's affections because she admires her niece extravagantly and foresees a brilliant future for her. But Tillie Kronborg is an "addle-pated" woman of thirty-five who has girlish ambitions to act and recite in public. Like Spanish Johnny she feels her art of recitation will bring her closer to communicating with other people. She remonstrates with Thea's younger brother on this point: " 'What are you going to do when you git big and want to git into society, if you can't do nothing? Everybody'll say, "Can you sing? Can you play? Then get right out of society" ' " (p. 25). Ray Kennedy, the old-maidish railway man, also holds a special place in Thea's world; he takes her on journeys out of Moonstone on the train, and he is a man whose honest and charitable disposition, despite so much bad luck, attests to something fundamentally good in human nature. But Ray is always a loser: he is not handsome, he has no family, and he seems to realize that his suit for Thea, like his ventures in stocks, will never prosper. Like Spanish Johnny and Aunt Tillie, Ray is concerned with communicating to others and he uses "bookish phrases" in his desire to express himself.

In this respect Thea's friends are not unlike the characters in Sherwood Anderson's *Winesburg, Ohio,* who tell their stories to the newspaper writer George Willard. Thea's friends quietly confide something of their romantic aspirations and fading dreams to her. In the determined, uncompromising girl they see the possibility of their own dreams being fulfilled, and in the lives of these characters Thea in turn catches a reflection of that elusive emotion which drives her relentlessly on with her music. But Thea's friends are failures and their frustrations sometimes find an outlet in bizarre and pathetic gestures: one night in a drunken orgy of self-pity and outraged innocence Professor Wunsch cuts down the Kohlers' dove house with an axe; Spanish Johnny is found lying under the railroad trestle cut up and bleeding after one of his escapades; Aunt Tillie humiliates the family with her ludicrous performances on stage; and Ray Kennedy, who pines for Thea's love, finally dies in an unnecessary railway accident, leaving an insurance policy which allows Thea to study in Chicago. Each of the characters is seen as contributing something special to Thea's growth as an artist whether it be talent, money, or dreams, but her complicity with these failures also suggests a source for her artist's drive in alienation from her peers.

Part I of *The Song of the Lark* crystallizes in episodic form the wonder and insatiable desire of a child called toward creativity. The structure, however, is not as casual as it may seem, for beneath the apparently loose arrangement of memories there is both conflict and a direct line of movement toward the resolution of that conflict. The choice for Thea is between staying in Moonstone (perhaps even conforming to its routine pattern of life) and leaving the familiar world for a career. On her thirteenth birthday she looks at the sand hills "until she wished she *were* a sand hill." But at the same time "she knew that she was going to leave them all behind some day" (p. 100). Later we read that "she felt as if she were being pulled in two, between the desire to go away forever and the desire to stay forever" (p. 177). Before Ray Kennedy's death Thea is neither going forward to a career nor consolidating herself in the town; she leaves school and devotes her time to giving piano lessons. The creeping death that threatens her imagination and creative desire is reflected in the moribund experiences that mark her daily life: the weekly prayer meetings with their resigned old women and sickly girls "already preparing to die"; her sister Anna's conversion and suffocatingly conventional views; then, finally, the suicide of the tramp, which brings typhoid and death to some of Moonstone's inhabitants. Ray's death makes it possible for Thea to go to Chicago, but the resolution of her dilemma—whether to go or whether to say—involves all the people she has known in Moonstone. In Part I we find Thea already assuming the artist's priestly role of expressing something for his people and of bringing them closer to spiritual fulfillment. She feels guilty for having turned away in disgust from the tramp when he appeared in Moonstone, but Doctor Archie urges her to forget the tramp and argues that by doing something great with her voice she can make amends. If she becomes a famous singer she will make the people she has known proud of her and that is the greatest thing she can do for them. " 'Take Mary Anderson, now,' " he says, " 'even the tramps are proud of her' " (p. 176). The artist's tie to the people of his past is also mentioned in relation to the faces of the old people at prayer meeting which, we are told, will some day come back to Thea in a very meaningful way. The idea of art giving meaning and dignity to humble lives is most pointedly dramatized in Ray Kennedy's death. Ray's vision as he lies dying is that Thea "wasn't meant for common men. She was like wedding cake, a thing to dream on . . . she was bound for the big terminals of the world" (p. 187). But prophetically he says to her that when you arrive " 'Then you'll remember me!' "

In Part II, "The Song of the Lark," Thea is alone in Chicago studying music; here she becomes more fully aware of her nature as an artist. From the time she could first remember there had always been "something" inside her, a secret presence like a friend, a presence which had shared her aspiration for achievement through music. Now in Chicago she realizes that her art is a process of self-discovery:

> Her voice, more than any other part of her, had to do with that confidence, that sense of wholeness and inner well-being that she had felt at moments ever since she could remember. . . . She took it for granted that some day, when she was older, she would know a great deal more about it. It was as if she had an appointment to meet the rest of herself sometime, somewhere. It was moving to meet her and she was moving to meet it. [P. 272]

Thea's awakening to herself as an artist is revealed in the Jules Breton painting *The Song of the Lark,* in which a peasant girl, on her way to work at dawn, stops to listen to a lark singing over the fields. Thea's intelligent and sympathetic piano teacher, Andor Harsanyi, also directs her toward her self-discovery as an artist when he urges her to study voice instead of piano. But Thea's first great experience of art comes when she hears Dvorák's *New World Symphony* performed. The first movement connects her with the moment of vision she had on the tableland above Laramie, while the "Largo" takes her home to "first memories, first mornings long ago" (p. 251). The two different moods of the symphony look forward to the two sources of inspiration in Thea's music: the heroic quest for ideal beauty, personal memories from the past.

The excitement she feels at the concert brings her to a decisive moment of commitment: "As long as she lived that ecstasy was going to be hers. She would live for it, work for it, die for it; but she was going to have it, time after time, height after height" (p. 254).

As Thea's desire to be an artist grows sharper and more defined, she feels an exuberance of physical energy: "She put her hand on her breast and felt how warm it was; and within it there was a full, powerful pulsation. . . . The life in there was rooted deep. She was going to have a few things before she died" (p. 274). Harsanyi tells Thea that great art has nothing to do with what is little, but with beauty and power (p. 267). And, as before, we find Thea associating art with heroic action: to decorate the wall of her room in the city she buys not pictures of the composers, but a photograph of the Naples bust of Julius Caesar ("she loved to read about great generals"); and in the Art Institute her favorite piece is "a great equestrian statue of an evil, cruel-looking general with an unpronounceable name" (p. 248). Thea's determination and drive stand in relief against the defeat and purposelessness of the people around her. Mrs. Andersen, one of her landladies, is a pale, anemic-looking woman of forty who has withered away since her husband's death. Thea finds her apologetic, shrinking manner peculiarly depressing. Mr. Larsen, the Swedish minister in Chicago, is a happy, contented man, but he is remarkable for his soft, indolent habits and his laziness. Thea's physical strength and well-being are most sharply accented by glimpses of sick and dying girls: on the train back to Moonstone she sits in front of a girl who is dying of tuberculosis, and when she arrives home she is told almost at once that one of the sickly girls from prayer meetings has just died.

But as Thea's sense of heroic purpose grows stronger, the gap for her widens between the claims of ordinary life and the desire to be an artist. Throughout Part II we are reminded of the necessary and often sordid details of everyday existence, which harass and impede the striving artist. When Thea and Doctor Archie look for lodgings they are depressed by the sleazy, unkempt wastes of Chicago and the ill-favored aspects of boardinghouses. The Swedish church where Thea sings is in "a sloughy, weedy district, near a group of factories," and her lodging house is an unpainted, gloomy-looking place in a damp yard where there is no running water; Thea has to carry both water and fuel to her room. But particularly when she is filled with the ecstasy of an imaginative experience she feels life around her becoming ugly and hostile. After the concert of Dvorák and Wagner has stirred in her all the emotions fundamental to her imaginative being, she believes that the world conspires to deprive her of that elevated ecstasy and sense of self: "There was some power abroad in the world bent upon taking away from her that feeling with which she had come out of the concert hall. . . . If one had that, the world became one's enemy; people, buildings, wagons, cars, rushed at one to crush it under, to make one let go of it" (p. 254). In this powerful scene, life is predicated as the natural enemy of art and imaged as a stream: "Thea was conscious . . . of the congestion of life all about her, of the brutality and power of those streams that flowed in the streets, threatening to drive one under." The image of the stream of life first introduced here subsequently becomes a leitmotif by which Thea's changing views are represented.

When Thea returns home to Moonstone for the summer, she is severely criticized for going to a dance in the Mexican Town, and again feels a conspiracy in the world against her. The Mexican dance is another imaginative ritual, like the trip into the desert with Ray Kennedy. Again Thea takes a journey out of Moonstone into the brightly-colored sand hills to a special place (an "adobe dance-hall") where there is music, dancing, and singing. There is an esthetic appropriation of natural detail in the scene: the moon-flowers over Mrs. Tellamantez's door are described as an unearthly white, while the moon is compared to "a great pale flower in the sky." But perhaps most interesting in this scene is the subtle association of art with religious initiation: three little girls are wearing their first communion dresses; the Ramas brothers (whose devoted attendance on Thea inspires Spanish Johnny to call them "the altar-boys") recall the time they had accompanied their mother when she went to help decorate the church for Easter and had told the other women "she had brought her 'ramas' "—the Spanish word for branches—instead of flowers; Thea herself is described by the brothers as "white and gold, like Easter!" When she sings for the music-loving Mexicans the completeness and intensity of their response is so overwhelming that she feels as if they have surrendered their very being to her—"as if all these warm-blooded people débouched into her" (p. 292). Thea momentarily has become their artist-priestess, and Spanish Johnny follows her performance with a teasing song which is a comic variation on that idea. As the author translates it: "Last night I made confession / To a Carmelite father, / And he told me do penance / By kissing your pretty mouth."

This scene with its "natural harmony" anticipates Thea's later view of art in terms of both natural and sacred obligation. But next morning when she is criticized by her older brothers and sister for associating with Mexicans she feels alienated from her family and betrayed by them, alone save for that secret companion inside herself. Taking refuge in her room, "she frowned at herself for a while in the looking-glass. Yes, she and It must fight it out together. The thing that looked at her out of her own eyes was the only friend she could count on. Oh, she would make these people sorry enough!" (p. 300). At this point Thea's commitment to art and isolation is motivated by revenge as well as self-discovery. That evening, talking with Doctor Archie, she asserts that " 'living's too much trouble unless one can get something big out of it.' " She doesn't mean money—" 'I only want impossible things. . . . The others don't interest me' " (p. 305). And in the final line of Part II Thea's commitment to art is defined as both heroic and irrevocable: "She was going away to fight, and she was going away forever" (p. 310).

In Part III, "Stupid Faces," Thea seeks, without fully realizing it, the companionship of other people in the arts. She tells her voice teacher, Madison Bowers, that she could never get along with girls of her own age, and it seems clear that she had hoped she would find in her fellow musicians both inspiration and friendship. Instead, she finds only shallow, self-seeking women who spend as much time on their appearance, " 'their frizzes and feathers,' " as their voice. What appalls Thea is the commonness of women like Mrs. Priest and Jessie Darcey who do not strive for artistic perfection but simply wish to please the whims of an essentially vulgar audience. Their sole measure of achievement is their popularity. Sorely disillusioned, Thea says of one of the singers whom she accompanies: " 'I hate her for the sake of what I used to think a singer might be' " (p. 331). Although her attitude is frequently cynical and contemptuous, like Madison Bowers's, Thea still feels the "challenge" of the stars in the heavens, still aspires to greatness for herself; but now she realizes more than ever that she must go the road alone. This is directly reflected in the Grieg song, "Tak for dit Räd," that she sings for Fred Ottenburg, a wealthy brewer's son. The reference in the song is to a heroic and strenuous journey undertaken alone: "Thanks for your advice! But I prefer to steer my boat into the din of roaring breakers. . . . I long to fight my way through the angry waves, and to see how far, and how long I can make them carry me" (p. 338).

In Part IV, "The Ancient People," Thea, after an exhausting and depressing second winter in Chicago, takes Fred Ottenburg's advice and with his help withdraws to the desert in the Southwest to be completely alone. Here even the landscape with its single mountain and sparse growth of pines—they stand at a distance from each other like the uncommunicative Navajos—mirrors the heroine's quest for complete solitude. Thea spends long stretches of time in the ancient cliff dwellings of one of the canyons, where she feels released from the tiresome sense of her individual personality and becomes attuned to a more primitive, fundamental sense of life and creativity. This sequence in the book is another imaginative ritual: the journey into the brightly painted desert, the canyon, cliff dwellings, and stream as *locus dramatis,* and the culminating vision of art Thea experiences standing in the stream. This time the author is more explicit about her intentions. She says Thea's bath in the stream came to have "a ceremonial gravity" and that "the atmosphere of the cañon was ritualistic" (p. 378). The significant difference in this scene from the picnic in the sand hills and the Mexican dance is that Thea experiences the art and music of nature rather than man. In the process of stripping away past memories and associations, she finds something like Keats's "negative capability" for identity through sensations: "She could become a mere receptacle for heat, or become a colour, like the bright lizards that darted about on the hot stones outside her door; or she could become a continuous repetition of sound, like the cicadas" (p. 373). This delving beneath personal identity to something elemental and universal about life prepares Thea for her vision of art as a sacred trust for the whole of mankind, rather than a struggle for individual achievement and recognition.

In a Joycean epiphany Thea contemplates for the first time a genuine synthesis of those formerly irreconcilable antagonists, art and life:

> One morning, as she was standing upright in the pool, splashing water between her shoulder-blades with a big sponge, something flashed through her mind that made her draw herself up and stand still until the water had quite dried upon her flushed skin. The stream and the broken pottery: what was any art but an effort to make a sheath, a mould in which to imprison for a moment the shining, elusive element which is life itself—life hurrying past us and running away, too strong to stop, too sweet to lose? The Indian women had held it in their jars. In the sculpture she had seen in the Art Institute, it had been caught in a flash of arrested motion. In singing, one made a vessel of one's throat and nostrils and held it on one's breath, caught the stream in a scale of natural intervals. [P. 378]

The Indian water vessels are functional utensils, but they also give expression in their careful craftsmanship and ornamentation to man's age-old desire for something beyond himself, that same desire Thea has experienced since she was a child. In reflecting and serving man's deepest needs (his need of water for physical life, his dream of a higher spiritual order) the pieces of pottery become for Thea a symbol of art and life conjoined in a purposeful harmony. The Indian pottery, moreover, reflects the communal aspect of art. For Thea, music had been the essence of her individuality, but in the presence of the ancient pottery and the cliff houses she feels her art no longer alienates her from other men, but connects her vitally to a tradition of human aspiration: "All these things made one feel that one ought to do one's best, and help to fulfil some desire of the dust that slept there. . . . These potsherds were like fetters that bound one to a long chain of human endeavour" (p. 380). The stream, too, is no longer "the stream of meaningless and undirected effort," but is the very stuff out of which art is made. A little later, as in her memory of the vision at Laramie, Thea sees an eagle fly over the canyon, and it again becomes a symbol of the continuity of human desire and the striving of art: "From a cleft in the heart of the world she saluted it. . . . It had come all the way; when men lived in caves, it was there. A vanished race; but along the trails, in the stream, under the spreading cactus, there still glittered in the sun the bits of their frail clay vessels, fragments of their desire" (p. 399). Thea's dedication to art is no longer conceived of as a selfish quest for power and recognition, nor as a means of revenge on a critical world, but as the fulfillment of a sacred obligation to both man's ancestors and his descendants.

Thea's re-entry into the mainstream of life comes when Fred Ottenburg joins her in Arizona and persuades her to run off to Mexico with him. Eventually she discovers that Ottenburg is already married; and in Part V, "Doctor Archie's Venture," she borrows money from her old Moonstone friend to leave America and study alone in Germany. At first it appears that Thea has been betrayed by her renewed contact with her fellow men, but, as Ottenburg himself finally makes her recognize, the experience was essential to Thea for further defining herself and determining her course. Their love affair never involved the submission of one to the other, but was more like a camaraderie; they were equals in all their adventures. Thea admired Ottenburg's physical energy and vied with him at throwing stones in discus fashion; to Henry Biltmer, the lodge keeper in Arizona, they looked like two boys moving about nimbly on the cliffs. On one of their expeditions Thea climbed to the top of a cliff, and Ottenburg, seeing her from below, thought of her as some wild creature from early Germanic times.

After Thea has broken off their affair, Ottenburg tells her that by going to Mexico with him she was simply driving ahead: " 'And you'll always drive ahead. . . . It's your way' " (p. 444). Thea loves Fred Ottenburg, but her desire to be a great artist is still strong. Their love has enriched her experience of life, and the fact that he is already married leaves her free to continue with her music and mesh that experience with her art. On the eve of Thea's departure for Germany he notices that her excitement, her eagerness "to get at it," is no longer colored by memories and personal struggles, but is now "unconscious,"—something selfless and instinctive.

The necessary isolation and impersonality of the artist is suggested in the title of Part VI—"Kronborg." The time is ten years later, and the distance we now feel from the great opera singer is effected by the author's changing the point of view from Thea's to Doctor Archie's. Thea's accomplishments and fame are rendered with appropriate awe by the limited vision of an old childhood friend, but he does not fail to perceive the remoteness which now invests the great artist's personality. When Doctor Archie first sees Thea again after a performance at the Metropolitan, she is tired and awkward behind her make-up and has lost much of the spontaneity and energy she once exuded. In later visits he cannot help but notice that she has grown hardened and impatient with those around her. Fred Ottenburg, still her admirer, realizes that only the challenge of her art brings back her vitality and zest for life: "It was only under such excitement, he reflected, that she was entirely illuminated, or wholly present. At other times there was something a little cold and empty, like a big room with no people in it" (p. 533).[24] In a sense Thea has died to life; on stage she looks to Doctor Archie like someone in the "next world"; her face (as her name suggests) is "shining with the light of a new understanding" (p. 500), and that "new understanding" has been the goal toward which Thea has been moving all her life.

Thea no longer has a life apart from the opera (she can talk only of herself and her work), but in her career art and life are still one because as Harsanyi suggests, her special gift is her passion. One of the final questions considered in the novel is the relationship of the artist to the people in his past. Doctor Archie always regretted that Thea did not get home when her mother was dying. Her failure to return appears callous and neglectful; and yet Oliver Landry, Thea's friend,[25] tells Fred Ottenburg that the special power in Thea's interpretation of Elizabeth in *Tannhäuser* derives from the anxiety and grief she felt over her mother's death: " 'The last act is heart-breaking. It's as homely as a country prayer-meeting: might be any lonely woman getting ready to die. It's full of the thing every plain creature finds out for himself, but that never gets written down' " (p. 540). Among other things we are reminded of those humble faces at the mournful prayer meetings which, for Thea, were so tedious, but promised to mean something some day. Through the "new understanding" of her art Thea appreciates those faces as she could not before; they are part of that passion, that vital enrichment in her art.

There is a tragic side to this relationship between the artist and her past; not only her mother but many of the people she once knew are now dead and cannot know that they have contributed to the growth of a great singer. But in this novel Willa Cather chooses to dwell on the positive aspect of that relationship and to show us how Thea's success fulfills the dreams of her childhood friends from Moonstone. At a performance which marks perhaps the pinnacle of her career, several of her old friends are present: her piano teacher, Harsanyi, who with his symbolic one eye has shared her singleness of vision and purpose; Fred Ottenburg, whom she will eventually marry; Doctor Archie; and by a rare accident of fate, Spanish Johnny, now an itinerant circus performer. Each reaps his own spiritual reward for the part he played in the development of Thea's voice. The triumph of art in life is presented (again embodying the image of the stream) in the figure of Spanish Johnny filled with happiness after Thea's performance: "Then he walked down Broadway with his hands in his overcoat pockets, wearing a smile which embraced all the stream of life that passed him and the lighted towers that rose into the limpid blue of the evening sky. If the singer, going home exhausted in her car, was wondering what was the good of it all, that smile, could she have seen it, would have answered her. It is the only commensurate answer" (p. 573). In the epilogue Willa Cather completes that vision of art's service to life by taking us, for a moment, back to Moonstone where Aunt Tillie "lives in a world of secret satisfactions" because the little girl she put all her faith in has given the world so much noble pleasure (p. 578).

Youth and the Bright Medusa and "Uncle Valentine"

Willa Cather's next fictional treatments of the artist figure are collected in *Youth and the Bright Medusa,* published in 1920.[26] Along with four stories reprinted from *The Troll Garden* ("'A Death in the Desert,'" "A Wagner Matinee," "The Sculptor's Funeral," and "Paul's Case"), it includes four later stories also concerned with art and artists. In all four Willa Cather is preoccupied in some way with the artist in relation to commercial success, a theme never previously developed in her fiction. Although Thea Kronborg is careful with money in the Moonstone way, her struggle for artistic greatness has nothing to do with possible monetary gain. The theme in these stories, however, is not that the artist struggles for wealth (that would automatically invalidate him as an artist for Cather), but that he becomes entangled unwittingly in the obligations that incidental riches bring to him. Thematically, Willa Cather was moving in her fiction toward the dilemma posed by material possessions (as explored in her critical novels *One of Ours* and *The Professor's House*) and the danger they posit for both human relationships and art.

The first new story in the collection, "Coming, Aphrodite!," is the most overtly erotic piece of fiction Miss Cather ever published.[27] A painter named Don Hedger, who is used to living alone in New York in a garret in Washington Square, finds his hermitlike existence completely upset when a beautiful young singer, who has taken the name Eden Bower, rents the room next to his. An open knothole in the partition between his closet and her bedroom allows him the voyeuristic pleasure of watching her exercise nude in front of a mirror. The scene is rendered through the painter's eye with an exquisite blend of the erotic and esthetic: "The soft flush of exercise and the gold of afternoon sun played over her flesh together, enveloped her in a luminous mist which, as she turned and twisted, made now an arm, now a shoulder, now a thigh, dissolve in pure light and instantly recover its outline with the next gesture" (p. 17). Hedger and Eden gradually come to know each other; after a wary courtship in which each struggles for power over the other, they become lovers. The nature of their relationship is dramatized in the story of the Indian Rain Princess; Hedger tells Eden the story to punish her after she has frightened him by a dare-devil balloon stunt on Coney Island. The Mexican Rain Princess, while still a virgin, becomes enamored of one of her father's captives, who is tattooed all over his body, and begs that his life be spared. She has the Captive tattoo her own body, but during the operation he violates her honor. His punishment is that he is gelded and has his tongue torn out; and he is made her slave. After her marriage to the King of the Aztecs, the Captive's special duty is to bring the Rain Princess lovers secretly and to lead them to their death in an underground river. The Captive, however, finally takes revenge; he calls the King to his wife's chamber when she has a lover there, and both she and her slave are put to death by fire. This story within a story suggests the bondage Hedger feels to the capricious Eden. In another image Hedger's enthrallment is related to Samson's subjection to Delilah: Hedger's dog sees that "the woman was pulling the long black hair of this mightiest of men, who bowed his head and permitted it."

But stronger than his enslavement to Eden is Hedger's commitment to his art. Eden wants him to make money and tries to arrange for him to meet some successful, influential artists; but Hedger resists and temporarily leaves her in order to regain the strength of his convictions. When he returns to New York she has gone to France, and Hedger is left alone again with his art. In a coda to the story, eighteen years later, Eden, now a successful prima donna starring in the opera *Aphrodite,* learns that Hedger is an important avant-garde painter, though still not commercially successful. The story openly dramatizes a number of the author's recurrent preoccupations and perhaps therein lies its greatest interest. The beautiful and desired woman is figured as a modern Venus, seen first in graceful nude movements in front of a gilt mirror, then rising above the waters, like Botticelli's Venus, on a balloon, and finally deified in neon lights on Broadway. The motherless male protagonist is frustated by the relationship, and art provides him with a noble, though lonely, retreat from the failure to fulfill and sustain the experience of love. But perhaps most significant are the identification of the beautiful woman with the perils and obligations of wealth and the dignity achieved by the artist who, for the sake of his art, resists this most powerful and insidious temptation.

The title of the collection refers most directly to "Coming, Aphrodite!": Don Hedger does battle with the Medusa of commercial success and only by contemplating the Gorgon in the reflection of art (like Perseus with Athena's shield) is he able to triumph over her. In the other three new stories the artist is at the Medusa's mercy, a victim of the financial bonanza that success brings. The story of Cressida Garnet in "The Diamond Mine" (1916) focuses not on the singer's career, but on the way she is exploited by the people around her—her brothers and sisters, her son, her accompanist, and her several husbands. The tragedy of Cressida's life is her failure to maintain any genuine human relationships. She herself says: " 'Somehow, my relations with people always become business relations in the end.' " This is best illustrated perhaps in the long account of her marriage to her third husband, an indigent Bohemian composer who saw her as a " 'great artist,' the common synonym for success. Her success, and the material evidence of it, quite blinded him." Her fourth husband regards her as a source of financial backing for a failing career, which he pursues until almost nothing is left of her fortune. The story ends with Cressida's death on the *Titanic,* and the family rapaciously dividing the spoils. The portrait of the constantly beleaguered, ill-fated singer has the authority of sympathetic and careful observation. There is genuine pathos in the artist's hopeless quest for love among the men who seek to exploit her. But the story as a whole is curiously flat; probably this is because, although it is told in the first person, the narrator never enters into the story's imaginative design.

The other two new stories, "A Gold Slipper" (1917) and "Scandal" (1919), are both about the vivacious opera singer, Kitty Ayrshire. Like Cressida Garnet, Kitty must also move in a world where art is honored less for its intrinsic qualities than for its prestige and commercial values. In "A Gold Slipper" Kitty is first seen through the eyes of a middle-aged Pittsburgh businessman who frankly admits his lack of interest in the arts. Forced by his wife and her friends to attend one of Kitty's concerts, he attracts the singer's attention by his visible boredom at her recital. By chance they are fellow passengers on a train to New York that same night, and in a lively dialogue they give voice to their mutual distrust of each other's worlds. For Kitty the arts help to satisfy her constant craving for what is new and exciting, which is precisely the reason why McKann, the businessman, finds them suspect—they subvert the perfect order of what is known and tried. Kitty follows up her verbal challenge to McKann's complacency by placing one of her gold slippers in his berth while he is asleep. Its effect is not lost: in spite of his vexation he still has it locked away in his safe many years later. "Scandal" is much less effective. In this story Kitty and a friend recall how a socially ambitious Jew, Siegmund Stein, once led the public to believe that he was keeping Miss Ayrshire's company. He would attend the opera faithfully when she sang and then escort around the city a woman who looked amazingly like Kitty, but was actually a girl from his factory. He even arranged to have Kitty herself give a private performance at a party in his home after he had married an heiress from California. Kitty's light-hearted reaction to the whole thing does not disguise the distasteful nature of Stein's manipulations. That she would choose a Jew for a villain perhaps reflects the difficult emotions Willa Cather experienced when Isabelle McClung married the Jewish violinist Jan Hambourg. "Scandal" is marred by this choice; instead of presenting the artist's age-old struggle with Philistia, it reduces the heroine at the end to complaining (with reference to her look-alike): " 'We are both the victims of circumstance, and in New York so many of the circumstances are Steins.' "

As a story about artists, "Uncle Valentine" (1925)[28] is unique in Willa Cather's fiction for it contains a character, Charlotte Waterford, who has successfully adjusted the opposing claims of art and life. We are told that "she cared more for music than for anything else in the world, and after that for her family and her house and her friends." But these two spheres of her life, the imaginative and the domestic, are never antithetical, rather they complement one another. She brings the intelligence and grace of an artist to the ordering of her home and at the same time her piano playing "was not an accomplishment with her, but a way of living." We are also told that "whatever it is that enables us to make our peace with life, she had found it." Charlotte Waterford is a special character in Willa Cather's fiction, an idealized character perhaps, certainly a still point in the unquiet world of her artists. In contrast to "Aunt Charlotte" are the Ramsays who live in the next house; theirs is a world in which the values of art (order, intelligence, sympathy) have not been integrated with their personal lives. The story takes shape around the return from Europe of Valentine Ramsay, a celebrated pianist and composer, to his family home at Greenacre. Like the other artists in Willa Cather's fiction, Valentine's personal life has not been successful: divorced from a wealthy and ambitious American woman, he has been having an extended affair with a peripatetic singer in Paris. He decides in the course of the story to make his home at Greenacre, since all his life he has been infatuated with "Aunt Charlotte"; but his former wife buys property in the area and he is driven back to Paris for peace of mind. We are told that two years later he was hit and killed by a motor car. The other members of the Ramsay family are unsuccessful artists. Valentine's Uncle Roland had been a child prodigy, a pianist, touring Europe and studying with Wagner, but now he has "broken nerves" and lives in an almost comatose state. Valentine's father is a happy enough man, indeed he is essentially complacent, but almost axiomatically the poetry he writes is worthless, sentimental stuff. The story of Valentine's return and defeat is presented through the eyes of a young girl in the Waterford household. It has Willa Cather's special charm of nostalgia for a gracious, civilized way of living in the past: life at Fox Hill is a world of spacious rooms, classical music, and well-cared-for gardens. Perhaps the best scene in the story is the description of a summer night when the garden is drenched in moonlight and all the characters feel the restless, romantic urge to transcend the limitations of their lives. Art promises escape, but the story suggests that only when art informs living itself with the values of intelligence and order (Aunt Charlotte's "good taste") can it provide a viable alternative to what is "ordinary"; otherwise art can lead to misery and madness. Willa Cather's fictional search for a right relationship between art and life never came any closer to resolution.

Notes

1. *Nebraska State Journal,* March 3, 1895; collected in *KA,* p. 124.
2. *Courier,* September 28, 1895, collected in *KA,* p. 392.
3. *Courier,* November 23, 1895; collected in *KA,* p. 409.
4. *Nebraska State Journal,* March 1, 1896; collected in *KA,* p. 417.
5. *Nebraska State Journal,* January 26, 1896; collected in *KA,* p. 120.
6. *Nebraska State Journal,* June 16, 1895; collected in *KA,* p. 153.
7. *Nebraska State Journal,* January 27, 1895; collected in *W&P,* pp. 175–76.
8. *Nebraska State Journal,* April 21, 1895; collected in *W&P,* p. 200.
9. *Courier,* November 9, 1895, and *Nebraska State Journal,* December 15, 1895; quoted in *KA,* p. 71.
10. *CSF,* pp. 405–10.
11. *CSF,* pp. 333–38.
12. *CSF,* pp. 411–23.
13. *CSF,* pp. 283–91.
14. The stories from *The Troll Garden* are reprinted in *CSF,* pp. 149–261.
15. Brown, *Willa Cather,* pp. 113 ff.
16. *KA,* pp. 93 ff. Bernice Slote also explains in detail the allusions behind the title and the epigraphs (from Christina Rossetti's "The Goblin Market" and Charles Kingsley's *The Roman and the Teuton*).

17. This view of the artist follows through an earlier observation Willa Cather made about literary people in the *Nebraska State Journal,* June 7, 1896: "It is gravely to be feared that literary people are rather mean folk when you get right down to the selfish little pericardiums that lie behind all their graceful artistic charms. They love humanity in the abstract, but no class of men can treat the concrete individual more shabbily." Quoted in *KA,* p. 68.

18. Some of the characters in this story are forerunners of types of figures which recur in Willa Cather's fiction. Arthur Hamilton, the quiet man of genuine good taste who is alienated from his unsympathetic wife and her clique of fashion-conscious friends, looks forward to Jim Burden, Godfrey St. Peter, Count Frontenac, Clement Sebastian, and Henry Colbert, to name only major characters. Imogen Willard, the honest, self-effacing observer, anticipates the shy, scholarly Nellie Birdseye of *My Mortal Enemy,* and there seems to be a direct line leading from the forthright "Jimmy" Broadwood to Cherry Beamish, the one-time music-hall performer in "The Old Beauty." The reappearance of so many character types suggests both the unity and complexity of the author's imagination.

19. "The Sculptor's Funeral" has been treated more fully in Part I as a form of pastoral elegy.

20. *CSF,* pp. 137–46.

21. *CSF,* pp. 125–35.

22. *CSF,* pp. 113–23.

23. *The Song of the Lark* (Sentry Edition; Boston: Houghton Mifflin, 1963). All quotations are from this text.

24. In a letter of April 22, 1913, to Elizabeth Sergeant, Willa Cather describes seeing Olive Fremstad getting into her car, glassy-eyed and drained after a performance; the image seems to have carried over to her presentation of Thea Kronborg. The idea of a great artist having little personal life apart from his art probably was also reinforced by Cather's seeing Fremstad's apartment, which she describes to Miss Sergeant as being both in bad taste and cheerless. (Copy of letter at University of Virginia Library.)

25. Landry is another of those weak, romantic men that Willa Cather's strong heroines find so attractive.

26. *Youth and the Bright Medusa* (New York: Alfred A. Knopf, 1920). All quotations are from this text. It is interesting to note that three of the stories ("The Diamond Mine," "A Gold Slipper," and "Scandal") all were written in the year 1916, although the two Kitty Ayrshire stories did not appear in magazines until the dates given in the text. In other words, after she finished *The Song of Lark* Cather went right on for a time writing about singers.

27. The erotic nature of the story can be appreciated fully by comparing "Coming, Aphrodite!" as it appeared in *Youth and the Bright Medusa* with a bowdlerized (or at least modified) version, entitled "Coming, Eden Bower!," which appeared in H. L. Mencken's *Smart Set,* August 1920, and

has been reprinted in *UVS,* pp. 141–76. For example, when Eden is described exercising in the nude in front of her mirror, the *Smart Set* version represses references to her thighs and breasts. Nearly one hundred variants are given in the appendix in *UVS.*

28. *UVS,* pp. 1–38.

CHAPTER SIX

The Last Four Books

Art and Life

We have seen that in her earlier novels Willa Cather explored the archetypal modes of the imagination—epic, pastoral, satire—and that the three novels written at the height of her career form something like a "mortal comedy." But what of the last four volumes, *Obscure Destinies, Lucy Gayheart, Sapphira and the Slave Girl, The Old Beauty and Others,* which most critics agree mark the decline of Willa Cather's art?[1] Are these books, from a writer of such depths, as undistinguished and insignificant as has been suggested? The answer, I believe, is at once affirmative and negative. With the exception of the long story "Old Mrs. Harris," the later writing lacks the same kind of imaginative energy which found expression in the earlier novels. The last fictions are subtle, intelligent, and artfully contrived, but the vision which underlies them is one which questions the old urge to expression through art. I believe the author came to feel in her later years that not art but life mattered most now; consequently, her last books occupy the paradoxical position of works of art suggesting their own devaluation.

As a romantic Willa Cather had believed strongly in the absoluteness of the artist's vocation, an attitude most directly expressed in *The Song of the Lark* and in "Coming, Aphrodite!."[2] In this light her major novels might be described as the egotistic expressions of an individual consciousness seeking both self-knowledge and recognition from others. But the last novels and stories posit quite a different relationship between art and its creator. No longer driven by the same urge to create, Willa Cather, I feel, came to view her lifetime dedication to art as placing selfish limitations on life, particularly on human relationships. Again the author was following a path well worn by (to use one of her favorite metaphors) the "pilgrims" of the imagination. Many writers before Willa Cather reached a point in their lives when they no longer felt art to be so very important. Some dramatized that feeling emphatically by arresting their work early or in mid-career: Rimbaud, for example, went to Abyssinia to make his fortune in the slave trade; Tolstoi turned his back on the world and the novel to become a recluse and social pamphleteer; and Hart Crane, in his quest for a transcendental ideal, despaired of the limitations of poetry and committed suicide. For Willa Cather the implications of her vision were never so definitive or tragic, yet instinctively she moved toward that same juncture where art terminates in the mute acceptance (or, in Crane's case, hopeful transcendence) of life.

Willa Cather's life changed irrevocably in 1927 with the disruption in her living arrangements caused by the loss of her Bank Street apartment and with the subsequent death of her parents. It was the long illness and the death in 1931 of her mother, I believe, which especially determined the direction of her writing for the remaining years. For her father, Willa Cather had felt much affection all her life, but her relationship with her mother had often been difficult; indeed, much of her youthful behavior seems to have been in deliberate contravention of her mother's wishes.[3] But with the passing of time and the prospect of her mother's approaching death, the author's attitude softened considerably. Edith Lewis's account is valuable here not only for suggesting the author's change of heart, but for giving an incisive portrait of the woman (Miss Cather's mother) who plays an important role in the last fiction:

> The long illness of Mrs. Cather . . . had a profound effect on Willa Cather, and I think on her work as well. She had come to understand her mother better and better through the years—her strong-willed, imperious nature, full of quick, eager impulses—quick to resent, quick to sympathize, headstrong, passionate, and yet capable of great kindness and understanding. She realized with com-

> plete imagination what it meant for a proud woman like her mother to lie month after month quite helpless.[4]

In her fiction Willa Cather had been moving closer to reconciliation with her mother. Myra Henshawe in *My Mortal Enemy* says to Nellie: " 'As we grow old we become more and more the stuff our forebears put into us. . . . We think we are so individual and so misunderstood when we are young; but the nature our strain of blood carries is inside there, waiting, like our skeleton' " (p. 82). Cécile Auclair in *Shadows on the Rock* strives to carry on her mother's ways of caring for the household; and in "Old Mrs. Harris" the neighbor exclaims: " 'Dat Vickie is her mother over again.' " With her mother's death a source of conflict integral to Willa Cather's imaginative life was gone, leaving her with a deep sense of her own thoughtlessness and perversity.[5] The subject matter of her fiction now changed; it was important to her to write about human relationships and about life and death, rather than art. And where her novels of the mid-1920s had found characters and settings in the world at large, the later fiction returns the author once again to her personal past in Nebraska and Virginia. But what is most significant is that these books are shaped throughout by a desire to see that world, at last, objectively and with compassion. The imaginative tension essential for great art is largely gone, but in its place we have the author's wisdom, her resolution—her testament to life which is poignantly simple and reassuring.

Obscure Destinies

The title of this collection of stories with its allusion to Gray's "Elegy" ("Let not Ambition mock their useful toil, / Their homely joys, and destiny obscure; / Nor grandeur hear with a disdainful smile / The short and simple annals of the poor") suggests the change in Willa Cather's art. No longer was she writing about artists or distinguished men and women, but about the ordinary people from her own past. Moreover, the value of great success and achievements is implicitly undermined by this allusion, for the next stanza of Gray's poem reminds us that "paths of glory lead but to the grave."

In "Old Mrs. Harris," the second story of *Obscure Destinies* (1932),[6] the author writes of her family (specifically, her mother and grandmother as she remembered them from the time of her adolescence) and a period in her life which she previously viewed with feelings confused by loyalty and bitterness. Although Thea Kronborg's mother is presented sympathetically, some of those memories emerge in *The Song of the Lark* where we find the nascent artist fleeing the suffocation and hostilities of family life by means of her music. Thea's sense of personal, family obligations is superseded by a dedication to the impersonal idea of ancient ancestors (the Indians of the Southwest) and "the chain of human endeavour" revealed in art: "She had clung fast to whatever was left of Moonstone in her mind. No more of that! The cliff dwellers had lengthened her past. She had older and higher obligations" (pp. 382–83). But in "Old Mrs. Harris" the artist returns to her personal past; the mood is not one of bitterness, nor is it escapist and nostalgic, but carries the purpose of examining objectively memories stored up for much of a lifetime.

"Old Mrs. Harris" is informed by quiet regret that youth in its self-absorption is so frequently cruel and indifferent. The effectiveness of the story derives from the subtlety with which point of view is managed. Although the controlling perspective is ultimately the author's—the grown Vickie remembering an episode of her adolescence—the story is narrated so that the three women in the family, while not understanding each other, emerge nonetheless as sympathetic individuals to the reader. Miss Cather in effect described the tragic undercurrent of this story in her essay on Katherine Mansfield, in which she singles out that author's ability to reveal the many kinds of relations which exist in a happy family: "Every individual in that household (even the children) is clinging passionately to his individual soul, is in terror of losing it in the general family flavour. As in most families, the mere struggle to have anything of one's own, to be one's self at all, creates an element of strain which keeps everybody almost at the breaking-point."[7] In "Old Mrs. Harris" sympathy at first appears to be reserved for the grandmother alone: the story begins with Mrs. Rosen's visit to Grandma Harris, and from the neighbor's vantage point the old woman appears to be the drudge in her daughter's household and the victim of her son-in-law's ineffectuality in business. But as we are taken inside Mrs. Harris's thoughts we find that as a Southerner reared in the old tradition she accepts her role in her daughter's kitchen and is grateful to be able to follow her daughter's fortunes in this customary way. Also, the view of Victoria Templeton as haughty and selfish, jealous of any attention paid to her mother, begins to soften as the old woman reflects that while her daughter is indeed proud, she has a "good heart." The old woman, moreover, admits to herself that because Victoria had been the prettiest of her children she had spoiled her. Mrs. Harris could have been wholly idealized if the author had retained only a granddaughter's perspective, but the tension in the family is felt from the daughter Victoria's point of view as well. At the Methodist social we are given a glimpse into her motives and feelings. We see her giving money spontaneously to the children of the poor laundress and know that the gesture is not intended to be patronizing; we feel the intended reproach by one of the meddlesome townswomen who implies that Victoria exploits her mother in the kitchen. Victoria could have been a negative character, but sympathy is elicited for her in exposing her vulnerability. When she discovers she is to bear yet another child, we have only sympathy for her feeling of misery and defeat. To balance Mrs. Rosen's critical view, Victoria is also seen through the neighbor's eyes in a radiant picture of maternity, happily giving nurse to her baby.

The portrait of Vickie is the most complex; because she is a projection of the author's younger self she is viewed at once most critically and most sympathetically. Vickie's desire to go to college, to escape from the cramped existence of an overcrowded family in a small midwestern town, blinds her to the feelings and needs of those around her. The measure of regret the author feels years later is suggested in the homely incident when the family cat dies. Vickie is so absorbed in her studies then that she pays little attention to the death of the cat, and her grandmother explains to the other children: " 'Vickie's got her head full of things lately; that makes people kind of heartless' " (p. 142). It is a seemingly trivial incident, but it is steeped in the self-recrimination which, I believe, underlies the story. When Vickie learns that although she has won a scholarship, there still will not be enough money for her to go to college, she sees everyone as her enemy; she even refuses her grandmother's comfort. Throughout the summer of the story Vickie turns away from her family to the Rosens, the cultured Jewish neighbors, who encourage her to be a scholar. We naturally feel sympathy for her desire to escape into the romantic world of the arts. But there is a complex dimension to this youthful self-absorption, imaged in the slight but telling details of Vickie's reading. In the Rosens' library, looking at an illuminated edition of *Faust* she pauses over a picture of Gretchen entering the church and Faustus gazing from behind a rose tree with Mephisto at his shoulder. Allegorically, the scene suggests the fundamental opposition between experience and abstract knowledge in the legend. Unaware of its implications, Vickie expresses an urgent desire to be able to read the German in which the text is printed, thus making a Faustian wish. Between the first and second parts of the book she finds the *Dies Irae* hymn, and while for Vickie it represents only a test of her Latin, the author suggests a perspective from the other end of life—the day of judgment.[8]

The failure of sympathy and understanding in the family reaches a dramatic crescendo at the end of the story, where the members of the family are so engrossed in their personal problems they do not realize the grandmother is dying; each of the women gives bitter expression to her frustration and despair as the grandmother looks helplessly on. Victoria asks her mother in an accusing tone if she is sick and says: " 'You ought to be more careful what you eat, Ma. If you're going to have another bilious spell, when everything is so upset anyhow, I don't know what I'll do!' " (p. 175). When Vickie hears that her grandmother is ill and her mother lying down in her room, she thinks, "Wasn't it just like them all to go and get sick, when she had now only two weeks to get ready for school, and no trunk and no clothes or anything?" (p. 185). But our sympathies are never one-sided, as this is a drama of the generations: Vickie's attitude throughout, we realize, is characteristically adolescent and her selfish indifference to her grandmother's plight is tempered by our knowledge that she is apprehensive and full of self-doubt about going away to school; and we learn that Victoria, so proud of her attractive appearance, is to bring yet another child into the crowded house. The interweaving of multiple viewpoint renders movingly the imaginative tension at the heart of the story: while the memories of hidden longings and isolation are powerfully recreated through Vickie's viewpoint, the narrative overview creates the mother and grandmother with sympathy and compassion.

In the last paragraph of the story the author observes that the attitude of the young to the old is universal, that some day in their turn Victoria and Vickie will come to understand Grandma Harris better and "regret that they heeded her so little." But despite the consolation of wisdom at the end, there is still a tragic feeling to the story. For the author the understanding and forgiveness have come too late because her mother and grandmother are now dead and compassion can be expressed only through art. The most moving image is that of the poor servant woman, Mandy, washing old Mrs. Harris's feet. The power of this image, in addition to its Christian connotations, relates to the Keatsian paradox that the servant's gesture of compassion is momentary but complete, while its artistic recreation must always be compensatory.[9] When Mrs. Rosen arranges for money so that Vickie can go to college, Grandma Harris assures her neighbor that Vickie will never forget it—and she has not. The homely details of childhood are nowhere else in Miss Cather's writing so lovingly described; but that affection is a quietly tragic emotion, because art, though timeless, can never restore life.

Although its origins are not so intimate or personal, "Two Friends" also derives from the author's Nebraska memories and contains the same theme of regret. In a painterly style which reflects the vivid, indelible quality of her memory (she cited Courbet as a model),[10] Willa Cather describes the friendship between two businessmen in a small pioneer town and a misunderstanding which separates them forever. The friendship has a rare and imaginative intimacy, and it gives the narrator, who as a child on moonlit summer nights listened to their sophisticated conversations about the world at large, an exciting sense of life's potential. At the same time the friendship suggests something "secure and established"; the feeling that it was one of life's "unalterable realities" is what inspires the adult narrator's recollection. The two men, however, eventually quarrel over politics and never speak to each other again. Both die a few years afterward, and this vignette from the narrator's childhood closes on a quiet note of regret for "something broken that could so easily have been mended; . . . something delightful that was senselessly wasted . . ." (p. 230).

"Neighbour Rosicky," in contrast, is an affirmative story: celebrating human relationships rather than success and accomplishments, it presents a picture of life lived fully and without regrets. The Rosickys have not been infected by the American urge to "get ahead" in the world; they refuse, for example, to sell the cream off their milk in spite of the profit it would bring. Mary Rosicky says: " 'I'd rather put some colour into my children's faces than put money into the bank' " (p. 25). The description of the Bohemian kitchen with the geraniums blooming on the window ledge, the plentiful food and strong coffee on the table, conveys a rich sense of life being lived fully in the present. The harmony and contentment that Rosicky himself feels is nowhere better conveyed than early in the story when he stops by the little country cemetery on his way home from the doctor's. He knows that he will not live much longer, but instead of feeling fear or regret, he is comforted by the knowledge that the graveyard is so close to his own fields and that he will lie beside old neighbors and friends. The description of the landscape, with the light snowfall binding together his barnyard and the little graveyard, mirrors the sense of unity in Rosicky's life. Before he dies he restores unity in his family's life as well. His eldest son has married an American girl from the town, who feels lonely and unhappy living in the country. By telling her the story of his own youthful discontent and by discreetly arranging for his son to take her to town more often, he wins his daughter-in-law's affection and makes her feel an important part of the family. The day before he dies she confides to him that there is a grandchild coming, an image of life coming full circle. In the story's final scene the doctor looks out over the graveyard where Rosicky is now buried and reflects that, with Rosicky's own horses working in the next field and the neighbors passing by on their way to town, "nothing could be more undeathlike than this place" (p. 71). Again the completeness and harmony of the Bohemian's life is suggested by the landscape with its "many-coloured fields running on until they met the sky."

In relation to Willa Cather's writing as a whole, "Neighbour Rosicky" is a kind of pendant, or coda, to her classic pastoral, *My Ántonia;* it gives us a later picture of the same Bohemian family that served as prototype for the characters of the famous novel. There is a significant formal difference, however, between the novel and the story: the highly self-conscious narrator, Jim Burden, who is undermined by a sense of personal failure, has been eliminated from the story, and life's failures and successes are measured by Rosicky himself. Rosicky is not a simple country peasant; as a Bohemian exile he spent his youth in London and New York and knows only too well the feelings of estrangement and individual worthlessness that a large city breeds. He also knows the depths of cruelty that human beings will sink to, cramped together in a city. He realizes that people in the country have the same capacity for meanness, but they are not "tempered, hardened, sharpened, like the treacherous people in cities who live by grinding or cheating or poisoning their fellow-men" (pp. 59–60). Rosicky's love for the country is a valid emotion because he has known its opposite. The living harmony between the graveyard and the countryside is emphasized when Doctor Ed compares it to city cemeteries where people are forgotten—"put away" in cities of the dead. At the end of the story we feel that Rosicky's grave must be snug and homelike, for his death does not leave regrets, a sense of life wasted; rather, it affirms the privilege of existence.

Lucy Gayheart: A Dance of Death

For what is perhaps her most complex novel philosophically, Willa Cather chose the commonest of narrative forms—the love story. *Lucy Gayheart* (1935)[11] has all the elements of a dime-store "romance"; a girl from a small town falls in love with a famous singer, their love is doomed from the outset, and they both eventually drown. The book has accordingly received more negative criticism than any of Willa Cather's other novels. Yet this mannered simplicity is deceptive; *Lucy Gayheart* is artfully put together and contains some of the author's most profound reflections on art and human relationships—above all, on the human condition as defined by mortality.

Many critics have dismissed *Lucy Gayheart* as a slight production from the author's later years. But there are two early short stories, one about life in the West and one about the world of the arts, which suggest that the germ for the novel had been in Willa Cather's imagination for many years. In "The Joy of Nelly Deane"

(1911) we find a heroine who anticipates Lucy Gayheart in several ways.[12] Both Nelly and Lucy have the same spontaneous vitality (they are always depicted in motion), and they are both the gayest, prettiest, and best-loved girls in their communities. Certain motifs in the plot of the story also carry over to the novel. Nelly, whose music is the essence of her vital nature, is, like Lucy, disappointed in love, is courted by a local businessman, and dies when she is very young. In the imagery of the story, Nelly's death is, like Lucy's, a kind of death by water. When Nelly is immersed in a pool of dark water in order to become a member of the Baptist Church, the narrator thinks "it will be like that when she dies," and simultaneously the church choir sings the hymn "Washed in the Blood of the Lamb." Nelly's unnecessary death in childbirth (which, like Lucy's, is caused by a mean-spirited man in a small town) fuses the images of baptism and the blood of the Lamb. The name of the town Riverbend in the short story also anticipates in its imagery a feeling of place important to the novel. Both the story and the novel likely had their source of inspiration in a real-life character who teased the author's imagination over the years; Willa Cather once met a spirited girl by the name of Miss Gayhardt in 1895, roughly the time in which the story and novel are set.[13]

A more direct clue to understanding the novel's form and theme (and proof that it was more than a whimsy) lies in the early story " 'A Death in the Desert' " where all the major characters in the novel can be seen to have their counterparts. In the short story we find a famous composer, Adriance Hilgarde, whose great zest for life, like Clement Sebastian's in the novel, is vitiated by a presentiment of his own death; there we find also a dying singer, Katharine Gaylord, who, like Lucy Gayheart, is in love with the musician but whose love goes unrequited; there is also a nonartist, Everett Hilgarde, whose love for the singer, like Harry Gordon's for Lucy, is thwarted. Life is tragic as set forth in the short story, but what is significant is the distinction the singer makes between her own plight and that of the composer she loves: Adriance Hilgarde's tragedy is "of the soul" because of his philosophical apprehension that individual life comes to an end with death, whereas Katharine Gaylord's is a tragedy "of passion" because her consuming love for the composer is never fulfilled. Tragedy thus delineated defines the relationship between Lucy Gayheart and Clement Sebastian, where the artist's preoccupation with death frustrates the romantic hopes of the woman who loves him. To these universal experiences of tragedy the author appended, in Harry Gordon's story, the theme of regret over the past. The controlling metaphor is also prefigured in " 'A Death in the Desert' ": as Katharine Gaylord, near death, listens to Adriance's latest composition, *Souvenirs d' Automne,* she says: " 'I lie here spent by the race-course, listening to the feet of the runners as they pass me—ah, God! the swift feet of the runners!' " Images of people in motion pervade the novel—people running, dancing, skating, hurrying from place to place. *Lucy Gayheart* is a kaleidoscope of movement, and its characters can be viewed as caught up in a dance of death.[14]

The "mortal" view of human experience adumbrates from Sebastian and his music. When Lucy first hears him sing in Chicago, she is struck by "something profoundly tragic" about the man. He sings Schubert's *Der Doppelgänger,* which brings to her mind an image of moonlight pouring down on the houses of an old German town: "moonlight, intense and calm, sleeping on old human houses; and somewhere a lonely black cloud in the night sky" (p. 30). The image is more than a romantic response to German *Lieder.* In the phrase "old human houses" the universe is separated into the human and nonhuman; the "double" vision of the song is life seen as comic, and life as tragic. Sebastian's singing is filled with the tragic conviction that all human effort is doomed to oblivion, that all desire must eventually return in death to a nonhuman void. The vision underlying Sebastian's song might popularly be called nihilistic or perhaps existential. As Lucy listens to him sing, "the outside world seemed to her dark and terrifying, full of fears and dangers that had never come close to her until now" (p. 31). In such a world all values are human and individual; but subject to time and change, they are fragile and fleeting. This is underscored in the encore, "When We Two Parted," which Sebastian sings at the recital; a song of separated lovers, it laments the frailty and the inevitable dissolution of human relationships. Lucy is profoundly moved by what she glimpses in Sebastian's singing, and she goes home that night "tired and frightened, with a feeling that some protecting barrier was gone—a window had been broken that let in the cold and darkness of the night" (p. 32).

Lucy had felt an omen for herself in the Byron song, and shortly after the concert she has the opportunity to work as Sebastian's rehearsal accompanist. Her fears of the singer are dispelled by his kindness, and after they have worked together for some time she finds herself falling in love with him. But Sebastian cannot return her love. Although the manner of the narration of Book I is such that we are looking mostly through Lucy's eyes, it is Sebastian's view of the world that engages our interest. When he sings Schubert's *Die Winterreise* we are given an insight into his feeling for Lucy. The Schubert song cycle presents a rejected lover who is psychically resurrected in winter to experience again and express the anguish of his loss. Sebastian sings the song without dramatic involvement. He does not identify with the melancholy youth, but presents him "as if he were a memory, not to be brought too near into the present. One felt a long distance between the singer and the scenes he was recalling, a long perspective" (p. 38). The emotional distance Sebastian establishes between himself and the youth of the songs defines his relationship to Lucy: she revives in him a memory of his youth, but romantic love is no longer a dramatic reality for him—his thoughts and emotions are preoccupied with much grimmer facts of life. In his studio Sebastian is always kind and courteous, but when Lucy, by chance, catches a glimpse of him walking alone in the street, she sees a man whose face is filled with a profound and forbidding melancholy—his other self.[15] Lucy ponders on Sebastian's relationship with his estranged wife and wonders if she is not the source of his unhappiness. But Sebastian is not a lover grieving over failure with a woman; rather, he is a man coming to terms with the knowledge that he must some day die. Lucy comes closest to understanding this when, unnoticed, she attends the funeral service for one of Sebastian's friends—a French singer who died suddenly while on tour in America. As the coffin is carried to the altar of the church, Sebastian follows it with a look of anguish and despair that strikes a chill in Lucy's heart. Unlike his rendering of *Die Winterreise,* Sebastian's involvement at the funeral is "personal and passionate," and Lucy feels, as at the first recital, that "a wave of black despair" had swept through the room—an image which recurs several times in the novel linking death with water. Lucy wonders if the woman had been dear to him, or whether death itself is so horrible to Sebastian; but when she remembers seeing him once before emerging from a church, she realizes that his despair has to do, not with the heart, but with "the needs of his soul" (p. 55).

The sequence at the church ends with the funeral procession and Sebastian walking rapidly away down the street. Images of people in motion, of life as a procession, inform almost every scene. The brief introductory chapter is a collage of remembered scenes from Lucy's life in Haverford, and we are told that the townspeople "still see her as a slight figure always in motion; dancing or skating, or walking swiftly with intense direction, like a bird flying home" (p. 3). Specific visual instances follow, one superimposed upon another: Lucy darting through a heavy snowstorm, her muff against her cheek; Lucy moving along just as swiftly in the breathless heat of an August noon; Lucy joyously coming along past lilac bushes and rows of jonquils in the springtime. Movement for Lucy is the essence of her vitality, the full measure of her pure, unconscious, physical joy in being alive. The first scenes in the novel are almost cinematic in their delineation of movement. On the last afternoon of the Christmas holidays Lucy is out with a party of young people skating on the river, the two ends of her scarf floating behind her, like "slender wings." Driving his horse into a lather to join the party is Harry Gordon, who, when he reaches the river, hurries into his skates and shoots past the others to take Lucy for a turn before sunset. They skate far down the river leaving the rest of the party behind; when they reach the end of an island they rest and watch the sun sinking below the horizon. The scene ends with Lucy and Gordon driving back to town in the sleigh, which is described as "a tiny moving spot on that still white country settling into shadow and silence" (p. 11). The image of the country in shadow and silence (Lucy describes it to herself as "the unknowing waste") foreshadows the vision of a cold, inhuman void that lurks beneath the surface of Sebastian's singing.

The next scene is similarly defined in terms of movement. Sleighs and wagons are driving from all directions to the railway station. The platform is crowded with "restless" young people watching for the train, when "a carriage drawn by two horses dashed up to the siding, and the swaying crowd ran to meet it" (p. 13). Fairy Blair, the town extrovert and tease, jumps out of the carriage and, throwing her coat in the air for the boys to catch, runs down the length of the station platform. When it is announced that the train will be twenty minutes late, she grabs two boys by the elbows and dashes into the street "doing an occasional shuffle with her feet." Soon she leads the whole group in a crazy chase: "She couldn't push the boys fast enough; suddenly she sprang from between the two rigid figures as if she had been snapped out of a sling-shot and ran up the street with the whole troop at her heels. They were all a little crazy, but as she was the craziest, they followed her. They swerved aside to let the town bus pass" (p. 14). In retrospect the image of youth being led in a mad dance is strongly suggestive. Movement continues: the Gayhearts alight from the bus and Harry Gordon drives up in his sleigh; then "a long line of swaying lights" moves across the countryside and the young people are soon on the train—"headed toward something." When she is alone, Lucy gives herself up to the train's rhythm which spells for her "escape, change, chance, . . . life hurrying forward" (p. 24).

The rhythm of movement forward never stops; the last image in the novel is of the sidewalk with Lucy's "light footprints, running away." Movement becomes a sober motif when Sebastian enters the story. The first piece that Lucy hears him perform is the song of a Greek sailor who has returned from a voyage and is acknowledging the protection of Castor and Pollux (the first image of the double). *Die Winterreise* is also structured on the idea of a journey, but Sebastian's interpretation of the songs is of a man at journey's end, from which perspective all of life's movement is seen as a hurrying forward to death. The image of all living things unwittingly caught up in a dance of death informs the novel throughout. In quasi-allegorical fashion, James Mockford, Sebastian's pianist, is a personification of Death. After listening to Sebastian sing *Der Doppelgänger,* which first gives her the tragic feeling, Lucy's attention is attracted by his accompanist, "a lame boy, who dragged one foot as he went across the stage" (p. 30). Mockford's physical infirmity is a reminder of human mortality, but the description of his person—his ghostly pallor, his red hair like a wig, and his green eyes—resembles the figure of Death made up for the old morality plays; Lucy, in fact, more than once thinks of him as someone made up for a theatrical performance. Other details are also suggestive: his age is indefinable, for at times he appears a boy and at other times he is clearly much older; his association with the color green (his eyes, his shirt and necktie, the green curtain of the stage) suggests perhaps the livid green of death; his impertinent manners and even his name suggest a rictus grin. Lucy instinctively hates Mockford, for she is his antithesis —an embodiment of Life with all its energy and desires. Fittingly, it is because of Mockford's diseased hip that Lucy is ensnared in the mortal chain that leads to her own death. While Mockford is resting for an operation, Lucy becomes Sebastian's pianist and falls in love with him. But, as we know from his singing, Sebastian is in death's train: he remarks to Lucy that Mockford is " 'one of the few friends who have lasted through time and change' " (p. 52). There is perhaps another grim double meaning intended when Sebastian says to Lucy at the piano, " 'Catch step with me' " (p. 41).

The action of Book I can be seen as a struggle between Life and Death for the possession of Sebastian's soul. At first the singer is simply courteous to Lucy, for he is completely absorbed by a sense of life's futility, but gradually he begins to respond to the freshness and spontaneity of Lucy's presence in his studio. As she would make her way along the lake front, the sharp air off the water "brought up all the fire of life in her," and she would take into the studio "the freshness of the morning weather." Sebastian watches for her from the window and delights in seeing her tripping along the street in the cold wind. Her figure hurrying along recalls to him a passage from Montaigne: " 'In early youth the joy of life lies in the feet' " (p. 50)—a passage which also reminds us of the *totentanz* motif. At the point when Sebastian and Mockford are about to leave Chicago for a series of concerts in Minnesota, Lucy accidentally comes upon Mockford alone in the studio. Her antagonist makes her feel how completely he has control over Sebastian. Lucy is repelled not only by his physical deformity and his white face, but by his insinuating familiarity and his jealousy of the man he calls "Clémont." Lucy "hurries" away, feeling she is a complete outsider and questioning the sincerity of Sebastian's friendship. Later that day she watches them, from a distance, leave the Arts Building on the beginning of their tour; Lucy feels completely alone in the world and takes comfort from the motion of the people rushing by in the wet, crowded streets.

When he comes back after ten days with Mockford, Sebastian is filled with morose thoughts to which he gives utterance in outbursts of sardonic humor. When Lucy admires a vase of flowers he says to her: " 'Yes, they're nice, aren't they? Very suggestive: youth, love, hope—all the things that pass' " (p. 69). Lucy asks him if he never got any pleasure from being in love, and he answers, " 'N-n-no, not much.' " News of an old companion's death ("it was like reading his own death notice") makes him reflect on all of life as a hopeless failure. But Lucy's eager sympathy revives his spirits, and he leaves her looking forward to the morning again. The following day he tells Lucy that he loves her, and although he confesses he has "renounced life" and will never share it with anyone again, he still believes in "the old and lovely dreams of man," which he will teach her and share with her. Sebastian is, in fact, falling in love with life again, with its movement and its ardor as embodied in Lucy. He says to her, " 'When I caught sight of you tripping along in the wind, my heart grew lighter. . . . When you knocked, it was like springtime coming in at the door' " (pp. 88–89). The scene is interrupted by Mockford who wants Sebastian to give him a ride in his cab, but Sebastian takes Lucy home first and on the way admits to her that he and "Jimmy" have been fighting over the accompanist's "rights."

When Harry Gordon comes to Chicago to pursue his courtship of Lucy, he brings back to her a world which has never looked at life's tragic side. Harry is the embodiment of self-confident youth and vigor: "He came to meet her with such a jolly smile, fresh and ruddy and well turned-out in his new grey clothes." And Lucy recognizes at once that the thing she liked best about him was "the fine physical balance which made him a good dancer and a tireless skater" (p. 97). But Lucy has "caught step" with Sebastian, and when she lies to Harry and tells him that she has "gone all the way" with the singer, that there is no going back, she unwittingly speaks a prophetic truth.

Images of life's irreversible flow increase when Lucy learns that Sebastian is to leave on his European tour earlier than planned. Giuseppe, the singer's faithful valet and Lucy's ally, brings her the news during the rush hour, and as they walk about the block they can scarcely hear each other for the clatter of truck wheels on the pavement and the troops of screaming children streaking down the sidewalk on roller skates. As she takes in what Giuseppe is saying, Lucy feels like a little boy's kite when the wind drops and it sinks "down in the dirty street, among the drays and roller skates" (p. 117). Sebastian and Lucy are together briefly before his departure, and though he tells her that he plans to get rid of Mockford and feels a revival of interest in his "heart," the foreboding of the song "When We Two Parted" weighs heavily on Lucy—"Surely that hour foretold sorrow to this." After he leaves Lucy, Sebastian too relapses into his old mood, and against the rumble of the wheels of his cab, he says aloud to himself, "A beautiful star goes out in my night." While he is on tour in the summer he keeps Lucy informed only of his itinerary (a stark image of movement); then in September comes the news of the fatal accident on the lake, with Mockford, the foreordained instrument of death, dragging Sebastian down into the cold waters.

Lucy had temporarily rekindled in Sebastian a desire to live (a revival of the heart), but having looked at life from a "long distance," he could not turn back and evade the terrible knowledge of death. She had brought sunlight to his studio, but he could not escape from death's shadow. Lucy fell under the shadow of Sebastian's vision temporarily (she is seated in the shadow of a pillar when he performs *Die Winterreise*), but hers is not a tragedy of death but of love's eternal frustration. When she goes back to Haverford she must discover not only a way of continuing to live, but a way of being able to love again.

Book II opens with an idyllic description of a "blue-and-gold autumn" on the plains. Then with Mrs. Ramsay, the elderly widow of one of the town's leading citizens, we watch from her window the procession of life moving past in the little town. The tender lyricism of the opening passage and the picture of the innocent children hurrying along as the school bell rings (" 'Run, Molly, run!' " Mrs. Ramsay calls to a little fat girl trailing behind) are poignantly moving in relief against "the tragedy of all effort and failure."[16] When the older people come along we are strongly reminded of Death leading the various estates, for each of the characters carries a reminder of mortality in his identification—the doctor's wife who walks to lose weight, the "Seventh-day Advent carpenter," the old Catholic priest, the flighty woman who sings at funerals: "One after another they came along the sidewalk in front of the house, under the arching elm trees, which were still shaggy with crumpled gold and amethyst leaves" (p. 145). The final figure to pass Mrs. Ramsay's window is Lucy Gayheart, her head bent forward and her shoulders drawn together, "as if she were trying to slip past unnoticed." Mrs. Ramsay reflects that in the past Lucy walked rapidly "as if she were hurrying toward something delightful," but now it was "as if she were running away" (p. 146).

It is Mrs. Ramsay who suggests to Lucy a way of finding happiness again. She says to her, " 'Life is short; gather roses while you may. . . . Make it as many as you can, Lucy. Nothing really matters but living. Get all you can out of it. I'm an old woman and I know' " (p. 165). Her advice is purposely a generalization, for happiness can only be sustained by life itself, not by an individual, perishable love. The importance of Mrs. Ramsay's words to Lucy is anticipated when Mrs. Ramsay's daughter observes the change that has come to her mother with the years. Once the older woman's sympathy for Lucy would have been passionate and very personal, now it was "more ethereal," like "the Divine Compassion" (p. 147). Earlier in the novel Professor Auerbach, Lucy's music teacher in Chicago, had given her the same advice: " 'You will learn that to live is the first thing' " (p. 134). Mrs. Ramsay also suggests to Lucy that in the end one's career comes second in importance to living, that accomplishments are only the ornaments of life. This repudiation of success and achievements as the chief purpose of one's life recalls Sebastian's bitter reflections after the death of his friend: "Life had so turned out that now, when he was nearing fifty, he was without a country, without a home, without a family, and very nearly without friends. Surely a man couldn't congratulate himself upon a career which had led to such results" (p. 78). Willa Cather does not reject art itself, but laments the lonely road the great artist must follow to achieve excellence.

Surprisingly, it is a concert at the town opera house which renews Lucy's desire to live. The author has chosen this symbolic turning point very carefully: what is important to note is that the work of art by itself—the often-sung opera *The Bohemian Girl*—does not inspire Lucy, but rather its rendition with such freshness and compassion by the aging soprano. "Her voice was worn, to be sure, like her face, and there was not much physical sweetness left in it. But there was another kind of sweetness; a sympathy, a tolerant understanding. She gave the old songs, even the most hackneyed, their full value" (p. 181). It is the woman's vitality and her human sympathy which transform the tired songs into a living, moving experience. In feeling the urge to live again, Lucy finds, as Mrs. Ramsay advised, that it is not an individual she loves, but that "Life itself" is the sweetheart (p. 184). Lucy feels she must go "back to a world that strove after excellence." But she is not a lonely artist figure like Thea Kronborg who would fight for a great career by denying herself life's pleasures; rather, she would return to a life of "flowers and music and enchantment and love," those things which symbolized the fullness of her life with Sebastian. Lucy would not return to "Art" (the jealous and exacting God Willa Cather describes in her early critical writings), but to "Life" enriched by the arts. The difference, I think, indicates the shift in Willa Cather's feeling in her later work.

The fact that life must end in death does not matter to Lucy; when she feels the renewed desire to go back into the world, her mind is filled with pictures of people in movement: "She could think of nothing but crowded streets with life streaming up and down, windows full of roses and gardenias and violets . . ." (p. 184). The words from Mendelssohn's *Elijah* that Sebastian sang for her in the beginning—*If with all your heart you truly seek Him, you shall ever surely find Him*—acquire their full value for Lucy as a description of living, not as a revelation after death; for seeking is finding or, as Willa Cather herself quoted, *Le but n'est rien; le chemin, c'est tout.*

Lucy's drowning when she goes skating on the river attests again to death's inexorable presence, but the image of the wagons crawling along the frozen land, taking her body home, initiates yet another tragedy in the novel—Harry Gordon's "life sentence" of guilt and remorse. Book III is narrated from Gordon's viewpoint, twenty-five years after the heroine's death. Gordon had loved Lucy Gayheart, but he had not understood her, and after her declaration of love for Sebastian his only thoughts were of revenging himself, of punishing Lucy. When Lucy came back to Haverford after Sebastian's death, he refused, in spite of her plea, to help or comfort her, withdrawing into the exclusive confines of his unhappy new marriage and the family bank. Indeed, on the last day of her life he had rudely denied Lucy a lift in his cutter. Book III opens on the winter afternoon of old Mr. Gayheart's funeral; during the services the townspeople feel "almost as if Lucy's grave had been opened" (p. 207). Harry Gordon, now fifty-five, reflects on the years since Lucy's death, and at last admits to himself his guilt. He had done everything possible to make Lucy suffer: the day on which she drowned "he refused Lucy Gayheart a courtesy he wouldn't have refused to the most worthless old loafer in town" (p. 220). He realizes that his guilt has been the preoccupation of his life since that day; he thinks of it and his barren marriage as a "life sentence." As an "act of retribution" he has kept up a friendship with Lucy's father, and when Mr. Gayheart is gone he takes possession of the Gayheart house with its sidewalk where Lucy's footprints are imprinted in the cement.

Harry Gordon's guilt is the result of his pride and possessiveness. He had not loved Lucy in a detached, selfless way; rather, he viewed her as a beautiful creature who would enhance his own life. Love that is possessive and self-regarding is destructive. Mockford's attachment to Sebastian is jealous and possessive, and both men drown. In contrast Sebastian grew to love Lucy because her feeling for him "seemed complete in itself, not putting out tentacles all the while. . . . In her companionship there was never the shadow of a claim" (pp. 80–81). Just as Lucy was forced to redirect her love from an individual to "life," so Gordon must replace passion with compassion. His love for Lucy finds expression in his solicitude for her father. Though Harry Gordon does not die in the novel, we know that, driving restlessly over the countryside in his automobile, he, too, has caught step with the three footprints in the sidewalk running away.[17]

Sapphira and the Slave Girl: A Winter's Tale

For her last published novel Willa Cather turned to Virginia and her memories of earliest childhood. Except for two stories with a southern setting ("The Elopement of Allen Poole" and "A Night at Greenway Court"), Virginia had not played a very large role in her fiction. The author was only nine-and-a-half years old when her family moved to Nebraska and she observed on occasion that an artist gathers his materials during the years between eight and fifteen. Most of her major novels are set in the West, which would seem to bear out this idea for Willa Cather. However, the epilogue of *Sapphira and the Slave Girl*[18] suggests to the contrary that, not only was Willa Cather gathering the materials of her art at an earlier age, but also that her imagination had begun to take its characteristic form very early. Book IX, "Nancy's Return," the epilogue of this last novel, might indeed serve as a prologue to Willa Cather's writing as a whole: it represents in fictional form some of the author's earliest memories; moreover, it suggests some of the psychological origins of her imaginative world. In a letter to Dorothy Canfield Fisher Willa Cather said the book began with a memory of Negro voices.[19] As a very small child she had been witness to the dramatic reunion of a runaway slave, Nancy, with Till, her mother, who had stayed on the family farm in Virginia after the Civil War. Since the novel developed out of this memory, for an understanding of its form and theme the epilogue is a suggestive place to begin this discussion.

"Nancy's Return" takes place twenty-five years after the main action of the novel. The author describes herself as a child, "something over five years old," who has been anticipating for days the return of the former slave girl to her Virginia home. Because she has a cold the child-narrator is kept in bed in her mother's room, but the women in the house have arranged that the reunion between Nancy and Till take place in the bedroom so that the child can be present. The scene has that vivid but incomplete quality of childish recall: certain details are markedly clear (it was a windy March day), while others, such as the whereabouts of the child's father, are shadowy and guessed at. There is also a dreamlike movement from one scene to the next without specific connections in time. These qualities which characterize a very early memory explain certain aspects of the novel's form; it is a curious combination of sharply etched scenes and vague suspicions and surmises. The indefinite nature of the drama itself—the refusal of Sapphira and the miller to let their differences show on the surface—has been explained in terms of the social mores of the period, when bitter feelings were hidden by good manners and an atmosphere of domestic comfort. There is doubtless period authenticity in this way of presenting the conflict in the novel, but this style also reflects the unknown or dimly perceived dimensions of experience from a child's point of view. The happenings in several of the most important scenes in the novel are only partially disclosed because they are presented as overheard or witnessed secretly from a distance: at the beginning, for example, Rachel Blake overhears Sapphira disciplining Nancy with a hairbrush (figuratively Rachel is a child eavesdropping at her mother's door); Sapphira overhears Bluebell accuse Nancy of an illicit relationship with the miller, and this sets in motion the novel's train of events; Rachel psychologically rejects her mother after overhearing the Bywaters discussing the evils of slavery; Sapphira, unnoticed, watches Nancy and the miller talking together at the cemetery; the miller overhears Martin harassing Nancy in the laundry cabin; and the schoolteacher, Fairhead, watching through a window sees little Mary drink a bowl of broth from the table while she is apparently walking in her sleep. The heightened, dreamlike quality of this last scene has the indelible yet at the same time elusive quality of earliest memories. Form for Willa Cather was always organic; here the weaving together of dramatic narrative with anecdote and descriptive scenes is shaped not simply by memory but by something much more shadowy and elemental—a memory of a memory, an intimation.

More important than the events witnessed on Nancy's homecoming is the special aura which surrounds the household and its inhabitants in the narrator's memory. The child's mother is energetic and impatient and dominates the scene; her father is altogether removed, probably in the basement, we are told, making shoes for the paws of his shepherd dog. In later portions of the epilogue the mother is absent and the narrator recalls the great pleasure she had in listening to the other women (her grandmother, the neighbors, and servants) telling stories over their work around the kitchen table. Although Sapphira and the miller, the main characters in the novel, have long been dead, there is a strong suggestion of their survival in the child's mother and father. Like the narrator's mother, Sapphira dominates her household with unchallenged authority, and, like the absent father, the miller spends most of his time at the mill, where he even has his bed. The most undisguised fictional treatment Willa Cather ever did of her parents was the Templetons in "Old Mrs. Harris" (Edith Lewis has suggested the story might well have been called "Family Portraits"),[20] and the essential nature of that couple reappears in

Sapphira and Henry Colbert. Rachel Blake's assessment of her mother in *Sapphira and the Slave Girl* could substitute for the description of Victoria Templeton without changing that character: "Mrs. Colbert, though often generous, was entirely self-centred and thought of other people only in their relation to herself. She was born that way, and had been brought up that way." Like the evasive and ineffectual Mr. Templeton, the miller concedes all authority to Sapphira: " 'You're the master here, and I'm the miller' " (p. 50). Edith Lewis's record supports the hypothesis that Sapphira and the miller are closely modeled on the author's parents. Though physically dissimilar to the miller, Mr. Cather is described as extremely gentle and courteous, and, like the father of the child narrator, he used to make little shoes for the paws of his favorite shepherd dog. Mrs. Cather is described as "a handsome, imperious woman, with a strong will and a strong nature. She was always the dominating figure in the family. . . . She ruled her children with a firm hand—when she punished them, it was no spanking or putting them in a corner; she whipped them with a rawhide whip."[21] The identification of these fictional characters with their real-life prototypes is not merely to satisfy idle curiosity; I believe that in her last books Willa Cather was making her peace with life, and chief among those who figured in it were her parents. The epilogue suggests that the story of Sapphira and the miller and the slave girl, Nancy Till, may well represent the fundamental psychological drama of Willa Cather's life—the child indulged by a gentle father and disciplined (perhaps in her own eyes rejected) by a strong-willed and unsympathetic mother. The pattern runs throughout Willa Cather's writing; the alienation that Nancy (and Rachel Blake) feel from Sapphira is prefigured in the many rejected and orphaned protagonists in her fiction. And it is from the emotional vantage point of a child, helpless in the face of capricious authority, that the novel's themes of power and justice derive their powerful, elemental character.

Willa Cather's preoccupation with power and possessiveness is nowhere as dramatically in the foreground as in this last novel focussed on the issue of slavery; the desire to possess and control determines both the characters and the plot. Submerged in the rich tapestry of descriptive scenes is a slow-moving but relentlessly straightforward narrative. Sapphira Colbert, the invalid mistress of the Mill House at Back Creek, is jealous of the affection that her husband, the miller, apparently feels for her mulatto slave girl, Nancy. When the miller refuses to allow Nancy to be sent away to Winchester, Sapphira invites her husband's nephew, Martin Colbert, a notorious rake, to come for a visit. Martin's prolonged attempts to seduce and rape Nancy finally move Rachel Blake, the Colberts' daughter, to help the girl escape to Canada. Her power thus challenged and checked, Sapphira formally requests her daughter never to visit at the Mill House again. But after one of Rachel's children dies from diphtheria Sapphira relents, knowing that death is not very far away for herself. The attitudes to slavery are a mirror of character: it is Sapphira, the slave owner, who feels jealousy, the passion of possession, in relation to her husband, whereas the miller and his daughter, who are essentially abolitionists, are indulgent and sympathetic toward others—the miller habitually overlooks the debts of the poor and Rachel is a Sister of Mercy at the bedside of the sick.

Sapphira's desire for complete control over the members of her family and the servants (slavery for Sapphira is a natural part of the social order) makes her behave frequently in a harsh, authoritarian manner, and results in a household fraught with jealousies and gross injustices. Sapphira's overbearing nature is evident in the first chapter, "The Breakfast Table, 1856," when she confronts the miller with the idea of selling Nancy. Her control over the household is so complete that she even marries Till to the eunuch, old Jeff, to ensure that she will not be deprived of the services of her personal maid by pregnancies and nursing babies. But it is through Nancy herself that we experience the full force of Sapphira's cruelty and vindictiveness because the girl is in bondage to Sapphira and has no way to escape. Nancy's affection for the miller is innocent, but Sapphira, immobilized in her wheelchair, has suspicions and punishes Nancy on every pretext. The injustice in Nancy's situation takes on a nightmarish quality when Martin Colbert begins to pursue her. He lies in wait for her at every opportunity, hoping to catch her off guard when she is making up his bedroom, or picking cherries in the orchard, or gathering laurel branches in the wood. Her hysterical fear of assault prevents her from sleeping at night (Sapphira has her sleep conveniently within Martin's reach); the psychological horror of her situation makes us see Sapphira as a monster of cruelty. Through Rachel Blake's eyes Sapphira's cruelty assumes an even more malignant cast, something perverse and unnatural. As a child Rachel always knew she was a disappointment to her mother; when she was older she pinned their resentment of each other on the moral question of owning slaves. Nancy's plight dramatizes for Rachel something she always felt herself in her relationship to her mother and motivates her to help Nancy escape. Rachel had been rescued from Sapphira when Michael Blake "dropped from the clouds . . . to deliver [her] from her loneliness," and we are told that afterwards "she no longer brooded upon real or imagined injustices" (p. 138). The moral problem of justice is pondered on philosophically by the miller who searches the Scriptures for a resolution to the question of slavery. Even minor characters like Mandy Ringer and her son Lawndis are preoccupied with the problem of justice in the world: when Mandy hears that the communion set stolen from the church was only silver plate, she is reassured that " 'there is a kind-a justice in this world after all' " (p. 126); and she is glad Rachel was able to free Casper Flight from his tormenters, because her crippled son cannot bear to see "a sparrow fall."

I have called *Sapphira and the Slave Girl* a winter's tale because, like the Shakespearean play of that title, it is a story of injustice and separation brought about through unfounded jealousy; more importantly, the novel is also a romance of forgiveness—the plot moves all the characters to a final point of reconciliation. This is in part brought about by the narrative viewpoint, which attempts to see the characters from as many sides as possible and to gain insight into the complexity of motive behind every act. Although the accent falls on Sapphira's harsh, reproving nature and the miller's religiosity, the characters are far from one-dimensional.[22] Sapphira is proud and vengeful and sets out to destroy Nancy in order to punish her husband, but at the same time we are made aware that her crippling illness is a heavy burden for a once active and ambitious woman. We see Henry Colbert poring over his Bible and reading Bunyan in his struggle to be a just and righteous man; but we are made to realize that if Sapphira is too domineering, the miller is too weak. He is fond of Nancy, as a father is fond of a daughter, but does nothing to protect her from his nephew's advances; his role in helping her to escape is a clandestine, non-committal gesture of leaving some money unguarded in his coat pocket. Sapphira and the miller are seen most objectively through Rachel Blake's eyes. All her life she has instinctively felt hostility towards her mother, but she nonetheless realizes that her mother is capable of great kindness as well as cold cruelty. She knows that Sapphira's respect and affection for old Jezebel, whose tempestuous energy parallels her own, is entirely genuine; and her indulgence of Tansy Dave, a youth deranged by a thwarted love affair, goes considerably beyond the master–slave relationship. Rachel is much more like her father in temperament, but sees clearly his moral cowardice. Rachel, too, is a fully rounded character: as a self-effacing nurse to the sick and a woman who suffers the loss of a beloved husband and three of her four children, she appears a benevolent and sympathetic character, and yet we are told that there was always something a little cold and sullen in her nature. For example, while she lives in Washington, she hurts her mother's pride deeply by never inviting her to visit there.

All the characters have their failings, but the plot works to bring them within the imaginative sphere of our forgiveness. Sapphira's punishment of Nancy is a wicked deed, but at the same time her crime is an instance of *felix culpa,* the fortunate fault: she sets out to harm Nancy, but by making her run away to freedom only succeeds in benefiting her. When Nancy takes her chance Till sheds tears of joy. Nancy's departure also comes at the right time for the miller because his innocent love for the girl is changing into guilty desire through a subconscious identification with his nephew. Thus Sapphira's dark scheme inadvertently benefits everyone, and we are reminded of the miller reflecting on the words of the hymn, "God moves in a mysterious way / His wonders to perform" (p. 111).[23] The design of forgiveness in the novel is specifically Christian in reference. The one person harmed by Sapphira is her daughter, Rachel, who is asked never to visit at the Mill House again; but the breach is healed by the hand of Providence. Rachel's two little girls get diphtheria: one recovers after a mystical sleepwalking scene in which the girl drinking broth reminds the schoolteacher of the Communion service (p. 259); but the other dies, and the two women are reconciled through mutual grief. The child's death seems a high price to pay to bring Sapphira to humility and repentance, but in the novel's Christian scope of reference we are assured that *"not a sparrow falleth to the ground"* without God's knowledge (p. 228). Little Betty, docile and meek, is God's innocent pawn sacrificed so that an incorrigible sinner might be saved.

Thus the characters in the novel are reconciled to each other and Sapphira is incorporated into the general atmosphere of forgiveness. The philosophical accord established between Sapphira and the miller is disclosed in their last scene together where they tell over their mutual failings and strengths. The miller says to his wife that she is a good woman because she has relented and offered Rachel their home for the winter, but Sapphira says: " 'Not so good as Rachel, with her basket!' " (p. 268). The miller responds that there are different ways of being good to people and sometimes keeping them in their place is also being kind. Earlier in the novel the miller had resolved the moral dilemma of slavery for himself by conceding the mysteriousness of God's design in human affairs and by telling himself that "in this world . . . nobody is altogether free" (p. 228). He had asked himself at the beginning: "If Lizzie, the cook, was in bonds to Sapphira, was she not almost equally in bonds to Lizzie?" (p. 110).

The spirit of harmony and forgiveness which prevails in this scene carries over into the epilogue. Many years have passed and we now view the characters from the sober perspective of human mortality. During the Civil War Back Creek people were divided in their political loyalties, but when their boys were injured or in danger, be they Union or Confederate soldiers, they were protected and cared for by the neighbors. The last glimpse we are given of Sapphira is through the eyes of Till, one of the servants most injured by Sapphira's autocratic ways, but that last view is colored by the same feelings of loyalty and Christian forgiveness. Sapphira's headstrong, indomitable nature is now seen as stoical dignity and courage in the face of death. We not only admire her at the end, but feel sympathy for her. Particularly affecting is the image of Sapphira with her candles reflected in the window; their religious connotations remind us of her final penitential confession to the miller: " 'We would all do better if we had our lives to live over again' " (p. 269).

The Old Beauty and Others: "Revelation, Revaluation"

One final volume of unpublished stories, *The Old Beauty and Others* (1948),[24] was put together and issued after Willa Cather's death. The story which gives the collection its title perhaps best illustrates what the author meant when she wrote in the essay "A Chance Meeting" that "an artist's limitations are quite as important as his powers . . . that both go to form his flavour, his personality."[25] If Willa Cather is faulted in her art for nostalgia and conservatism, then "The Old Beauty" could be cited as an example of this emotion and attitude evoked in excess. Written in 1936, the same year that the author published *Not Under Forty* with what amounts to a manifesto against the present in its Prefatory Note, "The Old Beauty" concerns a woman who yearns for an era which has passed and who withdraws in horror from the present. The story sketches briefly the life of Gabrielle Longstreet, who was the rarest flower in London's brilliant society of the 1890s. Recalling his acquaintance with her during those years is a very agreeable, nostalgic experience for Henry Seabury, the central consciousness in the story. Viewed from the 1920s those "deep, claret-colored closing years of Victoria's reign" appear a nobler, more gracious period in human history than the present. But nostalgia, as we have seen, is a complex emotion which involves troubled as well as beautiful memories, and the nostalgia of "The Old Beauty" when carefully considered contains some interesting revelations.

In this story the author touches again on what seems to me one of the major preoccupations of her last writing—the theme of regret and confronting one's past honestly. On renewing his friendship with Gabrielle Longstreet, now Madame de Couçy, widowed and living quietly in France, Seabury finds that her recollections of her London years are mixed with regrets. In her youth she had been surrounded by admirers; they were men of achievement, but she had simply taken them for granted. Now in her old age she has come to recognize their greatness and is saddened to think that she once held them so lightly. She says to Seabury: " 'My friends mean more to me now than when they were alive. I was too ignorant then to realize what remarkable men they were. I supposed the world was always full of great men' " (p. 32). She sees her youthful self as not simply ignorant but selfish as well, and it is this which fills her with regrets: " 'You may remember that I was a rather ungrateful young woman. I took what came. A great man's time, his consideration, his affection, were mine in the natural course of things, I supposed' " (p. 33). Now she bows to them in admiration and her chief pleasure is to read what those men wrote and what has been written about them. Cherry Beamish, Gabrielle Longstreet's spirited companion, gives Seabury a similar account of her friend: " 'Yes, . . . she gets very low at times. She suffers from strange regrets. She broods on the things she might have done for her friends and didn't,—thinks she was cold to them' " (p. 43). Nostalgia for the old beauty is complicated by disturbing memories. Even for Seabury the past has its disagreeable aspect. Gabrielle recalls to him that the last time they met he had rescued her from the embraces of a vulgar American businessman. For Seabury as well as for Gabrielle it had been "something quite terrible" (p. 52); Seabury had gone to China shortly after and their paths had not crossed again until the encounter at Aix-les-Bains.

Despite her troubled sense of the past, Gabrielle Longstreet clings fiercely to everything that the Victorian and Edwardian periods represented. She is repelled by the dress and manners of the Jazz Age. Seeing young couples tangoing in the hotel tea room, she says, " 'They look to me like lizards dancing—or reptiles coupling' " (p. 58). Seabury observes that he is grateful to have survived the holocaust of the war, to be sitting in a comfortable hotel " 'in a France still undestroyed.' " But the old beauty replies, " 'Are you grateful? I am not. I think one should go out with one's time' " (p. 46).

The denouement of the story is heavily symbolic. Seabury takes the two elderly women on a drive in the mountains to the Grande-Chartreuse. The lightness and purity of the air on a perfect autumn day gives Seabury and his friends "a sense of detachment from everything one had left behind 'down there, back yonder.' " They feel that there in the mountains "life would go on thus forever in high places," and we are told that Seabury would ever after remember that drive as "strangely impersonal" (p. 62). The autumnal journey seems to be almost a ritual preparation for death. The monastery, like the old beauty herself, is in ruins. (Earlier Seabury reflected to himself that "plain women . . . when they grow old are —simply plain women. Often they improve. But a beautiful woman may become a ruin" [pp. 24–25].) But it is also a "destination." In the stone courtyard, while the others are looking about the monastery, Gabrielle takes a mirror and casts a sunbeam down into the dark depths of the monastery well; Seabury, at a distance, notices that there is "a faintly contemptuous smile on her lips" (p. 64). The symbolism here is elusive. Does the deep well in the earth suggest to Gabrielle the grave? Is the contempt of her smile directed at man's mortal nature (contempt for her own fear of death); or is it a smile expressing contempt for men living in modern times?

On their return to the hotel the automobile in which the three friends are riding narrowly misses colliding with a small car driven by two young American women. The women are "bobbed, hatless, clad in dirty white knickers and sweaters"; they light cigarettes, swagger about giving orders to Seabury's driver, and call each other "Marge" and "Jim." Gabrielle is stricken by this encounter, and the next morning before dawn she dies in her hotel room. We are left to ask whether the incident on the road amounted for Gabrielle to a moment of self-confrontation: did she catch a glimpse in the two American women of her own cold and thoughtless youth? Or did the encounter with those " 'creatures' " confirm in her a desire to die, a desire to be with the people of her own time rather than to continue living in a discordant and vulgar present? Whether the last event in her life amounted to a brutal self-confrontation or whether it made the anachronism of her existence unbearable, we are assured that the old beauty has found peace at last. Seabury, viewing her body, observes that her face "had no longer need to muffle itself in furs, to shrink away from curious eyes, or harden itself into scorn," but lay on the pillow victorious—"like an open confession" (p. 70).

In "Before Breakfast" Willa Cather rehearses once again her theme of regret, occasioned by the proximity of physical death. The progatonist is Henry Grenfell, a self-made man who has worked his way up from a messenger boy with Western Union to a senior partner of a powerful corporation. Now as an old man he looks back on a remarkably successful life not with satisfaction, but with grave misgivings. What was it all for, he asks himself. His three sons have turned out well, two of them brilliantly, but he admits to himself despairingly that they are "as cold as ice." His best companions are old authors like Scott, Dickens, Fielding, and especially Shakespeare because, as he pointedly says to his son, " 'they're mighty human' " (p. 153). A vision of the world as nonhuman, as physical matter accounted for by science, and the nearness of his own extinction create havoc in Grenfell's soul. In the past he has always found solace from his cares on his island retreat in the North Atlantic, but this year a geology professor (two of Grenfell's "cold" sons are also professors) has spoiled the island for him by coming to study its formation and by drawing Grenfell's attention to its prehistoric age. The brevity and insignificance of human life strikes Grenfell at every turn thereafter. As he stands by the window, about to put in his eyedrops, he sees the morning star on the horizon in all its ageless and impersonal splendor, and thinks to himself, "Why patch up? What was the use . . . of anything?" (p. 148).

The geologist's presence on the island forces the crisis in Grenfell's soul; however, he does not rest the blame for his sense of failure and despair on forces external to himself: "The bitter truth was that his worst enemy was closer even than the wife of his bosom—was his bosom itself!" (p. 156). Grenfell devoted his life to a personal quest for power, which is now being mocked by the impersonal universe around him which will claim him in death. He reflects to himself that he had got ahead in the world—but on the wrong road. In the last part of the story he takes a very different road—a walk through the woods to another part of the island—and on his way he sheds his intensely personal response to everything for something akin to a transcendental feeling for life. The sight of the geologist's daughter out swimming in the Atlantic precipitates his reaffirmation of living. Her pink-skinned fragility in the "death-chill" water, coupled at once with her vitality, proclaims to him that life will continue to renew itself on the prehistoric rocks of the world. His acceptance of the human condition (his own rebirth to life) is evidenced in his awakened physical appetite and in his final reflection which good-humoredly turns on an image of evolutionary science over which he had despaired: " 'Anyhow, when that first amphibious frog-toad found his water-hole dried up behind him, and jumped out to hop along till he could find another—well, he started on a long hop' " (p. 166).

In the last story she was to write Willa Cather followed through her affirmation of life to the point of dissolving the dramatic conflict upon which her art was based. According to her biographers, "The Best Years," written in 1945, was inspired by a last visit with her brother Roscoe; and her purpose in writing the story was to recapture something of the pleasure and intimacy of their growing up together. It is easy to see this as the author's last nostalgic glimpse of her past—the description of the prairie with its horizon like "a perfect circle, a great embrace," is nowhere as idyllic; but in view of the direction in which her imagination was instinctively moving, its implications are more profound, more far-reaching. In this story of a young schoolteacher whose weekend visit at home is to be one of the last before her early death, the picture of a family which has certain characteristics of the author's own family has radically altered from earlier portraits. The mother, Mrs. Ferguesson, is a definite, energetic person, but the selfishness of Victoria Templeton and the cold authority of Sapphira Colbert have disappeared. There is no conflict here between mother and daughter; on the contrary, the mother's authority and management of the family are so benevolent that for Lesley Ferguesson being at home was a soothing feeling that went through her "like getting into a warm bath when one is tired" (p. 96). The father is recognizable as a failure in practical terms, but there is no sense of his dreamy nature being a source of real conflict. "Wide Awake Farm," where Mr. Ferguesson takes his regular afternoon siesta, is a purely comic rendering of Mr. Templeton's evasiveness and Henry Colbert's cowardice. In the last sequence of the story Lesley's school superintendent, Evangeline Knightly (a fictional portrait of a teacher whom Willa Cather loved), returns fifteen years after Lesley's death for a visit with Mrs. Ferguesson. The feeling of love and accord imaginatively achieved between mother and daughter is here consummated. Instead of writing a daughter's eulogy for her dead mother, Miss Cather reverses the situation and lets the mother speak words of love for her lost daughter. It affirms the deep feeling throughout the story that her mother truly loved her.

When Willa Cather died in 1947 she left an unfinished work which, in accordance with her wishes, was subsequently destroyed. It was tentatively titled "Hard Punishments," and its setting was the Avignon of the medieval popes.[26] Miss Cather had been working spasmodically on this long story after she finished *Sapphira and the Slave Girl;* however, after the death of her brother Roscoe in 1945 she never went back to it or any other writing. In a letter to a friend she says that she has no more interest in writing since her brother's death, because she realizes nothing in life really matters but the people one loves.[27] At this point in her life there is a very personal relevance to the author's reflections on the world's great artists and their last works.

> Art is too terribly human to be very "great," perhaps. Some very great artists have outgrown art, the men were bigger than the game. Tolstoi did, and Leonardo did. When I hear the last opuses, I think Beethoven did. Shakespeare died at fifty-three, but there is an awful veiled threat in *The Tempest* that he too felt he had outgrown his toys, was about to put them away and free that spirit of Comedy and Lyrical Poetry and all the rest he held captive—quit play-making and verse-making for ever and turn his attention—to what, he did not hint, but it was probably merely to enjoy with all his senses that Warwickshire country which he loved to weakness—with a warm physical appetite.[28]

An artist's abandonment or renunciation of his craft, however, does not invalidate his life's work. On the contrary, it places it in the more meaningful context of experience achieved, because the artist's path is a circuitous one which returns its pilgrim back to life. That Willa Cather, unlike many of her American contemporaries, traveled the full road is not always recognized. But the words of Wallace Stevens are a worthy reminder: "We have nothing better than she is. She takes so much pains to conceal her sophistication that it is easy to miss her quality."[29]

Notes

1. The popular critical consensus of Willa Cather's later fiction is reflected in James Woodress's critical biography, *Willa Cather: Her Life and Art.* While Professor Woodress sees *Obscure Destinies* as still in Miss Cather's best vein of writing, he finds *Lucy Gayheart* sentimental and not up to standard, considers *Sapphira and the Slave Girl* the work of a cool, disciplined intelligence but lacking the passion of the author's best work,

and the three stories published posthumously *(The Old Beauty and Others)* as interesting but distinctly minor pieces. Dorothy Van Ghent is more outspokenly negative in her assessment of the last books; she feels the novels show signs of the author's deep fatigue and believes that the posthumous stories seem "only the somewhat querelous writing of old age" (*Willa Cather,* pp. 41–42). For a more complete discussion of the critical consensus of these books, see the bibliographical essay by Bernice Slote in Jackson R. Bryer, ed., *Sixteen Modern American Authors* (New York: W. W. Norton and Co., Inc., 1973), pp. 29–73.

2. For a comprehensive discussion of Willa Cather's commitment to art see the second of two essays by Bernice Slote in *KA,* pp. 31–112. See also the chapter entitled "The Artistic 'Chain of Human Endeavour' " in Edward A. and Lillian D. Bloom's *Willa Cather's Gift of Sympathy* (Carbondale: Southern Illinois University Press, 1964), pp. 116–52.

3. Bennett, *The World of Willa Cather,* pp. 26–31.

4. Lewis, *Willa Cather Living,* pp. 156–57.

5. Willa Cather expressed some of these feelings in a letter to Irene Miner Weisz, dated March 12, 1931 (Newberry Library). See also Woodress, *Willa Cather: Her Life and Art,* p. 240.

6. *Obscure Destinies* (New York: Alfred A. Knopf, 1966). All references are from this text. The allusion to Gray's "Elegy" in the title was pointed out to me by Virginia Faulkner.

7. "Katherine Mansfield" in *Not Under Forty,* pp. 135–36.

8. The author gives us only the first three lines, but Vickie translates the whole hymn, which includes the following lines: "Thou, whom avenging powers obey, / Cancel my debt (too great to pay) / Before the sad accounting-day." The hymn underscores the theme of self-recrimination in the story. See Giannone, *Music in Willa Cather's Fiction,* pp. 210–12.

9. A number of critics, including Sergeant and Randall, have compared Mrs. Harris to Flaubert's Félicité in "Un Coeur Simple." The comparison seems to me erroneous: Mrs. Harris's background and her intelligent dignity make her quite another character from Flaubert's simple-minded servant woman. A much closer relationship exists between Félicité and Mandy, the superstitious but faithful servant who appears in other of Willa Cather's writings as "Poor Marty" and Mahailey. These characters all were based on the Cather family servant Margie Anderson, whose history (including a brief, unfortunate marriage) resembles Félicité's. See Bennett, *The World of Willa Cather,* pp. 57–59.

10. Brown, *Willa Cather,* p. 292.

11. *Lucy Gayheart* (New York: Alfred A. Knopf, 1961). All references are from this text.

12. *CSF,* pp. 55–68. In the introduction, p. xi, Mildred R. Bennett points out how Nelly Deane anticipates the character of Lucy Gayheart.

13. See Bennett, *The World of Willa Cather,* p. 217.

14. The Dance of Death motif appears in at least three of Willa Cather's fictions before *Lucy Gayheart.* She refers the title of *Death Comes for*

the Archbishop to Holbein's *Dance of Death.* There is the image of the runners in " 'A Death in the Desert' "; and Bernice Slote has pointed out that in the early story "On the Divide" the rude carvings Canute Canuteson makes on the window sills and boards of his house all depict designs from a Dance of Death (*KA,* p. 6). There is also a Death figure in the short story "Consequences" (1915), in which the decayed old man, dressed in theatrical clothes, follows the hero around until he chooses to commit suicide rather than live out his years and become like the old man (*UVS,* pp. 65–84).

15. The idea of a man or woman leading a double life fascinated the author from the beginning. In her earlier novels, her "tragedies of passion," the division in a man's nature is between his adult, social self and an instinctive, natural being connected directly to his childhood. Such is the double existence of Bartley Alexander, Jim Burden, Godfrey St. Peter, and Count Frontenac. For Clement Sebastian, however, the division in his soul is between the living man with his needs and pleasures, and the man haunted by the specter of inevitable death, a division brought about not by failure in love but by the failure of life. Many of the characters in *Lucy Gayheart* feel they have a second self which is hidden from public view but which is more real than the self they show to the world; even Lucy's officious sister, Pauline, feels she must always "put up a front" (p. 168). See also Willa Cather's description of the double life that goes on "even in harmonious families" in the essay "Katherine Mansfield" in *Not Under Forty,* p. 109.

16. The ringing of bells, which measure time, is a reminder of human mortality. Lucy feels that knowing Sebastian is "like tapping on a deep bell" because he has experienced life deeply and tasted the knowledge of death (p. 46). The singing of Harry Gordon's sleigh bells becomes cruelly ironic when he encounters the wagons taking Lucy's body back to town.

17. The final image in the novel perhaps suggests the origin of Lucy's name in Wordsworth's Lucy Gray. For Harry Gordon, Lucy is the embodiment of lost youth and happiness; as in Wordsworth's poem, she departs from life early and leaves only footprints which disappear at the edge of the walk.

18. *Sapphira and the Slave Girl* (New York: Alfred A. Knopf, 1961). All references are to this text.

19. Willa Cather to Dorothy Canfield Fisher, October 14, 1940 (Guy Bailey Memorial Library, University of Vermont).

20. Lewis, *Willa Cather Living,* p. 6.

21. Ibid., pp. 5–7. In *The Song of the Lark* Thea Kronborg's mother is also a strong, definite woman and her children are afraid of her rawhide whip (p. 22).

22. The complexity of the plot and the sympathetic treatment of the characters in *Sapphira and the Slave Girl* has been most fully appreciated by Lavon M. Jobes in her article "Willa Cather's Last Novel," *University Review* 35 (Autumn 1967): 77–80.

23. I am indebted to F. A. C. Wilson for the suggestion that the plot of the novel is conceived around the idea of the "fortunate fault."

24. *The Old Beauty and Others* (New York: Alfred A. Knopf, 1967). All references are to this text.

25. "A Chance Meeting" in *Not Under Forty,* p. 24.

26. See George N. Kates, "Willa Cather's Unfinished Avignon Story" in Willa Cather, *Five Stories* (New York: Vintage Books, 1956).

27. Willa Cather to Irene Miner Weisz, October 22, 1945 (Newberry Library).

28. From an undated fragment entitled "Light on Adobe Walls" in *Willa Cather on Writing,* pp. 125–26.

29. *Letters of Wallace Stevens,* selected and edited by Holly Stevens (New York: Alfred A. Knopf, 1966), p. 381.

Selected Bibliography

Works by Willa Cather

Date of first publication appears at the left except in the case of posthumous collections. Editions used in the text are indicated in the notes.

Published by the University of Nebraska Press

The Kingdom of Art: Willa Cather's First Principles and Critical Statements, 1893–1896. Selected and edited with two essays and a commentary by Bernice Slote. 1966. After first reference, cited as *KA.*

The World and the Parish: Willa Cather's Articles and Reviews, 1893–1902. Selected and edited with a commentary by William M. Curtin. 2 vols. 1970. After first reference, cited as *W&P.*

1903 *April Twilights (1903).* Edited with an introduction by Bernice Slote. Revised edition 1968.

Willa Cather's Collected Short Fiction, 1892–1912. Edited by Virginia Faulkner. Introduction by Mildred R. Bennett. (Includes *The Troll Garden,* first published in 1905 by McClure, Phillips & Co.) Revised edition 1970. After first reference, cited as *CSF.*

Uncle Valentine and Other Stories: Willa Cather's Uncollected Short Fiction, 1915–1929. Edited with an introduction by Bernice Slote. 1973. After first reference, cited as *UVS.*

Published by Houghton Mifflin Company

1912 *Alexander's Bridge.*
1913 *O Pioneers!* Sentry Edition, 1962.
1915 *The Song of the Lark.* Sentry Edition, 1963.
1918 *My Ántonia.* Sentry Edition, 1961.

Published by Alfred A. Knopf, Inc.

1920 *Youth and the Bright Medusa.*
1922 *One of Ours.*
1923 *April Twilights and Other Poems.*
1923 *A Lost Lady.*
1925 *The Professor's House.*
1926 *My Mortal Enemy.*
1927 *Death Comes for the Archbishop.*
1931 *Shadows on the Rock.*
1932 *Obscure Destinies.*
1935 *Lucy Gayheart.*
1936 *Not Under Forty.*
1940 *Sapphira and the Slave Girl.*
The Old Beauty and Others. 1948
Willa Cather on Writing. 1949

Willa Cather Letter Collections

I have consulted collections of Willa Cather's letters at the following libraries and archives:

Colby College, Waterville, Maine
Guy Bailey Memorial Library, University of Vermont, Burlington, Vermont
The Houghton Library, Harvard College, Cambridge, Massachusetts
Pierpont Morgan Library, New York, New York
Newberry Library, Chicago, Illinois
Yale University Library, New Haven, Connecticut
Nebraska State Historical Society, Lincoln, Nebraska
University of Nebraska Library, Lincoln, Nebraska
Willa Cather Pioneer Memorial, Red Cloud, Nebraska
University of Virginia Library, Charlottesville, Virginia
Huntington Library, San Marino, California

Willa Cather's will stipulates that her letters may not be quoted.

Writings about Willa Cather

Books

Bennett, Mildred R. *The World of Willa Cather.* New edition with notes and index. Lincoln: University of Nebraska Press, 1961.

Bibliography

Bloom, Edward A., and Lillian D. Bloom. *Willa Cather's Gift of Sympathy.* Carbondale: Southern Illinois University Press, 1962.

Brown, E. K. *Willa Cather: A Critical Biography.* Completed by Leon Edel. New York: Alfred A. Knopf, 1953.

Daiches, David. *Willa Cather: A Critical Introduction.* Ithaca, N.Y.: Cornell University Press, 1951.

Edel, Leon. *The Paradox of Success.* Washington: Library of Congress, 1960.

Giannone, Richard. *Music in Willa Cather's Fiction.* Lincoln: University of Nebraska Press, 1968.

Lewis, Edith. *Willa Cather Living: A Personal Record.* New York: Alfred A. Knopf, 1953.

Randall, John H. III. *The Landscape and the Looking Glass: Willa Cather's Search for Value.* Boston: Houghton Mifflin, 1960.

Schroeter, James. ed. *Willa Cather and Her Critics.* Ithaca, N.Y.: Cornell University Press, 1967.

Sergeant, Elizabeth Shepley. *Willa Cather: A Memoir.* Lincoln: University of Nebraska Press, 1963.

Van Ghent, Dorothy. *Willa Cather.* Minneapolis: University of Minnesota Press, 1964.

Woodress, James. *Willa Cather: Her Life and Art.* New York: Pegasus, 1970. Bison Book edition, Lincoln: University of Nebraska Press, 1974.

Articles

Charles, Sister Peter Damian. "Love and Death in Willa Cather's *O Pioneers!.*" *CLA Journal* 9 (December 1965): 140–50.

Cooperman, Stanley. "Willa Cather and the Bright Face of Death." *Literature and Psychology* 13 (Summer 1963): 81–87.

Edel, Leon. "Willa Cather's *The Professor's House:* An Inquiry into the Use of Psychology in Literary Criticism." *Literature and Psychology* 4 (November 1954): 66–79.

Gale, Robert. "Cather's *Death Comes for the Archbishop.*" *Explicator* 21 (May 1963): item 75.

Geismar, Maxwell. "Willa Cather: Lady in the Wilderness." In *The Last of the Provincials: The American Novel, 1915–1925.* Boston: Houghton Mifflin, 1947.

Gelfant, Blanche. "The Forgotten Reaping-Hook: Sex in *My Ántonia.*" *American Literature* 43 (March 1971): 60–82.

Helmick, Evelyn Thomas. "Myth in the Works of Willa Cather." *Midcontinent American Studies Journal* 9 (Fall 1968): 63–69.

Jobes, Lavon M. "Willa Cather's Last Novel." *University Review* 34 (Autumn 1967): 77–80.

Kates, George N. "Willa Cather's Unfinished Avignon Story." In Willa Cather, *Five Stories.* New York: Vintage Books, 1956.

Keeler, Clinton. "Narrative Without Accent: Willa Cather and Puvis de Chavannes." *American Quarterly* 17 (Spring 1965): 119–26.

Martin, Terence. "The Drama of Memory in *My Ántonia.*" *PMLA* 74 (March 1969): 304–311.

Miller, James E. Jr. "*My Ántonia:* A Frontier Drama of Time." *American Quarterly* 10 (Winter 1958): 476–84.

Slote, Bernice. "Willa Cather." In Jackson R. Bryer, ed. *Sixteen Modern American Authors: A Survey of Research and Criticism.* New York: W. W. Norton, 1973.

———. "Willa Cather as a Regional Writer." *Kansas Quarterly* 2 (Spring 1970): 7–15.

Stewart, D. H. "Cather's Mortal Comedy." *Queen's Quarterly* 73 (Summer 1966): 244–59.

Stouck, Mary-Ann. "Chaucer's Pilgrims and Cather's Priests." *Colby Library Quarterly* 9 (June 1972): 531–37.

Whittington, Curtis Jr. "The Stream and the Broken Pottery: The Form of Willa Cather's *Death Comes for the Archbishop.*" *McNeese Review* 16 (Spring 1965): 16–24.

Wilson, Edmund. "Two Novels of Willa Cather." In *The Shores of Light: A Literary Chronicle of the Twenties and Thirties.* New York: Farrar, Straus and Giroux, 1952

OTHER SOURCES CITED

Auerbach, Erich. *Mimesis: The Representation of Reality in Western Literature.* Translated by Willard Trask. New York: Doubleday and Co., 1957.

Brown, E. K. *Rhythm in the Novel.* Toronto: University of Toronto Press, 1951.

Delehaye, Père. *The Legends of the Saints.* Translated by V. M. Crawford. Notre Dame: University of Notre Dame Press, 1961.

Jessup, Josephine Lurie. *The Faith of Our Feminists.* New York: R. R. Smith, 1950.

Lewis, C. S. *A Preface to Paradise Lost.* New York: Oxford University Press, 1961.

Nims, Margaret F., trans. *Poetria Nova of Geoffrey of Vinsauf.* Toronto: Pontifical Institute of Medieval Studies, 1967.

Poggioli, Renato. "The Oaten Flute." *Harvard Library Bulletin* 11 (May 1957): 147–84.

Robertson, D. W. Jr. *Chaucer's London.* New York: Wiley, 1968.

Stevens, Holly, ed. *Letters of Wallace Stevens.* New York: Alfred A. Knopf, 1966.

Wolpers, Theodor. *Die Englische Heiligenlegende des Mittelalters.* Tubingen: Max Neimeyer Verlag, 1964

Acknowledgments

My first debt of gratitude is to my wife, Mary-Ann, who has co-authored the chapter on *Death Comes for the Archbishop* and whose appreciation of fiction has long been one of my critical touchstones. I wish to thank Mildred R. Bennett of the Willa Cather Pioneer Memorial and Educational Foundation, Red Cloud, Nebraska, who over the past several years has answered a multitude of questions about Willa Cather; F. A. C. Wilson, whose lively correspondence brought me to a keener and richer understanding of my subject; Professor Bernice Slote, University of Nebraska–Lincoln, and Professor John J. Murphy, Merrimack College, North Andover, Massachusetts, who read the book in manuscript and made important suggestions for revision; and Virginia Faulkner, University of Nebraska Press, whose editorship has been a creative force behind this book.

Two grants from the Simon Fraser University President's Research Fund enabled me to read Willa Cather's letters which are collected in libraries in various parts of the United States. My thanks are also due to my typists, Julie Knibb and Barbara Kantola, for their work in preparing the manuscript for the press.

Sections of this work have appeared in different form in the following periodicals: "Willa Cather and The Professor's House: 'Letting Go with the Heart,'" *Western American Literature* 7 (Spring 1972): 13–24; "Willa Cather's Last Four Books," *Novel: A Forum on Fiction* 7 (Fall 1973): 41–53; "*O Pioneers!:* Willa Cather and the Epic Imagination," *Prairie Schooner* 46 (Spring 1972): 23–34; "Perspective as Structure and Theme in *My Ántonia,*" *Texas Studies in Language and Literature* 12 (Summer 1970): 285–94, © 1970 by the University of Texas Press; "Willa Cather's Unfurnished Novel: Narrative in Perspectives," *Wascana Review* 6, no. 2 (1972): 41–51; "Hagiographical Style in *Death Comes for the Archbishop,*" *University of Toronto Quarterly* 41 (Summer 1972): 293–307; and "Art and Religion in *Death Comes for the Archbishop*" Arizona Quarterly 29 (Winter 1973): 293–302. I am grateful to the editors of these journals for their encouragement and for their permission to revise and reprint.

Grateful acknowledgment is extended to Alfred A. Knopf, Inc. for permission to quote from the following works of Willa Cather: *Youth and the Bright Medusa, Not Under Forty, The Old Beauty and Others,* and *Willa Cather on Writing;* and to Alfred A. Knopf, Inc. and Hamish Hamilton, London, for permission to quote from *One of Ours, A Lost Lady, The Professor's House, My Mortal Enemy, Death Comes for the Archbishop, Shadows on the Rock, Obscure Destinies, Lucy Gayheart,* and *Sapphira and the Slave Girl.* Also to Houghton Mifflin Company for permission to quote from *Alexander's Bridge* by Willa Cather; and to Houghton Mifflin Company and Hamish Hamilton, London, for permission to quote from *O Pioneers!, The Song of the Lark,* and *My Ántonia,* all by Willa Cather. Also to the University of Nebraska Press for permission to quote from the following Willa Cather collections: *The Kingdom of Art: Willa Cather's First Principles and Critical Statements, 1893–1896; The World and the Parish: Willa Cather's Articles and Reviews, 1892–1902; April Twilights (1903); Willa Cather's Collected Short Fiction, 1892–1912; Uncle Valentine and Other Stories: Willa Cather's Uncollected Short Fiction, 1915–1929.*

My debt to two friends, Pearl Kilpatrick and Phyllis Swan, lies outside formal acknowledgment.

D. S.

Index

This index is divided into two parts. Part I is an index to Willa Cather's titles; Part II is a general index. The italicized numbers in Part I indicate extended analysis or pointed discussion.

PART I

Index

PART II